THE MIRACULOUS MIRACLES AND SIGNS OF JESUS

The Study of the Eight Signs in John

DR. FRANK W. PARSONS

PUBLISHED BY FIDELI PUBLISHING, INC.

The Miraculous Miracles and Signs of Jesus

Unless otherwise noted, all Scripture is quoted from the
New American Standard Bible, 2020
by the Lockman Foundation, La Habra, Calif.

ISBN: 978-1-970730-86-9

Published by

Fideli Publishing, Inc.
119 W. Morgan St.
Martinsville, IN 46151

www.FideliPublishing.com

This book is dedicated to Pastor Roger Sellen,
a faithful colleague and co-laborer
in the Kingdom of our Lord Jesus.

Preface

The Gospel of John is similar to other three Gospel writers, but the apostle John is distinctive in his presentation and purpose for writing. In summation of John's Gospel, the apostle John declares to us why he wrote his particular Gospel. The apostle John says,

> Now Jesus performed **many other miraculous signs** in the presence of the disciples, which are not recorded in this book. [31]But these [*miraculous signs*]a are recorded so that you may believe that Jesus is the Christ, the Son of God, and that **by believing you may have** [*eternal*] **life** in his name.
>
> (John 20:30, 31 NET)

> aNote: "*miraculous*" [John 20:30 NET] is not in the GK text, but the contortion is likely implied. Also, John only uses the word "*life*," but the thought is definitely "*eternal life*". The meaning then implied is "*eternal life*" through faith in Jesus Christ as Lord. For example, see 1 John 5:10-13.

The above Scripture, John 20:30, 31, is the most significant topic and striking emphasis throughout the Gospel of John. The apostle John is writing "these decisive 'signs" in order to prove to the reader that Jesus (Yehoshua in HEB) is indeed unequivocally the promised Messiah and the Redeemer of the entire world.John 1:29; 1 John 2:2 In so doing as noted in the above two verses, John lays out *three distinct evidences* to every reader that trusts and receives Yehoshua as Lord and only Redeemer shall be given eternal life today in Christ.

1. John has selected particularly eight signs in his Gospel that prove beyond any doubt that Yehoshua is the Messiah (the Christ) and the Redeemer of the world.

2. John declares he and the other apostles chosen by Christ were *eyewitnesses of all the miraculous miracles and signs* and that these signs by Jesus are true and authentic from God.

3. Yehoshua laid own His life on the cross for our sins, He was buried and arose from the dead on the third day in *fulfillment of the Scripture*.[1 Cor. 15:3, 4]

John wrote a very pungent introduction [John 1:1-18], in which he establishes conclusively that Yehoshua is the Designer, Creator, and Sustainer of the entire universe and all life and all things. Christ the Lord is indeed Almighty God and only Redeemer. John says in his Gospel,

> [1]In the beginning was the Word, and the Word was with God, and the Word was fully God. [2]The Word was with God in the beginning. [3]All things were created by him, and apart from him not one thing was created that has been created. [4]In him was life, and the life was the light of mankind. [5]And the light shines on in the darkness, but the darkness has not mastered [overtake] it.　　　　John 1:1-5 (NET)

The apostle Paul also says similarly as given by the paraphrased Amplified Bible,

> [15]He [Christ] is the exact living image [the essential manifestation] of the unseen God [the visible representation of the invisible], the firstborn [the preeminent one, the sovereign, and the originator] of all creation. [16]For by Him [Christ] all things were created in heaven and on earth, [things] visible and invisible, whether thrones or dominions or rulers or authorities; all things were created *and* exist through Him [that is, by His activity] and for Him. [17]And He Himself existed *and* is before all things, and in Him all things hold together. [His is the controlling, cohesive force of the universe.] [18]He is also the head [the life-source and leader] of the body, the church; and He is the beginning [origin], the firstborn from the dead [preeminent over the dead], so that He Himself will occupy the first place [He will stand supreme and be preeminent] in everything. [19]For it pleased the *Father*[b] for all the fullness [of deity--the sum total of His essence, all His perfection, powers, and attributes] to dwell [permanently] in Him (the Son), [20]and through [the intervention of] the Son to reconcile all things to Himself, making peace [with believers] through the blood of His cross; through Him, [I say,] whether things on earth or things in heaven.　　　　Col. 1:15-20 (AMP)

> [b]Note: verse 19, the phrase, "*For it pleased the Father—*" is not the GK text. The NET is correct, "*For God* was pleased to have all his fullness

dwell in the Son." The NRS also reads, "For in him [Christ] **all the fullness of God was pleased to dwell**."

The Hebrews writer equally declares,

> God, after He spoke long ago to the fathers in the prophets in many portions and in many ways, ²in these last days has spoken to us in His Son, whom He appointed [GK *tithemi, established, destined*]c heir of all things, through whom also He made the world [GK *aion, universe* NIV]. ³And He is the radiance of His glory and the exact representation of His nature, and upholds all things by the word of His power. When He had made purification of sins, He sat down at the right hand of the Majesty on high,   (Heb. 1:1-3)

> ᶜ*Tithemi* does not mean that the Son has now become the heir. The meaning is that **Christ is the Heir**. The Son is the Origin and Source from which the universe came into being; He is the Creator and Sustainer of all things. The Triune Eternal God (blessed Trinity) worked in consort in the creation of all things. Christ is heir is likely a reference to His humanity.

The apostle John reminds his readers that Christ the Lord entered this world to redeem humankind from their sin. Yehoshua came into this world to save us from our sin and deliver us from the coming wrath of God which is Hell, the Lake of Fire. Yehoshua came into this world to *give eternal life to everyone* that will truly receive and trust Him as LORD and only Redeemer. Those who genuinely place their trust in Him, He gives them the _absolute authority_ to become "children of God," John 1:12. However, those who reject, deny, or do not receive Yehoshua as Lord and Savior, the apostle John warns,

> "He who believes in Him is not condemned; but **he who DOES NOT BELIEVE IS CONDEMNED ALREADY**, because he has not believed [*trusted*] in the name of the only begotten Son of God."
>
> John 3:18 (NKJ)

Therefore, those who are without Yehoshua as their personal Lord and Savior or Redeemer **stand condemned already for Hell** due to their sin before a holy and righteous God. The wrath of God presently abides over every unsaved. The wrath of God continues to rest upon all those without Yehoshua as personal Lord and Savior.

> Whoever believes in the Son has eternal life. Whoever doesn't believe in the Son won't see life, but the angry judgment of God remains on them."   John 3:36 (CEB)

While there are many similarities between all four Gospels (Matthew, Mark, Luke, and John), each Gospel writer has their unique emphasis and purpose for writing. For example, Matthew's emphasis addresses Yehoshua as the Messiah fulfilling of all prophecies of Scripture. Yehoshua the Messiah has come to fulfill the prophetic promises of God.[Matt. 5:17, 18; Rom. 15:8] Matthew gives special emphasis of Yehoshua as the Redeemer and King and the coming Kingdom of God.[Matt. 19:28] This will be very evident as God regathers the nation Israel and reestablishes Israel as His covenant people.[Matt. 25:31; Luke 22:24, 30; Rom. 11:24-27; Rev. 3:21] However, Israel must believe and receive Yehoshua as Messiah and only Redeemer or else they shall perish in their sin like everyone.[John 8:24]

Mark seems to give little attention to the fulfillment of the prophecies and Scripture in the OT. Mark is likely writing more to the Roman and Greek minds, the Gentile audience. Mark present Jesus a man of *authority*. Jesus is a man of *action*. For instance, Mark gives emphasis that the devil and all the evil angels (demons) *fear* Him. Demons immediately *obey* Him. Therefore, all demons are *subject* to the Yehoshua and even to His Name. Holy angels are all under Jesus' *authority* and *serving* Him and *obeying* His every command. The holy angels are Jesus' messengers doing His bidding and will. Everything in creation obeys Him, even the "wind and waves" obey Jesus. Yet, Mark presents Yehoshua as a merciful and loving Servant and Redeemer to all mankind to save wicked humankind from pending wrath of Almighty God.

Luke was written for apostle Paul's defense at Roman. Luke writes particularly to a Roman official. Luke refers to the Roman official with cryptic name, "*most excellent Theophilus*." (The cryptic name may have been used to give some protection from any persecution.) *Theophilus,* meaning "*Beloved-Loved of God*."[Luke 1:1-3] Luke gives a particular emphasis to the Holy Spirit. Luke seems to stress that *the Kingdom of God is here but not yet.* [Luke 22:24, 30; Acts 1:6-8]

The three Gospels (Matthew, Mark, and Luke) mentioned above are sometimes referred to as "synoptic Gospels." The meaning of the word synoptic is to "*see together*." That is, the synoptic Gospels give similar emphasis. The synoptic Gospels place an emphasis on Jesus' northern ministry in Israel, which were Galilee and Perea areas.

Ah, but John seems to give more emphasis to Jerusalem and Judea areas, Jesus' southern ministry to Israel. As it has been noted, the apostle John is **distinctly evangelistic**. He writes to convince his readers, especially Jews, that Yehoshua is truly the Son of God. Yehoshua is the promised Messiah and Redeemer (Savior) of the World. The Good News is that by trusting in Yehoshua as Messiah and Redeemer who died on a cross for our sins, you shall be given eternal life.[John 1:12, 13; 20:31; 1 John5:13]

Sometimes overlooked, John is writing particularly to the most zealous Jews living under the Mosaic Law, the Jews in Jerusalem and Judea. (Many zealous and hardcore Jews then and even now are indeed very hostile to Yehoshua and the Gospel.) This is why John uses the word "**signs**" frequently throughout his Gospel. The apostle John has in mind his unbelieving Jewish brethren whom he wants to reach with the Gospel. Signs are less emphasized in some of the other Gospel writers. KJV uses the word *miracles* perhaps due the Latin Bible. The GK word is _semeion_, *signs*. In fact, John gives (as noted above) *eight* very distinct signs to establish that Yehoshua is the Anointed One, which is the Messiah or the Christ. Yehoshua is indeed the Lamb of God, the Redeemer of the world.

> The next day he [*John the Baptist*] saw Jesus coming to him and said, "Behold, **the Lamb of God who takes away the sin of the world!**" Johr. 1:29

Allow me to say again, John writes his Gospel for evangelistic purposes. This is very evident throughout his Gospel. Here are some of the key words John frequently uses which emphasis for evangelism: _believe_ (or trust); _signs_ (or miracles); _life_ [e.g., eternal life] ; _light_; the "**I AM**" (HEB name for God, **YHWH**),[Exo.3:13-15] _witness_; _truth_; and _glory_ to mention a few.

John is very direct and forceful in his writing. One might even say John is feisty in his words. John is ready to confront the ardent cynic, the unbelievers. The apostle John is bold and brassy. He even takes a poke at those who profess to believe in Him but do not openly and publicly declare Yehoshua as Lord and only Redeemer. "For they loved the praise of men more than the praise of God."[John 12:43 KJV] In one incident when the Samaritan did not receive Jesus, James and John wanted to call fire from Heaven on the Samaritan.[Luke 9:54-62] At Jesus' arrest, I am certain that if James and John had a sword like Peter, they would have sought to cut off some heads. John is intensely *bold*, *brassy*, and *a fighter* for God. How desperately the church needs bold men like the apostles. Would you dare to be bold for Jesus: 'Go out into the highways and hedges, and compel *them* to come in, that my house may be filled.'[Luke 14:23 KJV]

Table of Contents

Part One
John's Prologue
The Word Became Incarnate

Part Two
The Miraculous Signs of Jesus

The First Miraculous Miracle and Sign
Jesus Transformed Water into Wine

The Second Miraculous Miracle and Sign
Jesus Heals a Nobleman's Son

The Third Miraculous Miracle and Sign
Jesus Heals a Paralytic of Thirty-Eight Years

The Fourth Miraculous Miracle and Sign
Jesus Feeds 30,000 with 2 Fishes and 5 Barley-cakes

The Fifth Miraculous Miracle and Sign
Jesus Walks on the Sea of Galilee

The Sixth Miraculous Miracle and Sign
Jesus Heals a Blind Man from Birth

**The Seventh Miraculous Miracle and Sign
Jesus Raises Lazarus from the Dead**

**The Eighth Miraculous Miracle and Sign
Jesus Raises His Body from the Dead**

ABBREVIATIONS AND ACRONYMS

ABPE = Aramaic Bible in Plain English

AFV = A Faithful Version

AKJV = American King James Version 1999, by Michael Peter (Stone) Engelbrite

AMP = Amplified Bible

ARA or ARC = Aramaic

ASV = American Standard Version

BSB = Berean Study Bible and BLB = Berean Literal Bible

BYZ = Byzantine manuscripts

CEB = Common English Bible

CEV = Contemporary English Version

cf. = clarified

Coptic = referring Egyptian text; Egyptian Christians

Coverdale Bible = Miles Coverdale Bible 1535

CSB or HCSB = Holman Christian Standard Bible

1 Chro. = 1 Chronicles, OT

2 Chro. = 2 Chronicles, OT

1 Cor. = 1 Corinthians, NT epistle

2 Cor. = 2 Corinthians, NT epistle

CJB = Complete Jewish Bible

DBT = Darby Bible Translation,

Deut. = Deuteronomy, OT

Ecc. or Eccl. = Ecclesiastes, OT

ENG = English

Eph. = Ephesians, NT epistle

ERV = English Revised Version, 1885

ESV = English Standard Version

Ezek. = Ezekiel, OT

Ex. or Exo. = Exodus

f = the following verse

ff = the following verses

Gal. = Galatians, NT epistle

Gen. = Genesis, OT

GK = Greek NT

GNV = Geneva Bible (1599 edition) Bible Gateway

GNT = Good News Translation

GWT = God's Word Translation

HEB = Hebrew language of the OT

Heb. =Hebrews, NT epistle

Isa. = Isaiah, OT

ISV = International Standard Version

James = NT epistle

Job = book of the OT

John = the Gospel of John, NT

1 John = the First Epistle of John, NT epistle

2 John = the Second Epistle of John, NT epistle

3 John = the Third Epistle of John, NT epistle

Josh. = Joshua, OT

Jude = NT epistle

Judges = book of the OT

1 Kings = book of the OT

2 Kings = book of the OT

KJV = King James Version; NKJV = New King James Version

lit. = literally

Latin = LAT.

Latin/English = LAT/ENG

LSV = Literal Standard Version 2020

LET = Literal Emphasis Translation 2017

Luke = the Gospel of Luke, NT

LVE = Latin Vulgate in ENG

LXE (& LXA) = GK OT (Septuagint) in ENG

LXX = Septuagint, GK OT

Mark = Gospel of Mark, NT

MSS = manuscript(s)

Matt. or Mat = Gospel of Matthew

MSG = The Message

NAS = New American Standard 2020 and Update 1995

NCV = New Century Version

NEB = New English Bible

NEH = Nehemiah, OT

NHEB = New Heart English Bible,

NIV = New International Version

NKJV = New King James Version, Thomas Nelson, 1982

NLT = New Living Translation

NRS = New Revised Standard 1989

NT = New Testament

OT = Old Testament

p = page

pp = pages

OJB = Orthodox Jewish Bible

1 Peter = NT epistle

2 Peter = NT epistle

Psa. = Psalm, OT

Phi. Or Phil. = Philippians, NT epistle

PTL = Praise the Lord

PNT or Philips NT = J B Philip's NT

Prov. = Proverbs, OT

Rev. = Revelation, NT epistle

Rom. = Romans, NT epistle

1 Tim. = 1 Timothy, NT epistle

2 Tim. = 2 Timothy, NT epistle

1 Sam. = 1 Samuel, OT

1 Thess. = 1 Thessalonians, NT epistle

2 Thess. = 2 Thessalonians, NT epistle

TNT = Tyndale New Testament, 1534

Titus = NT epistle

TRE = Textus Receptus in ENG (GK text of the KJV)

VUL = Latin Vulgate

WBT = Webster's Bible Translation

WEB = World English Bible

WNT = Weymouth NT

WYC = Wycliffe Bible

YLT = Young's Literal Translation

Introduction

Thex style and study of this volume by the author is similar to his other writings. There is no significant change in the formatting. Yet, the style is different as he lays out the primary text of Scripture for discussion in each chapter. (There are no memory verses) The author establishes a brief introduction and a short conclusion at the end of each chapter. At the top of each page, there will be the *chapter title* on one side of page and *on the opposite page there is the chapter subtitle*. Hopefully, this style of formatting shall help guide the reading and working through "*The Miraculous Miracles and Signs of Jesus*" more effectively.

As in previous writings by the author, there are occasional footnotes, which the reader should find informative and helpful in the study of the Gospel of John. These footnotes have been placed at the end of each chapter. In addition, you find a list of abbreviations and acronyms starting on page xv, as well as an index, and list of other books, tracts, and songs by Dr. Parsons.

As many may know, Scripture quotations are from various translations. The various translations have been used for variety of purposes but especially for clarity in some texts. When Scripture is quoted in a separate paragraph, the texts will be indented and in smaller fonts. When Scripture quotations are within the paragraph, the font size remains the same size within the paragraph. The Scripture quotations will be from the New American Standard, 2020 and the 1995 *updated* edition unless noted in the text. Some of the other major Scripture quotations are from the Geneva Bible (GNV) 1599; King James Version (KJV) 1611; American Standard Version (ASV) 1901; New Revised Standard (NRS) 1989; New English Translation (NET) 2005; the New International Version (NIV) 2011; English Standard Version (ESV) 2011; the Common English Bible (CEB) 2011; the Berean Study Bible (BSB) 2016;

the Majority Standard Bible (which uses the BYZ text, 2022). Also, there are quotes from the Literal Standard Version (LSV) 2022.

If a Hebrew (HEB) or a Greek (GK) word is given, the word is spelled out phonetically in English (ENG). Small and large brackets (⁰, []) are used to indicate a word or phrase is added to clarify the Scripture text, but the insertion is not part of the original text or translation. The GK OT is quoted in the ENG from Septuagint [LXX] by Brenton (1851). When the author uses personal paraphrases, the word(s) are placed in *italics* and indented.

There are occasional footnotes at the end of the chapter as noted above. The footnotes are placed at end of each chapter for quick reference but to avoid distraction of the reading. The footnotes are for those who are inclined to probe more into the subject.

Similarly, for the clarity of a word, there are inserted *like footnote fashion* within the Scripture texts, which the reader should also find informative. These footnotes are located immediately below the Scripture text. In addition, occasionally, the author has added notes in brackets within the main text of Scripture but in a reference format. These occasional footnotes have been marked by letter, e.g., [a]. Often brackets "⁰" are sometimes used to alert the reader, but sometime brackets may be omitted. Please keep in mind that annotations are placed in the text similar to footnotes but remain in the text for immediate and quick clarity. For instance,

> But as many as received him, to them gave he [the] power to become the sons[a] of God, *even* to them that believe on his name: Which were born, not of blood, nor of the will of the flesh, nor of the will of man, but of God.　　　　　　　　　　　　　　　　　　John 1:12, 13 (KJV)

[a]The word "son" is GK *teknon*, meaning is *children*.

Here is another example,

> "I and my Father, We are One[b]."　　　　　　　　　John 10:30 (ABPE)

[b]"We are One" is the most literal translation. The expression "*we are One*" is the meaning, but while this is understood by translators, the expression is not translated in ENG.

The insertions are to keep the flow going for reader by providing an immediate clarity without disrupting the flow and reading.

For those who are a little more meticulous, the HEB OT and GK NT with various readings and difference by variance in translations are utilized. This includes consulting various HEB and GK lexicons. The Holy Spirit is precise in what He reveals. Nevertheless, there are words declared in Scripture that are significant in meaning. So, sometimes these words are essential to probe further. For instance,

> "The thief comes only to steal and kill and destroy; I came that they may have life, and have *it* abundantly. I am the good shepherd; **the good** **shepherd lays down His life for the sheep.**"   John 10:10, 11

> ᵍThe word "good" is the GK *kalos*. The emphasis of *kalos* is that the Shepherd *does good things for His sheep*. Another GK word for "good" is *agathos*, but *agathos* means relatively good person.^Rom. 5:7

So, let us give careful attention to the Scripture text and especially the more difficult texts and issues. Thus, challenging each of us to pay close attention to the verse(s) at hand.

This study is divided into two main divisions.

The first is "Part One. This is the **prologue** or the apostle John's **introduction**. The introduction is John 1:1-18. Please give careful attention to this section. This is because it is from the introduction that John lays the foundation and purpose for writing his Gospel. John is indeed very transparent in his purpose for writing.

> But to all who have received him [Jesus Christ]_ those who believe in his name– he has given the right [GK *exousia*: legitimate authoritative] to become God's children– children not born by human parents or by human desire or a husband's decision, but by God.   John. 1:12, 13 (NET)

There are many things revealed in John's introduction (the Gospel of John). There are four things that loom out to the forefront in his prologue.

First, John declares that Messiah Yehoshua is "**the Creator**" of everything. In fact, without Messiah Yehoshua there is absolutely nothing that would exist even the entire universe and all that is in it. The Messiah Yehoshua created it and sustain it all by His power and authority.

Second, John declares the **Word** (the **Logos**) came to **Illuminate** or enlighten mankind. In Yehoshua, there is **light**, but without Him, a person gropes in darkness. (Listen, without Jesus as Lord and Savior, a person can only grope in this world for God.) Ah, but those who genuinely received and personally know Him as Lord and Redeemer and walk in obedience to Him, He **enlightens** and even delivers them from the evil forces of darkness.^Acts 26:16, 17; Col.1:13, 14 All outside Yehoshua's redemption (all of fallen humanity) come up short of the mark. For "In whom [Christ Jesus the Lord] are hid all the treasures of wisdom and knowledge."[Col. 2:3 KJV]

Third, John is very clear that God is the invisible God, but God has **tabernacled** in flesh and blood in Yehoshua the Messiah and Redeemer. Yehoshua came, and He has come to explain and make the invisible God known to mankind. All those that personally trust and receive Yehoshua as Lord and Savior are given the absolute guarantee of **eternal life** with Him **today**. The Messiah will give eternal life with Him in Heaven. However, if you do not trust and receive Him, you shall most assuredly perish eternity in the wrath of God in the Lake of Fire.

Fourth, John presents Yehoshua the **Revelator** and **Revelation** of God. Yehoshua is the complete embodiment of all truth.[Col. 2:3] Yehoshua does not possess some truth; **Yehoshua is indeed the Revelator of ALL TRUTH**. To declare that Yehoshua is the possessor all truth, many unbelievers cannot bear to hear such declaration. For them, truth is relative and continuingly changing. Hence, there is no absolute truth.

The other division is "Part Two;" this is the eight signs (or miracles) in the Gospel of John. Some only note seven signs. Why do some expositors chose just seven signs instead of eight? I do not know. However, there are clearly and distinctly eight signs in the apostle John's Gospel. The eighth sign is the resurrection of Jesus Himself and by His own enate power and authority. However, some put forth the notion that John 21:1-14 is the eighth sign, but the text in John 21 is not classified as a sign. Scripture is explicit that Yehoshua intrinsically raise His physical body from the dead. Hence, the resurrection of Jesus Christ is unequivocally and indisputably the eighth sign.

The first sign (miracle) by our Lord occurs at a wedding. The wedding host ran out of wine. (This is probably due to an over-extended and unexpected large crowd.) Mary tells Jesus that host is out of wine. Though Jesus already knew this occurred, He responded by declaring,

> Jesus said to her, "Woman, what does your concern have to do with Me? My hour has not yet come."   John 2:4 (NKJ)

Jesus' response, 'My hour has not yet come.' Perhaps His statement suggest that this is not the precise time now to begin His public ministry. This was especially true since His ministry to Israel included signs, wonders, and miracles.[Heb. 2:1-4] Nevertheless, Jesus in His mercy performs His first sign by transforming water into wine. Yet, because Jesus said, 'My hour has not yet come,' this amazing sign seems to have been done *incognito*. No one knew or even aware of the amazing miracle except the disciples and the servants who drew the water, which was transformed into wine. Yet, it seems the rest of those at the wedding are oblivious this sign. Still, as we shall see, this miracle must have been made known later to some servants serving the wine.

The second sign is the healing of nobleman's son. Apparently, the nobleman was very distraught and feared his son would die. The nobleman implores and begs Jesus to come immediately to help. The nobleman asked Jesus to come with him at once for fear his son will die. Jesus told the nobleman to go home to his son: 'Your son lives [*now*].'John 4:50

The third amazing sign is when Jesus instantly heals a man who had been a paralytic for thirty-eight years. The religious leaders were angry with Jesus because He heals the paralytic on the Sabbath. The Pharisees were very upset that Jesus not only violated the Sabbath by healing the paralytic, but Jesus refers to God as His Father. Hence, Jesus declares *Himself to be equal with God*. (The cults stumble over Jesus declaring Himself equal to God.)

The fourth astonishing sign is when Yehoshua feeds five thousand men, and this is not counting all women and children present who were also fed. Thus, a conservative estimate would probably be nearly thirty thousand or perhaps more. The multitude was fed with just five small loaves of barley (perhaps like five small barley-cakes) and two small fish by Jesus' miracle. This is an astonishing miracle. This sign leaves the critics dumbfounded and in denial.

The fifth amazing sign that apostle John records is Yehoshua walk on the Sea of Galilee. Our Lord walks on the water during a violent wind storm and at night. Incredible! This is indeed a remarkable, miraculous sign. Yehoshua (Jesus) is Lord over all natural physical Laws of nature. This is certainly understandable when we realize Christ the Lord is the Creator and Sustainer of all things.

Also, I include the miracle of Peter walking on the Sea of Galilee during very turbulent storm. (This miracle is only recorded in Matthew; so, this miracle is omitted in John's Gospel.) The disciples were all in the boat during violent storm, and Peter sees who he thought was the Lord. Then, he says, "Lord if that is really You, command me to come to You on the water." Jesus tells Peter, 'Come,' and incredibly, Peter steps out of boat and walks on water. There are very important lessons we need to learn here. Therefore, don't overlook these lessons.

The sixth sign is Jesus heals a man who has been blind since birth. The blind man is completely healed. Pharisees interrogate the man *twice* who was healed of his blindness. Yet, the Pharisees were so angry with the man's response that the religious leaders throw the man out of the temple. It is also, one of rare encounters with Jesus where He openly declares that He is the Messiah, the Son of man, the Son of God.

The seventh astonishing sign is when Jesus raise Lazarus from the dead. Jesus delays in going to heal Lazarus, and so, when Jesus arrives at Lazarus' home, Lazarus is already in the grave. Lazarus had been dead four days. His body had already begun to decompose, to rot. This amazing miracle and sign was performed before the unbelieving Jews. This miraculous sign could not be denied or refuted by the unbelieving Jews. So, the leading Jewish leaders plan to kill both Lazarus and Jesus.

This is a special added chapter once this manuscript was completed. I thought there was a critical need to discuss *where was Lazarus while his body lie in the tomb*? There are some very grim errors that have creeped into the churches as Jude warns.[Jude 1:3, 4] Therefore, this added chapter is very important; please study it well.

The eighth sign is when Jesus lays down His life on the cross and dies; He raises His own body from the dead three days later. There are very many things we could all learn concerning the death and the resurrection. We shall note particularly three things. One, Jesus declares His death and resurrection numerous times to the disciples. Yet ironically, the disciples did not perceive or grasp what Jesus was telling then. Still, the disciples did not ask Him what He means.

Secondly and conversely, some of the unbelieving Jewish leaders actually perceived Jesus' prediction of His death and resurrection. True! Surprisingly, Jesus prediction of His death and resurrection was *not* concealed from the unbelievers Jews leaders, which seems to me to be very ironic indeed. For example, we read,

> The next day, the one after Preparation Day, the chief priests and the Pharisees went to Pilate. [63]"Sir," they said, "we remember that while he was still alive that **deceiver said, 'After three days I will rise again.'** [64]So give the order for the tomb to be made secure until the third day. Otherwise, his disciples may come and steal the body and tell the people that he has been raised from the dead. This last deception will be worse than the first." [65]"Take a guard," Pilate answered. "Go, make the tomb as secure as you know how." [66]So they went and made the tomb secure by putting a seal on the stone and posting the guard.
>
> Matt. 27:62-66 (NIV)

Thirdly, it is very important to note and fully realize that the **shed blood** and **death are intricately interwoven** together in our Lord's redemption of humankind. Some men of the faith allege the death Christ is sufficient in our redemption. However, the shed blood is equally very important in connection of our redemption.

> And almost all things are by the law purged with blood; and without shedding of blood is no remission [*forgiveness of sin*]. Heb. 9:22 (KJV)

> For I delivered to you first of all that which I also received: that Christ died for our sins according to the Scriptures, and that He was buried, and that He rose again the third day according to the Scriptures.
>
> 1 Cor. 15:3, 4 (NKJ)

Friend, our redemption was completed at the cross. This is why Jesus said when He laid down His life upon the cross for our sins,

> Therefore when Jesus had received the sour wine, He said, **"It is finished!"** And He bowed His head and gave up His spirit. John 19:30

Part One

The Word Became Incarnate

PART ONE

John's Prologue

In the beginning was the Word, and the Word was with God, and the Word was God. ²He was in the beginning with God. ³All things came into being through Him, and apart from Him nothing came into being that has come into being. ⁴In Him was life, and the life was the Light of men. ⁵The Light shines in the darkness, and the darkness did not comprehend[a] it. ⁶There came a man sent from God, whose name was John [the Baptist]. ⁷He came as a witness, to testify about the Light, so that all might believe through him. ⁸He was not the Light, but *he came* to testify about the Light. ⁹There [the Word] was the true Light which, coming into the world, enlightens every man. ¹⁰He was in the world, and the world was made [created] through Him, and the world did not know Him. ¹¹He came to His own [people], and those who were His own [but many of His covenant people] did not receive Him. ¹²But as many as received Him, to them He gave the right [legitimate authority] to become children of God, *even* to those who believe in His name, ¹³who were born, not of blood nor of the will of the flesh nor of the will of man, but of God. ¹⁴And the Word became flesh, and dwelt among us, and we saw His glory, glory as of the only begotten from the Father, full of grace and truth. ¹⁵John [the Baptist] testified about Him and cried out, saying, "This was He of whom I said, 'He who comes after me has a higher rank than I,[b] for He existed before me.'" ¹⁶For of His fullness we have all received, and grace upon grace. ¹⁷For the Law was given through Moses; grace and truth were realized through Jesus Christ. ¹⁸No one has seen God at any time; the only begotten God[a] who is in the bosom of the Father, He has explained *Him*.   (John 1:1-18)

[a]Note: "*comprehend*" is the GK word is *katalambano*. The full import *katalambano* can also mean that the darkness could not "*overpower*" or "*overtake it*." This is the preferred meaning.

[b]"Higher rank than I" [v 15 NAS]: the translation by NAS might be misunderstood. Literally, "*He* was before me." The NIV the NET, and CEB is preferred "he *existed* before me." Though word "*existed*" is not in the GK text, this is likely closer to the meaning in the context since the Word *existed* before all eternity.[John 1:1-3]

'"-- *the only begotten God*" is preferred GK text even though this a difficult textual statement. While the phrase, "The only begotten Son" is acceptable as well, the more difficult textual reading is preferred, "-- *the only begotten God*". Therefore, there is a variance in the GK texts. So, there is debate among scholars. Yet, the translation preferred is: "*monogenēs Theos*, the only begotten God."

CHAPTER 1

Christ the Lord
is the Creator of all things

In the beginning was the Word, and the Word was with God, and the
Word was fully God. The Word was with God in the beginning. All
things were created by him, and apart from him not one thing was
created that has been created.   John 1:1-3 (NET)

Introduction

All four Gospels focus mainly on Jesus public ministries to Israel, [Matt. 15:24;
Rom. 15:8] which was perhaps three and half years. There is a difference of emphasis
by each of the Gospel writers to Jesus' ministry. Matthew, Mark, and Luke, place
their emphasis upon Jesus' northern ministry, the Galilean and Perea regions. John
places his emphasis upon the southern ministry, Judea and Jerusalem regions.

As noted earlier, Matthew's writing is likely directed more towards a
general Jewish audience. Matthew seems to emphasize Jesus as the *King* and
rightful *Messianic Ruler* to his Jewish audience. It is natural therefore for
Matthew to use key words such as: *"kingdom of heaven"* (Kingdom of God)
or *"to fulfill* or *fulfillment,"* *"it is written."* *"This was to fulfill —"* Matthews
traces the genealogy through Joseph through Solomon's lineage. However, the
rightful lineage line is through Mary's lineage. Joseph's lineage traces back to
Solomon, but the lineage through Solomon was cut off from the royal line.[Jer.
22:20] Luke traces Jesus' lineage back to Nathan (another son of David) through
Mary. Both Solomon and Nathan were born through Bathsheba. Since Jesus
lineage is traced back to Bathsheba, this in itself demonstrates to me the won-

derful and very great mercy and longsuffering God gave to Bathsheba and mankind. David had committed adulty with Bathsheba. In attempt cover up the adulty, David had Uriah the Hittite, the husband of Bathsheba, appears as though he was accidently killed in battle. Still, David having Uriah on the *frontline of the battle* was a murderous act on his part. I say this because Bathsheba may not have had any power to refuse David since he was the king.

Matthew's emphasis is that the Messiah came to "fulfill" the Scripture and the promises of God.[Matt. 5:17, 18] For example, Matthew records that Jesus' early life living in Egypt is a direct fulfillment of the Scriptures as Messiah. For example,

> When he arose, he [Joseph] took the young Child [Jesus] and His mother [Mary] by night and departed for Egypt, and [*the child Jesus*] was there until the death of Herod, **that it might be <u>fulfilled</u> which was spoken by the Lord through the prophet**, saying, "Out of Egypt I called My Son."
>
> Matt. 2:14, 15 (NKJ) [See Hosea 11:1]

Mark maybe appealing more to the Roman or Greek (Gentile) mindset (which I also mentioned earlier). Mark gives little emphasis in quoting from the HEB Scripture and prophetic fulfillment. (The GK mind would have little interest in fulfillment of Scripture like the Jews who would surely have keen interest in fulfilling prophetic prophecy.) The Greek and Roman mind is more interested in Jesus' <u>authority</u>, <u>power</u>, and a man of decisive <u>action</u>. Key words in Mark are: *"immediately* (KJV, *straightway*)," *"Gospel* or *Good News*," and *"teaches with authority."* Mark portrays or depicts Jesus as a man with *absolute authority* and *power*.

> [21]Then they went to Capernaum. When the Sabbath came, Jesus went into the synagogue and began to teach. [22]The people there were amazed by his teaching, because he taught them like one who had **authority**, not like the experts in the law. [23]Just then there was a man in their synagogue with an unclean spirit, and he cried out, [24]"Leave us alone, Jesus the Nazarene! Have you come to destroy us? I know who you are – the Holy One of God!" [25]But Jesus rebuked him [the spirit]: "Silence! Come out of him!" [26]After throwing him [demon possessed man] into convulsions, the unclean spirit cried out with a loud voice and came out of him. [27]They were all amazed so that they asked each other, "What is this? A new teaching **with authority**! He even **commands the unclean spirits** and **they obey him.**" [28]So the news about him spread quickly throughout all the region around Galilee.　　　　Mark 1:21-28 (NET)

2

Luke's Gospel (as I have said) was written by one of Paul's closest companions, which the apostle calls, "beloved physician."[Col. 4:14] So, Luke may have written the Gospel of Luke and Acts as possible defense for Paul in Rome.[Luke 1:1-4; Acts 1:1, 2]

Luke does not necessarily seem to follow the chronology timeline of the of Matthew and Mark. Luke seems to focus on "detail account information of some events" rather than a strict chronological timeline. For example, Luke records the beheading of John the Baptist death sometime after the event.

Luke's Gospel key words are: *"salvation," "the Holy Spirit,"* emphasis on the *poor*, Jesus as the *Son of man*, and *"repentance."* Luke gives detail in his Gospel such as, Jesus' birth, death, resurrection, and ascension. Luke's writings (Luke and Acts) are somewhat equal in size to Paul's writings of his epistle. Thus, Luke's and Paul's writings encompasses two/thirds of the NT. This alone illustrates the importance of Dr. Luke's and the apostle Paul's contribution to the NT. Furthermore, Luke may have been the only Gentile given authority as a scribe to pen Scripture. (If indeed Luke was not of Hebrew descent or ethnic heritage, this gives Luke a unique distinction.)

There is an emphasis in Luke in which he stresses *"the kingdom is already but not yet."* One aspect of this emphasis is noted with the presence of the Holy Spirit throughout Luke's writing. Luke presenting the idea of **"the kingdom already but not yet"** is noted with Luke's unique future for Israel.

> They [*Israel as a nation*] will fall by the edge of the sword and be led captive among all nations, and Jerusalem will be trampled underfoot by the Gentiles, **until the times of the Gentiles are fulfilled**.
>
> Luke 21:24 (ESV)

> So when they had gathered together, they began to ask him, **"Lord, is this the time when you are restoring the kingdom to Israel?"** [a] [7]He told them, **"You are not permitted to know the times or periods** that the Father has set by his own authority. [8] But you will receive power when the Holy Spirit has come upon you, and you will be my witnesses in Jerusalem, and in all Judea and Samaria, and to the farthest parts of the earth." Acts 1:6-8 (NET)

[a]Note: Jesus' answer was **neither**, *"yes"* or *"no."* 'You are not permitted to know the times or periods that the Father has set by his own authority.'[V6 NET] So, there is nothing implied in *canceling*, *replaying*, or *postponing* God's promise to Israel.[Luke 22:28-30; 21:24; Rom. 11:24-27]

Again, Paul refers to Israel as covenant people (see Rom. 11:24-27) which yet to be fulfilled. Unfortunately, perhaps as high as ninety percent of the professing Christians see no restoration of Israel. This is likely do to the Romanist's and traditionalist's influences against any future restoration of the nation Israel. (Unfortunately, *Somatic prejudices* still continue to loom over the theological world.) Many in the professing Christian leaders allege that the church is now "*spiritually the new Israel.*" Therefore, many have alleged there is no future reign of Isreal on earth or a future kingdom in Jerusalem. Thus, many are alleging that the Church is now spiritually Israel. Hence, Christ's reign is in Heaven and not on earth.

However, Isaiah declares that Israel shall be taught by the Lord God Himself, "All your children will be disciples of the LORD— I will make peace abound for your children."[Isa. 54:13 CEB] See John 6:45. (Prophecy may have some application to Jesus' tthree- and half-year ministry, but this is indeed a future prophecy.) There are a host of promises of the regathering of Israel from the nations, which promises comes from God who cannot lie.[Isa. 10:20; 11:11f; Jer. 23:3; Zech. 10:10; etc.]

John's Gospel presents **Jesus as very God incarnate**. Thus, Jesus is indeed Almighty God who tabernacles Himself in humanity, and the Word continues fully as God and fully man in one person, Jesus Christ. Jesus came to redeem fallen mankind that will genuinely receive Him as Messiah and Redeemer. Nevertheless, each individual must genuinely trust and personally receive and make the commitment and relying on Jesus as the Messiah and the only Lord and Savior.

> But as many as received him, to them gave he [the] power to become the sons[b] of God, *even* to them that believe on his name: Which were born, not of blood, nor of the will of the flesh, nor of the will of man, but of God. John 1:12, 13 (KJV)

[b]The word "son" is the GK *teknon*, meaning *children*.

John's Gospel, as I have said, is strongly Evangelistic. The apostle John emphasis on evangelism is more so than the other Gospel writers. Thus, some of John's key words are: "*father*" nearly 120 times. The word "*believe*" is used nearly 100 times. Other significant words in John are: *life* (often implying *eternal life*), *word, love, witness* (or *record* or *testimony* which is the same in the GK) to mention a few. John is *clear* and *upfront* for his purpose for writing the Gospel of Gospel:

> And many other signs truly did Jesus in the presence of his disciples, which are not written in this book: But these are written, that ye might

believe that Jesus is the Christ, the Son of God; and that believing ye might have [*eternal*] life through his name.   John 20:30, 31 (KJV)

Similarly, in his first epistle, John writes,

> If we receive the witness of men, the witness of God is greater: for the witness of God is this, that he hath borne witness concerning his Son. [10]He that believeth on the Son of God hath the witness in him: he that believeth not God hath made him a liar; because he hath not believed in the witness that God hath borne concerning his Son. [11]And the witness is this, that God gave unto us eternal life, and this [eternal] life is in his Son. [12]He that hath the Son hath the [eternal] life; he that hath not the Son of God hath not the [eternal] life. [13]These things have I written unto you, that ye may know that ye have eternal life, *even* unto you that believe on the name of the Son of God.   1 John 5:9-13 (ASV)

A. The Word was fully God

Let us parallel the text in John's Gospel between the KJV and the NET. Note that they are practically identical.

In the beginning was the Word—and the Word was with God—and the Word was God. 1:1 KJV	In the beginning was the Word— and the Word was with God— and the Word was fully God. 1:1 NET

1.   "In the beginning was the Word—"

As John uses the word "*beginning*," he has in mind creation of all things. There are two things we do not want to overlook in the apostle's meaning of word "*beginning*." John uses the expression to refer to Christ as "the **Word**." "The **Word**" is indeed a unique expression that John uses to refer to Christ [v] [14]. John presents Christ the Lord as the Eternal One Himself (the Self-Existent One or the Eternal One) with the Father and the Holy Spirit.

> Jesus said to them, "Most assuredly, I say to you, before Abraham was, **I AM**."   John 8:58 (NKJ)

Jesus applies the sacred name "**I AM**" [HEB **YHWH**] to Himself.[Exo. 3:13-15] (This is known as the *Tetragrammaton*: the four HEB letter referring the Lord our God, **YHWH**.) Therefore, the apostle John comes outright and plainly declares that Christ the Lord is indeed Almighty God.

The second thing we must grasp or understand is that Christ the Lord is then equal within the Trinity of God. There is no false assertion of *subordinationism* or evil doctrine of the "Oneness doctrine."[1] There is but one God, but God is Triune (the Father, the Son, and the Holy Spirit), which is a mystery hidden in God alone.

So then, John is declaring the Word (which is Christ the Lord) has existed from all eternity. The Word is without beginning or ending, from everlasting to everlasting, He is the Eternal God. Hallelujah!

2.   "and the Word was **with** God—"

The express that "the Word was *with* [GK *pros*] God" has the emphasis of be *face to face* and completely equal within the Triune of God as noted above. Thus, implying there is an equality: *face to face* within the Trinity of God. Christ is *face to face* within the Godhead because Christ the Lord is fully God Himself.

This is very evident with Jesus' teaching and dialogue with Philip who requested to see the Father.

> If you have known me, you will know my Father too. And from now on you do know him and have seen him." [8]Philip said, "Lord, show us the Father, and we will be content." [9]Jesus replied, "Have I been with you for so long, and you have not known me, Philip? The person who has seen me has seen the Father! How can you say, 'Show us the Father'? [10]Do you not believe that I am in the Father, and the Father is in me? The words that I say to you, I do not speak on my own initiative, but the Father residing in me performs his miraculous deeds. [11]Believe me that I am in the Father, and the Father is in me, but if you do not believe me, believe because of the miraculous deeds themselves.   John 14:7-11 (NET)

As noted above, this is not the false doctrine of the Oneness doctrine, or also known modalism. (See note # 1 at end of the chapter). Jesus did not say He is the Father or the Father is the Son. Jesus said, 'Believe me that I am in the Father and the Father is in me.'[John 14:11]

This is excellently illustrated in the translation of [John 10:30].

> "I and my Father, **We are One**.'"   John 10:30 (ABPE)

> '"**We are One**" is the most literal translation. The expression "**We are One**" is the meaning, but while this is understood by translators, the expression is not translated in ENG.

3. "and the Word was God."

John seals his intention conclusively in his last phrase. Let us note the complete opening sentence once again,

> In the beginning was the Word, and the Word was with God, and the
> **Word was God**.   John 1:1 (KJV)

Whether some believe God's Word is inerrant, the Bible, well friend rest on them. However, disbelief is the same as declaring God a liar. Friend, God has given us His Word, the Bible, that we can know Him personally and receive eternal life through Jesus Christ.[John 3:18, 36] In addition, we may have fellowship with the living in the "here and now." So, only a fool would dare call God and His Word a liar.

> - **Let God be true, and every human being a liar**. As it is written: "So
> that you may be proved right when you speak and prevail when you
> judge."   Rom. 3:4 (NIV)

If anyone dare to deny Christ is Almighty God after the truth has been explicitly make known to them through God's Word the Bible, then, they have condemned themselves to Hell. Jesus' warning is very true.

> "Enter through the narrow gate; for the gate is wide and the way is
> broad that leads to destruction, and there are many who enter through
> it. [14]"For the gate is small and the way is narrow[d] that leads to life, and
> **THERE ARE FEW WHO FIND IT**. [15]"Beware of the false prophets,
> who come to you in sheep's clothing, but inwardly are ravenous wolves.
>   Matt. 7:13-15

> [d]The GK word "_thlibo_" (_narrow_) does not mean in context _difficult_ or
> _hard_. Jesus is explicit, _His yoke is easy or burden is light_.[Matt. 11:28-30] So,
> perhaps the NAS is perhaps a little closer to the intended meaning: "For
> the gate is small [GK _stenos_] and the way is narrow [GK _thlibo_] that leads to life,
> and there are few who find it."

As noted above, have we forgotten Jesus words of comfort?

> "Come to Me, all who are weary and heavy-laden, and **I will give you
> rest**. Take My yoke upon you and learn from Me, **for I am gentle** and
> **humble in heart**, and **YOU WILL FIND REST FOR YOUR SOULS**.
> For My **YOKE IS EASY** and **MY BURDEN IS LIGHT**."
>   Matt. 11:28-30

7

Unfortunately, some translators look at the words as religion rather than as in relationship. Friend, without Jesus as Lord and Savior, then, the road is difficult and hard. Jesus has all power and authority, and He promises never to leave you or forsake you.^{Heb. 13:5} Jesus is the only Savior.^{Acts 4;12; John 14;6} Jesus is the Great Shepherd.^{Psa. 23; Heb. 13:20, 21} Praise God, we have two abiding Comforters: the **risen Lord Jesus** and **the Holy Spirit**. Jesus promises He and the Holy Spirit will be with us forever.^{John 14:16; 15:26} Hallelujah! There is only victory in Jesus. We overcome by the blood of the Lamb.

Jesus warns those who may be foolish and reject Him as the only Lord and Savior, as given by the Literal Standard Version,

> I said, therefore, to you, that you will die in your sins, for if you may not ^[do not] believe that **I AM,**^e you will die in your sins." John 8:24 (LSV)

^eThe "*he*" is not in the GK text, but many translators think it is implied. So, some translators place the "*he*" in the text, but the pronoun is not in the GK text.

B. The Word was with God in the beginning

The next sentence by John is similar, which may be John's Hebraic background being repetitive. For example, David says by Spirit of God,

> Who is this majestic king? The LORD who is strong and mighty! The LORD who is mighty in battle! ⁹Look up, you gates! Rise up, you eternal doors! Then the majestic king will enter! ¹⁰Who is this majestic king? The LORD who commands armies! He is the majestic king! (Selah)
>
> Ps. 24:8-10 (NET)

Similarly, the apostle John says,

In the beginning was the Word, and the Word was with God, and the Word was God.
1:1 KJV

The same ^[lit. *this One*] **was in the beginning with God.** 1:2 KJV

Christ the Lord remains the same, and He does not change. Christ is immutable, unchangeable. The same Christ the Lord who spoke the world into beginning, is the same Christ the Lord who is within blessed Trinity of God, and He Himself is fully Eternal God. Christ the Lord is not like a chameleon, He does not change.

> [1]God, formerly multifariously and abundantly having spoken to the fathers in [by] the prophets, [2]At these last days spake [spoken] to us in [by] the Son, whom he set [established] heir of all things, by whom also he made the times [GK *aion, universe* NIV]; [3]Who being the brightness of glory, and the figure of his foundation, and bearing all things by the word of his power, having made by himself the purification of our sins, he sat down on the right hand of the Majesty among the highest ones; [4]Being so much better than the angels, inasmuch as he has inherited a more distinguished name than they.   Heb. 1:1-4 (SLT)

Again in verse 12,

> Like a robe you will roll them up, like a garment they will be changed. But you [*Lord*] are the same, and your [*Lord*] years will have no end [e.g. *You are eternal*]."   Heb. 1:12 (ESV)

Hebrews also says concerning Christ Jesus,

> Jesus Christ *is* the same yesterday, today, and forever.   Heb. 13:8 (NKJ)

This is why the angels told the disciples as the Lord Jesus ascended to Heaven,

> As they were still staring into the sky while he was going, suddenly two men [*angelic beings*] in white clothing stood near them and said, "Men of Galilee, why do you stand here looking up into the sky? **This same Jesus** who has been taken up from you into heaven **will come back in the same way** you saw him go into heaven."   Acts 1:10, 11 (NET)

Christ did not take on flesh and later discard the flesh. Neither did Christ the Lord set aside His eternal Deity during incarnation, but He did veil is glory during His time as the Servanthood. Christ the Lord is the eternal God that tabernacles Himself in flesh. It is impossible for Christ the Lord that He somehow discard His Deity or discard His humanity at any time. This is one of *"hairbrained nonsense"* that Christ somehow *disrobed Himself of His Deity or humanity*. This is perpetrated and concocted by many electric church preachers today. Listen to me, the Lord is **immutable forever**. Friend, Christ the Lord remains eternal God and He remains fully human as High Priest before the Throne of God on our behalf.

> But we see him [*Christ*] who for a little while was made [condescended] lower[f] than the angels, namely Jesus, crowned with glory and honor because of the suffering of death, so that **by the grace of God he might TASTE DEATH FOR EVERYONE**. [10]For it was fitting that he, **for whom**

and by whom all things exist, in bringing many sons to glory [a reference to Heaven], should make the founder [GK archegos, author NAS] of their salvation perfect through suffering.

[14]Since therefore the children share in flesh and blood, he himself likewise partook of the same things [e.g. same human nature], that through death he might destroy the one who has the power of death, that is, the devil, [15]and **deliver** all those who **through fear of death** were subject to lifelong slavery. [16]For surely it is not angels that he helps, but he helps the offspring of Abraham [that is the children humankind]. [17]Therefore he had to be made like his brothers in every respect, so that he might become a merciful and faithful high priest in the service of God, to **make propitiation for the sins of the people**. [18]For because he himself has suffered when tempted, he is able to help[g] those who are being tempted.

Heb. 2:9-10, 14-18 (ESV)

[f]Christ was **not** "*made lower than the angels*." The meaning is that our Lord humbled Himself, *condescending* and taking on flesh to save mankind. (See Phi. 2:5-11.)

[g]The meaning of the word "*help*" in GK is "*boetheo*" "[*the Lord*] *aids* the believers" [Heb. 1:14] when we pray when we are tempted or troubled. Keep in mind this a present ministry of our Lord, "a merciful and faithful high priest in the service of God." (See Heb. 4:14-16.)

What a pity, some hyper-dispensationalists do not rightly recognize the Epistle of Hebrews is for the body of Christ, the church.

Friend, at times, our prayers are often meaningless, empty, and futile. Therefore, it is also certain our prayers are unfortunately infrequent before the throne of God. Ah, but Jesus *knows all about are sorrows and all about trouble and all about our weaknesses*. Friend, Jesus Christ *is* the same yesterday and today and forever [Heb. 13:8]. Jesus is indeed "a merciful and faithful high priest in the service of God."[Heb. 2:18]

C. The Word created all things

The NAS 1995 gives the literal translation, which is excellent, but the import is far greater in meaning as given by the apostle John,

All things **came into being** through Him, and apart from Him [*without Christ the Lord*] **nothing came into being** that has come into being.

John 1:3

The meaning **is not** that the Christ was some agent being used to create for God. The meaning is that the universe and all that is in it was sovereignly **designed**, **created**, and yea, all things are continually to be **sustained** by Christ the Lord. As Hebrews says concerning Christ the Lord, "**he upholds the universe by the word of his power.**"[Heb. 1:3 ESV]

This is clearly evident as Paul declares,

> The Son is the image [the extract essence of His being] of the invisible God, the firstborn [Sovereign] over all creation. ¹⁶For in him all things were created: things in heaven and on earth, visible and invisible, whether thrones or powers or rulers or authorities; **all things have been created THROUGH HIM and FOR HIM**. ¹⁷He is before all things [He is eternal], and in him all things [are] hold together [and sustained]. ¹⁸And he is the head of the body, the church; he is the beginning [Source] and the firstborn [Preeminent One] from among the dead, so that in everything he might have the supremacy. ¹⁹For God was pleased[h] to have all his fullness [Deity] dwell in him, ²⁰ and through him to reconcile to himself all things, whether things on earth or things in heaven, by making peace **through his blood, shed on the cross**.
>
> Col. 1:15-20 (NIV)

> [h]"-please *the Father*-" (*the Father*) is not in the GK text; it is an insertion. The ESV is preferred, which reads, "For in him all the fullness of God was pleased to dwell." [Col. 1:19 ESV]

The atheism, evolution, and much of the world's higher education have been *steamrolling* over the educational systems to where life emerged from a *big bang*. Even if there is included a *god* with such non-sense thinking, e.g. evolution, God is only a *tack-on*. The Sovereignty of the Lord our God and His deliberate acts in His creation is nothing more than mockery.

Listen to me! Christ is not only the Designer, the Creator and the Sustainer of the universe, He is Sovereign and rules over His creation. As the apostle Paul says,

> With a view to an administration suitable to the fullness of the times, *that is*, the summing up of all things in Christ, things in the heavens and things on the earth. In Him also we have obtained an inheritance, **having been predestined according to His purpose who WORKS ALL THINGS AFTER THE COUNSEL OF HIS WILL**.
>
> Eph. 1:10, 11

Humanity is nothing more than compared a young chick which just cracked its shell and discovered a worm to eat. Now the young chick imagines he has got the world by the tail and knows all things. Yet, the newly hatched chick: little does it know that it is only a little morsel for the chicken hawk just above him.

Like the little chick, many Pastors have completed some studies in biblical doctrine, but they have little or no **on-going** *in-depth study* in all of God's Word except for their tradition that they may zealously follow. If we are faithful in the study of His Word, the Bible, we ought to *probe* and *unveil* our knowledge and illumination by the Spirit and not by tradition. Many Pastors have going awry and forsaken the Sacred Truth. Hence, they have forsaken the genuine Biblical Theology rather than following God's Word, OT and NT. All who faithfully preach and teach God's Word ought to be fervently and faithfully and continually studying of all of God's Word to know and do God's will. Therefore, theological tradition <u>must</u> always be subordinate to God's Word.

Why some Pastors give so little emphasis in personal study of God's Word other than perhaps their sermon preparation? Many Pastors are just *following tradition* (their doctrine of men) that taught them. They are not zealously studying the whole Bible for their own enlightenment and understanding walk of faith and obedience. Our hearts have become <u>hardened</u> by sin and <u>disbelief</u>. Heb. 3:12, 13 We have become <u>calloused</u> to God's Word. We have become <u>calloused</u> to the illuminating of the Spirit. Many do not even know the mighty miracles and great lessons in the Bible which most Sunday school children know. What a shame! Jesus rightly said of teaching of Pharisees which apply to our day,

> This people *honor* me with their lips; But **their heart is far from me.** [9]But in vain do they worship me, **Teaching *as their* doctrines the precepts of men**. Matt. 15:8, 9 (ASV)

The NET is correct in its rendering of the text below.

> In the beginning was the Word, and the Word was with God, and **the Word was <u>FULLY GOD</u>**. [2]The Word was with God in the beginning. [3] All things were **<u>CREATED</u>**[i] by him, and apart from him not one thing was created that has been created. John 1:1-3 (NET)

> [i]Note: the GK word is *ginomai* not usual for "made;" *ginomai* means "came into being." Hence, *created* is a more precise connotation in the context here.

There is a very great difference what Gospel some people are preaching nowadays. Many have a **different JESUS** from what the Bible plainly declares. Also, many are teaching a **different Gospel** from the Gospel given in the Bible.

We ought to expect such deficiency or error from the cults, the aberrant or deviants, the unbelievers, and ardent critics. They have a different Jesus or a different Gospel. This is because they come up short on Biblical Theology, and they do not allow Scripture to interpret Scripture. Jesus and the Gospel is seen through the imagination and reasoning the natural man.[1 Cor. 2:14]

Pastors, teachers, and Christian workers need continue in on-going study and letting the Scriptures speak for themselves. Some are so deficient in studying and knowing all of God's Word they do not know how to present the Gospel to the unsaved. Tragically, many behind pulpit or teaching classes do not know how to draw in the net.

Conclusion

The Gospel of John is plain and very clear. Yes, the apostle is so clear and simple that even a child can receive the Gospel. Jesus is the Eternal Creator that entered this world to save humankind for the penalty of sin. God did so by **extending** or **offering** His love to rebellious humanity. The Lord wants to forgive us of our sins and give us reconciliation and lasting peace with Him. Nevertheless, since the Lord is infinitely in holiness and righteousness, **sin** and **the sinner** God shall pour out His wrath upon all who are not under the blood of Christ.

Watch it! God is **offering** His love. The world is not yet the benefactor of the love of God. God is offering reconciliation or peace through Jesus Christ. If the world was already a recipient of the love of God, there would be no fear of the pending wrath of God in Hell. However, all of mankind is alienated and separated from God do to their sin before a holy and righteous God. Therefore, the consequence of rejecting the love of God in Christ is catastrophic, eternal condemnation to those without the reconciliation offered in God's love in Christ the Lord. As John says so clearly,

> For **GOD SO LOVED THE WORLD**, that he gave his only begotten Son, that whosoever believeth in him should not perish, but have everlasting life. [17]For God sent not his Son into the world to condemn the world; but that the world through him might be saved. [18]He that believeth on him is not condemned: but **HE THAT BELIEVETH NOT IS CONDEMNED ALREADY**, because he hath not believed in the name of the only begotten Son of God.   John 3:16-18 (KJV)

> He that **believeth on the Son hath everlasting life**: and **he that believeth not the Son** shall not see life; but **the wrath of God** *abides* **on him**. John 3:36 (KJV)

Footnotes:

1. *Subordinationism*: this is the false doctrine teaching that Christ and the Holy Spirit are subordinate to God the Father. It is even alleged that God Father's essence being is different from the Son and the Holy Spirit. Hence, fracturing the Trinity's oneness. However, God is one; there is but one God. Yet, God is Triune: the Father, the Son, and the Holy Spirit. Therefore, God is only one essence of being. Hence, the Trinity of God is without beginning or end, co-eternal and co-equal.

2. *Oneness doctrine*: the false doctrine is also known as the *Doctrine of Modalism*. The doctrine endorses Unitarianism, and thus, adamantly rejects the NT teaching of the Trinity. The false doctrine maintains that God has taken upon different *modes* or *forms*. For instance, God revealed Himself as "the Father" in the OT, and He manifest Himself as the "Son" in the Gospel, but now God has revealed Himself as the "Holy Spirit." However, Jesus is clear with literal translation of *John 10:30*, "I and the Father **we are one**."

CHAPTER 2

Christ Illuminates every person coming into the world

In him [*the Word*] was **life**, and the life was the **light** of all people. ⁵The light shines in the darkness, and the darkness did not overcome it. ⁶There was a man sent from God, whose name was John [*the Baptist*]. ⁷He came as a witness to testify to the **light**, so that **all might believe** through him. ⁸He himself was not the light, but he came to testify to the light. ⁹The true **light**, which **enlightens everyone**, was coming into the world. ¹⁰He was in the world, and the world came into being [made, *created*] through him; yet the world did not know him. ¹¹He came to what was his own [*people Israel*], and his own people did not accept him. ¹²But to all who received him, who believed in his name, he gave power to become children of God, ¹³who were born, not of blood or of the will of the flesh or of the will of man, but of God.   John 1:4-13 (NRS)

Introduction

The subject (or person) the apostle John refers to in his prologue he designates as "the **Word**." The **Word** is referring to Christ the Lord entering into the world of sin and woe to save sinners. In this portion of John's introduction, he unveils five salient benefits when a person genuinely put their genuine saving faith in the Word, Jesus Christ as Lord and Savior. These five benefits are far more important than most of us fully realize concerning the Word, Christ the Lord.

> ➢ First, Christ the Lord, the Word, is *Life*. The meaning is not just intrinsic life: Christ the Lord is the *source* and *sustainer;* He is the *Life*.

The Word is life now, but more importantly Christ Lord is the *source* and *sustainer* of all life for eternal life to come in Heaven. Without the Word as our Redeemer, there is only darkness, condemnation, and eternal separation in Hell.

➤ Second, the Word is **Light**. The world and the demonic force are full of darkness. Humankind can only grope through the darkness of this present world without the Light, Jesus Christ as Lord and Savior. There are endless dangers and unforeseen pitfalls without the Light of Christ the Lord. Many are unfortunately unaware of the dangers and helpless against such dangers. John is equally implying Christ the Lord wants to be your Friend and Guide through this darkened world and through demonic force surrounding us. Yes, Jesus wants to be a Friend that will be closer than a brother or sister. The Word will be your greatest Friend now and your Friend in eternal life to come.

➤ Third and amazingly, John reveals the Word as the **Illuminator** to the whole world. (The Word brings light to world that is in full of darkness.) To be delivered from the darkness in this world, we must individually commit our life to Him and walk in faith and obedience to Him and His will. While there is commonality between light and illumination, there is an important distinction and purpose. Light helps us see our way as we move through this world of darkness. Ah, but Illuminator is one that guides. This means the Word, Christ the Lord, must be the master or the controller of our life in all we say and do. This means we must be willing to follow His lead.

➤ The fourth point by John is that the Word is our **Maker**. (This is in reference to Lord our God as the *Maker* of all things.) The expression "Maker" has nearly dropped from people's vocabulary today in the world of so-called evolution and the world of atheism. John reminds us that the Word, Christ the Lord, is indeed our *Maker*, and as such, we shall all indeed stand before Him.

➤ Fifth and lastly, John points concerning the Word as the **Sovereign** *Authority*. Christ the Lord's judgment is absolutely final. This is no appeal after Christ makes His sentence and judgment without Him as your Savior! Friend, there is no higher authority. The Word's authority (Christ the Lord) is final. His authority is Sovereign. There is nothing or anything in all creation that is able to override the Word's Sovereign

Authority. This means that everyone who will genuinely receive the Word, Christ the Lord, He Sovereignly grant the authority or the legitimate right to become children of God just by believing in His Name.[John 1:12, 13] Hallelujah!

Therefore, with this brief introduction, let us dive into John's marvelous Gospel as he unveils various rolls or aspects of the Word and benefits of knowing Him. I hope it shall be as exciting and spiritually informative for you, the reader, as it was to me in studying this masterpiece in the prologue of the apostle John's Gospel.

A. The Word is the Life

The apostle John says,

In him was life, and the life was the light of all people. John 1:4 (NRS)

The phrase is "In Him was Life." John uses the word *"life"* (GK *zoe*) 47 times in his Gospel. The meaning is not that *the Word came to life* or *the Word had life*. The thought being conveyed is real life comes alive when a person commit their whole being over to the Word, Christ the Lord. Friend, and Christ is Lord over our lives whether we believe it or not. However, you must choose to receive the Lord over your way of life. The wise will eagerly seek the Lord while He may be found, but the fool goes about his way of life without instruction,

> [5]Trust in the LORD with all your heart And do not lean on your own understanding. [6]**In all your ways acknowledge Him**, And He will make your paths straight. [7]Do not be wise in your own eyes; **Fear the LORD and turn away from evil**. Prov. 3:5-7

> Come now, you who say, "Today or tomorrow we will go into this or that town and spend a year there and do business and make a profit." [14]You do not know about tomorrow. What is your life like? For you are a puff of smoke that appears for a short time and then vanishes. [15]You ought to say instead, "**If the Lord is willing**, then we will live and do this or that." [16]But as it is, you boast in your arrogance. All such boasting is evil. [17]So whoever knows what is good to do and does not do it is guilty of sin. James 4:13-17 (NET)

Please listen to me! Without Jesus as your Lord and Redeemer over your way of life, you will only grope through this world. (Did you get that? Christ must be <u>over</u> your life and not just <u>in</u> your life.) Tragically, all those without

17

Christ as their Redeemer will end up in Hell. They never received Jesus as Lord and only Savior. There are those who know Christ as Savior, but they fumble and stumble through this world since Christ is not the Lord of their lives. They will be empty handed and have no trophies to lay at the feet of the King, the Word, Christ the Lord.

Do you know what is sad? Some people have the Good News presented to them, and intellectually, they acknowledge the cross of Christ as true. Yet, here is the kicker: they never get around to make a genuine commitment and trust in Christ even though they know the Gospel is true. How sad is that?

Unfortunately, the majority of people that hear the Gospel shall reject it. They had within their grasp the **PEARL of GREAT PRICE**, but they foolishly rejected the Word, Christ the Lord. No wonder, Solomon said,

> Do you see a man wise in his own eyes? *There is* more hope for a fool than for him.   Prov. 26:12 (NKJ)

Unfortunately, even sadder, there are millions that never heard the Gospel. Sadly, they shall perish in their sin. They shall perish not because they rejected the Gospel; they will perish in their sin without a Redeemer. No one has never shared with them the Good News. Will there be friends you know that will say to you at the Judgment, *"Why didn't you warn me of Hell and the free gift of eternal life in Christ?"*[Matt. 10:28; Rom. 6:23] Some believers do not truly believe the Gospel is for everyone.[John 3:16] Listen, the Gospel is indeed for everyone that will believe and receive Jesus Christ as Lord and Savior. The Bible is clear, God is not willing that any perish.[2 Peter 3:9] Yes, eternal life is indeed available to everyone.

In the synagogue in Capernaum, Jesus said,

> "Do not labor for the food which perishes, but for the food which endures to everlasting life, which the Son of Man will give you, because God the Father has set His seal on Him."   John 6:27 (NKJ)

> This is that bread which came down from heaven: not as your fathers did eat manna, and are dead: he that *eats* of this bread shall live forever.
>
> John 6:58 (KJV)

> "It is the Spirit who gives life; the flesh profits nothing; the words that I have spoken to you are spirit and are life.   John 6:63)

Jesus does not mean we are to literally consume Jesus' flesh, but that if we want **eternal life** in Heaven, we must personally receive Jesus Christ by faith and walk in faith and obedience to Him.

This is "life" that Jesus gives, and this life, in the here and now, starts right now **today** if you truly trust and receive Jesus. If you truly receive Him, then, He needs to be the Lord of your life and you must seek to walk in His will and not your will. This life with Christ Jesus continues in Heaven. However, you must genuinely trust and receive Him right now.

> "The thief comes only to steal and kill and destroy; I came that they may
> have **life**, and have *it* [*life*] abundantly.   John 10:10

This is not the evil and false doctrine, "Name it and Claim it." Jesus, the Word, **will never leave you** or **forsake you**.[Heb. 13:5] In addition, the Lord will provide for those who trust Him and walk in His will.

As Jesus talked with Mary and Martha, their brother Lazarus had been dead for four days, and his body was in the state of decomposition.

> Martha said to Him, "I know that he will rise again in the resurrection
> on the last day." [25] Jesus said to her, "I am the resurrection and the life;
> he who believes in Me will live even if he dies, [26] and **everyone who
> lives and believes in Me will never die**. Do you believe this?"
>
>   John 11:24-26

The cults just do not get it even though Jesus is very clear. The cults are fixated on evil doctrine of *soul sleep*, which is very misleading in the phrase "*soul sleep*." By the phrase "*soul sleep*," the cults mean that the person no longer exists except in the memory of God. So, such cults allege, God will call everyone back in existence again for judgment.

The believer's body will indeed be risen and glorified like our Lord in the rapture. Yet, at death, the dead in Christ will immediate ascend to Heaven being escorted by His mighty angel in their souls to Heaven.[Luke 16:22; 2 Cor. 5:8; Phi. 1:21-23; 3:20f]

What a shame! Many profess faith in Christ, but many are ignored or give little thought or commune with prayer throughout the day. Yet, He tells us,

> Jesus said to him, "I am **THE WAY**, **THE TRUTH**, and **THE LIFE**.
> No one comes to the Father except through Me.   John 14:6 (NKJ)

The word "*way*" (GK *hodos*): the early Christians were known "people of the **Way**"[Acts 19:23] because genuine faith in Christ is not a religion; it is a genuine personal *relationship* with Christ as lifestyle, *the way of life*.[Acts 19:9]

Jesus is not just a truth or one of the truths. The Word, Christ the Lord, is **THE TRUTH**. The world hates that there is the absolute Truth. To the world, truth is relative and changing, and so, truth is whatever you want to be.

Yes, our Lord is indeed "**THE LIFE**." There is no real life without Jesus. Real life is having a "little talk with Jesus" because He will surely care for you. Yes, as Jesus said,

> 'My sheep hear My voice, and **I know them**, and **they follow Me**. And I give them eternal life, and **they shall never perish; neither shall anyone snatch them out of My hand**. My Father, who has given *them* to Me, is greater than all; and **no one is able to snatch** *them* **out of My Father's hand**.'
> John 10:27-29 (NKJ)

Finally, the apostle John says,

> But these [*things*] are written, that ye might believe that Jesus is the Christ, the Son of God; and that believing ye might **have** [*eternal*] **life through his name**.
> John 20:31 (KJV)

B. The Word is the Light

The apostle John uses the word "light" at least twenty-three times in the Gospel of John. There is a contrast between "*light*" and "*darkness*," but there is no idea of Dualism or Zoroastrianism.[1] The devil and evil spirits are created beings and very finite compared to God. Satan is depicted like *a force of darkness* and powerful in the Bible.[e.g. Eph.2:1-3;6:10-17] (Evil spirits exist at the mercy of God.) So, evil spirits are very finite in comparison to the Word, the Light, Christ the Creator. Evil angels fear the Light, Christ shall cast them into the Lake of Fire.

> In him was life, and that life was the **light of all mankind. The light shines** in the darkness, and **the darkness has not overcome**[a] it [the Light].
> John 1:4, 5 (NIV)

> [a]The word "*overcome*" is "*katalambano*." The meaning is more than "unable to *comprehend*" or "unable to *apprehend*." The more preferred meaning in the context is "unable to *seize* or *overtake the Light*." The Light overtakes the darkness and bring illumination.

"*Unable overtake the Light*" is a marvelous portrait of the Word. *Strike a match* in a very dark room, and the light from the match shall immediate give light to the entire room. If only the church understood this principle and carried the Light to every home in their church community: **door to door, house to house**. Just think, what a glorious change would occur because of the Light? My friend, do you know I have offered to go door to door to all the homes in the community of the church with the various Pastors in different communities.

(Getting around nowadays for me is indeed very difficult.) Still, amazingly, more than one has responded, "No one is interested." I have had to laugh, and I remark, "Of course my brother, they are not interested; they are not yet saved." Only the genuine saved are eager to hear the Word.

Listen carefully my brother: "We do not knock on doors to invite them to church." **NO, NO**! Pay close attention: we knock on doors to **INVITE THEM TO <u>RECEIVE</u> JESUS AS LORD AND SAVIOR**. Let us first seek to get people into the Kingdom of God.[Matt. 6:33] Neither do we invite people to Bible study (this is the cults method); we invite people to receive Jesus Christ.[John 1:12] Our focus must be in presenting Jesus Christ in the home, business places, or wherever. Inviting people to church is **not** the Gospel. Inviting people to Bible study or inviting people to church is **not** the biblical pattern. We must invite people to receive Jesus and enter the Kingdom of God.

Many Christians still do not get it! We do not invite people to church. We must invite them to receive the Good News. We are all sinners deserving Hell due to our sin, but Jesus has come as Light in the world to save every sinner that will repent and trust Jesus as Lord and Savior.

Believing the facts of the Gospel only means "*you are not stupid*," but it does not mean you are saved and have the new life in Christ. We do not invite people to believe in a particular dogma. Please get it right: we are to invite people to receive Jesus as personal Lord and Savior and enter into the Kingdom of God. Friend, everyone must make a personal commitment that Jesus is Lord to save them. Jesus Christ must be the Lord of your life! Otherwise, you may have made only a profession of faith but remain void of genuine saving faith Jesus Christ. You must place your sole (total reliance) in Christ for your salvation.[2 Tim. 1:12]

Once again, John says concerning the Word, Christ the Lord "[He] was the Light of men."[John 1:4b] Many Christians stumble because we must only believe in Him, **we must follow and let Jesus lead us**. We do not just believe the facts of the Gospel and then go our way. We need to believe in Jesus as Lord and walk with Him in the dark, dark world. This is the whole point of King David's point in Psa. 23. Jesus said,

> **"I am the Light of the world; he who <u>FOLLOWS</u> ME will <u>NOT</u> walk in the darkness, but will have the Light of life."**   John 8:12

What good is it if someone professes faith in Christ, but he does **not** walk in the Light? His faith is dead.

Jesus declared to a man who has been blind from birth and which He heals the blind man. He says to the blind man, 'I am the Light of the world.'[John 9:5] The apostle John says in his first letter,

> [5]This is the message we have heard from Him and announce to you, that **GOD IS LIGHT**, and **in Him there is no darkness** at all. [6]If we say that we have fellowship with Him and *yet* walk in the darkness, we lie and do not practice the truth; [7]but **if we walk in the Light as He Himself is in the Light**, we have fellowship with one another, and **the blood of Jesus His Son cleanses us** from all sin. `   1 John 1:5-7

Sorrowfully, many claim to be children of Light, but they are walking with the world: they are still walking in darkness.

C. The Word is the Illuminator

This point in John's Prologue is so subtle and easy to overlook. John says as given by the Literal Standard Version,

> He was the true Light, which enlightens every man, coming into the world   John 1:9 (LSV)

Here the Holy Spirit is working in harmony with Christ the Lord in order to illuminate mankind. The Holy Spirit comes and dispenses illumination, but the Father and Son work in concert to achieve the illumination with the Holy Spirit. (See Luke 24:49; John 14:16, 26; 15:26; 16:7.)

The root word for "*light*" (is a noun, and it is a reference to Christ.) The root word in v4 is the same root word is used as a verb "enlightens" in v9 NAS. (Others translate the word as "*light*.") Here the NSA is commended because it strongly illustrates the action of the Light. The two ideas of "light" and "enlightens" supplement one another, but there is a subtle distinction that must be noted.

There is a slight distinction in my mind. (Some will dismiss the distinction for sure.) The Light in [v 4] helps us to see our way. Here in v9, but there is the idea of guidance through the darkness of this world. Hence, the Word, Christ the Lord, is being the Illuminator to the world.

Some will object, "Hey, that is the ministry of the Holy Spirit!" My reaction is, "*Exacta mundo!*" (exactly). This is equivalent today to the expression, "no problem." Ha, ha! Christ's ministry supplements the Holy Spirit's ministry, and the Holy Spirit supplements Christ's ministry.
Jesus said,

"And I will pray the Father, and he shall give you another [GK *allos*, another of the same] Comforter [GK *parakletos*], that he may **abide with you forever**."

John 14:16 (KJV)

The GK word *allos* implies **another the same**. The GK word "**Comforter** or **Helper**" is the same word in First letter John,

My little children, these things write I unto you, that ye sin not. And if any man sin, we have an **Advocate** [GK *parakletos*] with the Father, Jesus Christ the righteous: 1 John 2:1 (KJV)

If you still have doubt, let us look at a parallel.

In the same way, the Spirit helps us in our weakness, for we do not know how we should pray, but **the Spirit Himself INTERCEDES for us** with inexpressible groanings. And he who searches our hearts knows the mind of the Spirit, because the Spirit intercedes on behalf of the saints according to God's will. Rom. 8:26, 27 (NET)	Who will bring any charge against God's elect? It is God who justifies. Who is the one who will condemn? Christ is the one who died [died in our place] (and more than that, he was raised), who is at the right hand of God, and who **ALSO** is **interceding** for us. Rom. 8:33, 34 (NET)

While many smile and dismiss this added kicker, the Word of God says, 'In the mouth of two or three witnesses shall every word be established.' Deut.19:15; Mat. 18:16; John 8:17; 2 Cor. 13:1; 1 Tim. 5:19; Heb. 10:28 Well, if anyone still doubts, let us note once more below.

Watch out and do not miss this point here! In John 1:4, the Word, Christ Lord, gives Light to see your way when you trust Him. Amen? Ah, but in John 1:9 the Word, Christ the Lord, will give enlightenment to the mind of the believers. Christ gives counsel and wisdom. Col. 2:3 Please note as David said,

The LORD is my shepherd, I lack nothing. ²He takes me to lush pastures, he leads me to refreshing water. ³He restores my strength. **He LEADS ME down the right paths** for the sake of his reputation. ⁴Even when I must walk through the darkest valley, I fear no danger, **FOR YOU ARE WITH ME**; your rod and your staff reassure me. ⁵You prepare a feast before me in plain sight of my enemies. You refresh my head with oil; my cup is completely full. ⁶Surely your **GOODNESS** and **FAITHFULNESS WILL PURSUE ME ALL MY DAYS**, and I will live in the LORD's house for the rest of my life. Psa. 23:1-6 (NET)

Let me explain as if you were a child, which we are all children in the eyes God who are genuinely saved. Did you ever lose something, and you have looked everywhere but you could not find it? Then you prayed, and *eureka*, you found it. (The GK Archimedes shouted *"heureka"* or *eureka* after discovering a way to determine when the metal is purity of gold.[2]) It is not until we look up, then we might pray and get the illumination.

Listen, Jesus is the one who has all the answers. Right? (If you didn't know that our Lord has all the answers, then, you know it now.) Yes, Paul says,

> In whom [*Christ the Lord*] are hid **ALL** the **TREASURES** of **WISDOM** and **KNOWLEDGE**.   Col. 2:3 (KJV)

Yes, yes, you say! The world does not know that the Word, in Christ the Lord, *are hidden all the treasures of wisdom and knowledge*. Like looking for something you lost, the Lord knows where the item is, correct? Then, talk to the Lord in pray for help. "Why in the world do we wait until we get to the bottom of the *barrel* before we look up?" Don't you know Christ the Lord is able to unlock the mysteries of life and even the mysteries of Cosmos, the universe? If only scientists that are Christians would know and avid themselves in prayer to Christ, what a difference this would make.

Do you know that because Daniel and his three companions chose to not to defile themselves and remain obedient to the Law of Moses, the Bible says,

> As for every matter of expertise and understanding about which the king consulted them, he found them **ten times better** than all the soothsayer priests *and* conjurers who *were* in all his realm.   Dan. 1:20

Laugh and call the above a hyperbole if you want, but do you know that many imagine the apostles as a little more than *"country bumpkins,"* ignorant men. Well, Daniel and his companions were literally ten times greater in knowledge and wisdom. Similarly, Christ open the apostles' minds,

[45]Then opened *He* their understanding [GK *nous, mind*], that they might understand the scriptures, [46]And said unto them, Thus it is written, and thus it behooved [*necessary*] Christ to suffer, and to rise from the dead the third day: [47]And that repentance and remission of sins should be preached in his name among all nations, beginning at Jerusalem. [48]And ye are witnesses of these things. Luke 24:45-48 (KJV)	[45]Then **He OPENED THEIR MINDS so they could understand the scriptures**, [46]and said to them, "Thus it stands written that the Christ would suffer and would rise from the dead on the third day, [47]and repentance for the forgiveness of sins would be proclaimed in his name to all nations, beginning from Jerusalem. [48]You are witnesses of these things. ,Luke 24:45-48 (NET)

If you are still wondering, the Word, Christ the Lord, is able to _Enlighten_ you and me. I <u>do</u> <u>not</u> mean that we will be ten times smarter. But Christ the Lord does have the answers to all questions of life, even every area of life. If we are looking for something or looking for answer, well, you can go to AI (artificial intelligence, a computer) like Google and can certainly find help and solutions. But why go to artificial intelligence when you can go to the Source of all knowledge and wisdom?

> He is the image [the extract reflection] of the invisible God, the firstborn [Preeminent, Sovereign] of all creation. [16]For by him all things were created, in heaven and on earth, visible and invisible, whether thrones or dominions or rulers or authorities— all things were created through him and for him. [17]And he is before all things [Eternal], and in him all things hold together [and sustained]. [18]And he is the head of the body, the church. He is the beginning [GK _arche_ also: _origin_ or _source_], the firstborn [Supreme over all] from the dead, that in everything he might be preeminent [of all things]. [19]For in him all the fullness of God was pleased to dwell, [20] and through him to reconcile to himself all things, whether on earth or in heaven, **making peace by <u>the</u> <u>blood</u> of his cross.**   Col. 1:15-20 (ESV)

Next time you are seeking help (whether simple or very complexed), go to the real _Source_, Christ the Lord. You might be delightfully surprised. After all, the Word, Christ the Lord, He Enlightens us as the Illuminator. Do you think Jesus can give wisdom and knowledge to your ministry? Well, do you think Jesus can Enlighten your ministry? But wait! Friend, you cannot walk with the world and walk with Christ and claim fellowship the Lord.

D. The Word is the Maker and Sustainer of all things

Now John says of the Word, Christ the Lord,

> He was in the world, and the world was **made** [came into being, created] through him, yet the world did not know him.   John 1:10 (ESV)

The Logos, the Word, Christ the Lord is the Designer, the Maker, and yes, the Sustainer of all life and all things. Christ is the reason all things existing and, if I may add, continue to exit in the universe. As David declares,

> Certainly you made my mind and heart; you wove me together in my mother's womb. [14]I will give you thanks because your deeds are awesome and amazing. You knew me thoroughly; [15]my bones were not hidden from you, when I was made in secret and sewed together in the depths of the earth. [16]Your eyes saw me when I was inside the womb.

All the days ordained for me were recorded in your scroll before one of them came into existence. [17]How difficult it is for me to fathom your thoughts about me, O God! How vast is their sum total! [18]If I tried to count them, they would outnumber the grains of sand. Even if I finished counting them, I would still have to contend with you.

Psa. 139:13-18 (NET)

Hence, Christ the Lord is indeed our Maker and Sustainer. Hallelujah! The world imagines that we are freaks of nature through the process of evolution through *natural selection*. Even their reasoning is insane since they assume all life just started with a "Big bang." Ironically, admitting to "the Big bang" implies some **One** heard it. Hello! Who heard the Big bang? The atheist is pointing to God without them realizing it. All the theories of evolution are nothing more than an endless hypothesis and a farce.

My friend, we are precious in the sight of the Lord. He ought to know; He made us. Even in death, we are precious in the Lord's sight,

> Precious in the sight of the LORD *is* the death of his saints.

Psa. 116:15 (KJV)

So, what then is the purpose of all mankind? Friend, what is the chief end of man? The chief of humankind is to worship the Lord, the only God and enjoy Him forever. Or as every Jewish child learns at an early age, the *Shama*!

> "Hear, O Israel! The LORD is our God, the LORD is one! You shall love the LORD your God with all your heart and with all your soul and with all your might."
> Deut. 6:4, 5

Everything today is so generic. The Lord is addressed as pronoun *"He, Him, You,* and so on." Oh, yes, people say, "I worship God." How nice and so quaint, but what is your *god's* name? "Uh, God?"

Joshua gave this charge to Israel, but this charge has fallen on deaf ears today even among many churches,

> "Now, therefore, **fear the LORD** and serve Him in sincerity and truth; and **put away the gods** which your fathers served beyond the [*Euphrates*] River and in Egypt, and serve the LORD. If it is disagreeable in your sight to serve the LORD, choose for **yourselves today whom you will serve**: whether **the gods** which your fathers served which were beyond the [*Euphrates*] River, or **the gods of the Amorites** in whose land you are living; **BUT AS FOR ME AND MY HOUSE, WE WILL SERVE THE LORD.**"
> Joshua 24:14, 15

Many in the churches do not get it when Jesus said,

> "If anyone comes to Me and does not hate his own father, mother, wife, children, brothers, sisters, yes, and even his own life, he cannot be My disciple." Luke 14:26

Let me make it plain! The Word, Christ the Lord, He is our **Maker**. Hello! The term "Son of God" does not mean Christ is a second generation "*god.*" Perish the thought! The word "*son*" identifies or declares "*relationship*" or "*to whom one belongs.*" Messiah is referred to "Eternal Father," but the Messiah is not God the Father. Messiah is *the Eternal Father* [Isa. 9:6, 7] in the sense that the Messiah is the Father is of Creator, His is our **Maker**. So, the word "*son*" as it used of angels and redeemed does not mean offspring. The holy angels and redeemed are sons of God through relationship in the family of God. So, "*son*" is used of holy angels or the true believers (of both men, women, and children in Christ).

Pay attention! Holy angels are "sons of God," but holy angels are not offsprings of God. Holy angels are son of God by **relationship**. Holy angels are sons of God by relationship, holy unto the Lord. Fallen angels are **not** sons of God since the evil angels are alienated from God and have no relationship with God.

Christ is the Son in relationship within the Triune God: the Father, the Son, and the Holy Spirit. The unregenerate are not sons of God. The unsaved are sons of the devil.john 8:44; 1 John 3:10 Everyone that is truly redeemed in Christ (men, women, and children) are "sons of God" by relationship through faith in Christ. *Son* in relationship with God does not mean or imply gender. *Son* implies family or relationship.

Even in the root meaning of the word "son" as to the redeemed, we are not literally offspring as though we are "gods." This is ignorance of the "Name it and Claim it." The root word for adoption in the Bible is *son*, GK *huiothesia*: from the words, *huios* (*son*) and *thesia* (*placing*). Hence, *huiothesia*, meaning, "*the placing as sons.*" This cannot be explained any plainer then when Paul says,

> For **you are all SONS** [GK *huios*] of God through faith in Christ Jesus. [27]For all of you who were baptized [*ingrafted by the Holy Spirit, (1 Cor. 12:13)*] into Christ have **clothed yourselves with Christ**. [28]There is neither Jew nor Greek, there is neither slave nor free man, there is **NEITHER MALE NOR FEMALE**; for you are all one in Christ Jesus. [29]And if you belong to Christ, then you are Abraham's descendants, [sons, Gal. 4:7] **heirs according to promise**. Gal. 3:26-29

The feminist movement though they have good intentions are raising havoc in the translations of the Bible. For example, the Lord sought a man. [HEB _ish_, e.g.; married man, _man, male_] Again, Jesus said, 'Follow Me, I will make you fishers of men.'Matt. 4:19 Yes, the GK word is _anthropos_ (which can mean all of mankind), but the **paradigm** our Lord is using He means reaching men, the heads of families. Unfortunately, many in the church are oblivious to the paradigm Jesus established or blatantly disobedient to His command. God does not use women or children to fight a war. We are at war! Yet, many churches are using women and children, and God did not design women or children to fight wars. Testosterone is not only for reproduction; testosterone is for aggression to fight wars.

God uses men to fight the spiritual war that we are up against. Unfortunately, this a very big error using the word "man" in reference to all men and women. Many churches have swallowed this delusion _hook, line, and sinker_. There is little spiritual discernment or spiritual zeal today. Women negotiators; women were not designed to be fighters.

Still, many do not get it. In Paul rebuffs of Israel and their present spiritual blindness and failure to see the infinite mercy of the Word, Christ Lord, when the apostle says,

> But who are you, O man, to answer back to God? Will what is molded say to its molder [your Maker], "Why have you made me like this?" Has the potter no right over the clay, to make out of the same lump one vessel for honorable use and another for dishonorable use?
>
> Rom. 9:20, 21 (ESV)

Don't you know that the Lord has now consigned everyone to unbelief, Jew and Gentile. God consigned everyone to disbelief in order that He may have mercy upon all humanity? (_Electionists_ don't get either!)

> For God hath concluded them all [Jew and Gentile] in unbelief [disobedience to the Gospel], that He [our Maker] might have mercy upon all. 33O the depth of the riches both of the wisdom and knowledge of God! how unsearchable _are_ his judgments, and his ways past finding out! 34For who hath known the mind of the Lord? or who hath been his counsellor? 35Or who hath first given to him, and it shall be recompensed unto him again? 36 For of him, and through him, and to him, _are_ all things: to whom _be_ glory _forever_. Amen. Rom. 11:32-36 (KJV)

E. The Word is the Sovereign One in Authority

Finally, the apostle John says concerning the Word, Christ the Lord,

> He came to His own, and His own did not receive Him. [12] But as many as received Him, to them He gave the right [GK *exousia, legitimate authority*] to become children of God, to those who believe in His name: [13]who were born, not of blood, nor of the will of the flesh, nor of the will of man, but of God. John 1:11-13 (NKJ)

That is, Christ came to His *own* possession, Israel, but many of His *own* (among the Jews) do not receive Him as the Messiah and Redeemer. This is because Israel was spiritually blinded by God. Shocking but true that the nation Israel became spiritually blinded to the Gospel, but there are still many Hebrew Jews that did and do believe in Yehoshua as Messiah and Lord. Praise the Lord! The apostle explains the mystery of God,

> [22]Take notice, therefore, of the kindness and severity of God: severity to those who fell [*Israel*], but kindness to you [*Gentiles*], if you continue in His kindness. Otherwise you also will be cut off. [23]And if they [*Israel*] also do not persist in unbelief, they will be grafted in, for God is able to graft them in again. [24]For if you [*as Gentiles*] were cut from a wild olive tree, and contrary to nature were grafted into one that is cultivated [*which is Is-ael*], how much more readily will these, the natural branches [*Israel*], be grafted [*again*] into their own olive tree! Rom. 11:22-24 (MSB)

So, many Israelites did not receive Jesus as Messiah and Lord. Therefore, God opened the floodgate of His **mercy** to everyone without going through the nation of Israel as the Covenant Nation, which includes the Jews and the Gentiles. Therefore, the Lord has concluded both Israel and Gentile in unbelief in order that Christ might have mercy upon all that will believe and receive Jesus as Lord and only Savior. Hallelujah!

> For God hath concluded them [*Jews and Gentiles*] all in unbelief,[a] that he might have mercy upon all. (Rom. 11:32 KJV)

> [a]The word "unbelief" can also imply "disobedient," (GK *apeitheia*). That is, disobedient, meaning disbelief concerning the Gospel. Note the example below.

> Since then, it remains for some to enter into it, and those who first heard good news did not enter in because of unbelief.[b] Heb. 4:6 (LSB)

[b]The word *"unbelief"* can also imply *"disobedient"* (GK *apeitheia*), but the LSB uses the connotative implied meaning is *unbelief.*

As to the future regather of Israel in their land, the apostle continues as he says,

> So that you may not claim to be wiser than you are, brothers and sisters, I want you to understand this **mystery: a hardening has come <u>UPON PART OF ISRAEL</u>, UNTIL** the full number of the Gentiles has come in. [26]And so all Israel will be saved; as it is written, "Out of Zion will come the Deliverer; he will banish ungodliness from Jacob." [27]**"And THIS IS MY <u>COVENANT</u> WITH <u>THEM</u>, when I TAKE AWAY THEIR SINS."** [28]As regards the gospel they are enemies of God for your sake; but as regards election they are beloved, for the sake of their ancestors [*patriarchs*]; [29]for the gifts and the calling of God are irrevocable. [30]Just as you [*Gentiles*] were once disobedient [*apeitheo, debrief*] to God but have now received mercy because of their [*Israel's*] disobedience [*apeitheo, debrief*], [31]so they have now been disobedient [*apeitheo, debrief*] in order that, by the mercy shown to you, they too may now receive mercy. [32]For God has imprisoned [*shut-up or closed, concluded*] all in disobedience [*apeitheo, debrief*] so that he may be merciful to all.　　　　Rom. 11:25-32 (NRS)

I am emphasizing Israel's place in the plan of God since 90% of the professing church allege that the church has replaced Israel, and the church is the new Israel. I mean, some are so given over to spiritualizing Scripture that they are telling spiritual lies. God has not cast aside Israel. The same grace that calls the Gentiles will indeed summon Israel, though it will be only- remnant by grace.

Others are so given over to the doctrine of *the election* that salvation is only for the elect, and salvation is not for the entire world. Friend, the floodgate of God's mercy is open to all who will believe and receive the Word, Christ Lord, as their Savior. Friend, this comes from God who cannot lie.[Titus 1:2] Praise the Lord!

Please note again my friend, this is indeed the Good News,

> But as many as received him, to them gave he [*the*] power to become the sons [GK *teknon*, children] of God, *even* to them that believe on his name: Which were born, not of blood, nor of the will of the flesh, nor of the will of man, but of God.　　　　John 1:12, 13 (KJV)

"By the blood," meaning we cannot be a child of God because you are Jew or that your Mom or Dad is a Christian. Neither can *"through the will of the flesh;"* that is, no one can become a child of God by works. We are wicked sin-

ners and Hell-bound unless we are born from above through personal faith by the Spirit of the living God. Finally, John says neither can we become a child of God "*by the will of man*;" water baptism, the laying of hands, or church membership **cannot** make you a child of God. However, the apostle John **does not** mean that the will of human is uninvolved. The meaning is that no outside power or authority by human intervention can give anyone new life in Christ. A person must believe and receive Christ to be saved, [John 1:12]. How else shall a person be saved unless we each exercise our will to trust and receive Jesus as Lord and Savior? So, we must each individually personally be born from above through faith Jesus Christ.[John 3:3, 7]

The apostle John says

> But as many as **RECEIVED HIM**, to them He **GAVE THE RIGHT** [GK *exousia, the authority or legitimate right*] to become children of God, *even* to those who believe [*trust*] in His name.   John 1:12

I beg you my friend, listen to me. The Word, Christ Lord has all authority. The power rests in Jesus Christ. No one, and I mean no one else has the authority over Him. Christ Lord has Sovereign Authority. Sadly, many in the churches do not even know that all Sovereign Authority resides with Jesus Christ. The text below is inference to Jesus' humanity; as to His deity, He has always possessed all power and all authority.

> [18]Jesus came up and said to them, "All authority (all power of absolute rule) in heaven and on earth has been given to Me. [19]Go therefore and make disciples of all the nations [help the people to learn of Me, believe in Me, and obey My words], baptizing them in the name of the Father and of the Son and of the Holy Spirit, [20]teaching them to observe everything that I have commanded you; and lo, I am with you always [remaining with you perpetually--regardless of circumstance, and on every occasion], even to the end of the age."   Matt. 28:18-20 (AMP)

Some churches are so **full of self** (the carnal minded) that they have little room for following Jesus' mandates, and many in the church's leaders do not even know what His commands are for the church. The churches are no longer going out "*door to door*" (7/24) to share the Gospel. Those who do go out "door to door" is nothing more than a *dripping faucet*. Many are just too lazy. Sadly, some churches do not even *have a drip*: they are spiritual dead and there is no spiritual life in them. Shame, shame! We have been given the Greatest Command and complete authority from Heaven with power, authority, and even with the assurance of Jesus' presence with us. That is, we go "door to door" to share the Good News that Jesus *saves to the uttermost.* [Heb. 7:25] As I have said, our Lord even goes right along with us. We are not alone.

Unfortunately, many are fearful and have little faith of our Lord's presence. In addition, the Holy Spirit is present and convicting the unbeliever as we share the Word of God.[John 16:7-11, Heb. 13:5] Everyone has the right to hear the Good News. As saints in Christ, we are expected to 'Go out into the highways and hedges, and compel *them* to come in, that my house may be filled?'[Luke 14:23] Why then are we not following His commands? Friend, this more than disobedience. Friend, men are fearful and have no faith. Their faith is not coupled with a strong commitment and action. It's dead faith.

The Lord gives everyone the right to enter His Kingdom. Listen! The door into the Kingdom of God is open to everyone, regardless of your sin and unbelief. The Door is open to everyone through Jesus. Jesus the Lord has given everyone the right to be made a child of the King. Yes, even those who just trust in the Word, Christ the Lord. Yes friend, just believe in His Name! Friend, we have the greatest message to the world. Will you go and compel *them* to come to Jesus as Lord and Savior?

Conclusion

John's message is simple and plain so that a child is able to receive it. But the Gospel message is also so profound and deep that the greatest minds cannot comprehend it all. Friend, it cannot be any plainer when Jesus said,

> "For God so loved the world, that He gave His only begotten Son, that whoever believes in Him shall not perish, but have eternal life."

> John 3:16

Here is short hymn in which yours truly has written.

Infinite grace and mercy, He died on Calvary

[1]"How can it be that the Lord our God should die in our place for you and me?" In His infinite grace and mercy, He died on Calvary.

Refrain
How can it be that our God died for you and me?
How can it be? In His love He went to Calvary.

[2]"How amazing and infinite love, the Lord God died for you and me on Calvary?" In His infinite grace and mercy, He died on Calvary.

[3]"How can it be anyone would delay in this love, the Lord our God even died for you?" In His infinite grace and mercy, He died on Calvary.

[4]"Amazing love, How can it be if you will only believe, He died for you on Calvary?" In His infinite grace and mercy, He died on Calvary.

Song by Dr. Frank Parsons, 2025

The hymn is adapted to, *"And Can It Be That I Should Gain?"* by Charles Wesley.

Watch out now! Jesus is offering His love to you, but you do not have the love of God until you believe and receive Jesus as Lord and Savior, and then, you become a recipient of the love of God that will never leave or forsake you. You become a recipient by **repenting** of your sins and genuinely **receiving** and **trusting** in the Word, Christ the Lord, as your personal Redeemer. Delay or dare to put the decision off, then you have condemned yourself to an eternal Hell.

> "He who believes in Him is not condemned; but **he who DOES NOT BELIEVE IS CONDEMNED ALREADY**, because he has not believed in the name of the only begotten Son of God."
>
> John 3:18 (NKJ)

John sums up again at end of chapter three,

> "He who believes in the Son has everlasting life; and he who does not believe the Son shall not see life, but the wrath of God abides on him."
>
> John 3:36 (NKJ)

Please understand my friend, without Jesus as your Lord and Savior, you stand already completely condemned due to sin without the Redeemer. Therefore, come to Jesus as Lord right now while there is still time.

The Philippian jailer asked Paul and Silas what he had to do to be saved, and they said to him,

> They said, "Believe in the Lord Jesus, and you will be saved, you and your household." Acts 16:31

The apostle Paul and Silas meant that all his household can also be saved by just trusting Jesus Christ as well, the Word. That is, the jailer and everyone in his house can be saved if they each will personally trust in Jesus as Lord and Savior. Yes, it is truth my friend,

> But as many as received Him, to them He gave the right to become children of God, *even* to those who believe in His name, who were born, not of blood nor of the will of the flesh nor of the will of man, but of God. John 1:12, 13

Footnotes:

1. Zoroastrianism: "An Iranian religion, founded c600 B.C. by Zoroaster, the principal beliefs of which are in the existence of a supreme deity, Ahura Mazda, and in a cosmic struggle between a spirit of good, Spenta Mainyu, and a spirit of evil, Angra Mainyu." https://www.dictionary.com/browse/Zoroastrianism

2. "*Heureka*:" Google search.

CHAPTER 3

The Word Tabernacles in humanity

And the Word became flesh, and dwelt among us, and we saw His glory, glory as of the only begotten from the Father, full of grace and truth.

John 1:14

Introduction

Do you know what is so amazing to me? There are many people that allege to believe the Bible, which is good. Yet incredibly, many in the same breath blatantly deny the miracles in the Bible. There are endless ways that people even deny the incarnation, and there are too many avenues to discuss in this study. Still, in simple terms, many reject the testimony of God's Word in one form or another. Listen and please imprint this indelibly in your mind forever: **CHRIST THE LORD** entered this world **born of a virgin**, was **crucified on the cross for our sins, buried and risen from the dead on the third day**, and **our Lord is coming to judge the world in righteousness**. Hallelujah!

These glorious truths mentioned above are not only denied by many Jews, but these precious truths are even denied, as I have said, by individuals that espouse to believe the Bible. These are people who act like a *chameleon*, and they masquerade as believers. However, make no doubt about it, they are as Jude warns:

These men are **dangerous reefs** at your love feasts, **feasting without reverence** [GK *aphobos, without fear*], feeding only themselves. They are **waterless clouds**, carried along by the winds; autumn trees without fruit– **twice dead, uprooted**. Jude 1:12 (NET)

35

These are very dangerous predators and enemies of our Lord. These are wolves in sheep skins. There is no spiritual light in them, and some are difficult to spot such characters. At the other extreme or antithesis, there those who indorse paganism in one form or other. These are people unfortunately that may have been seduced by demons and deceived. Friend, *I kid you not!* Well, let me clear the desk and make this very plain! The Bible is very, very explicit that there is but **one God**, and His name by translation is "**the Lord**." (For by Jewish brothers and sisters, I shall refrain from spelling out the Blessed Name, "Tetragrammaton," which is the four HEB letters or the spelling in ENG.) The Shama is clear,

> "Hear, O Israel! The LORD is our God, the LORD is one! You shall
> love the LORD your God with all your heart and with all your soul and
> with all your might."   Deut. 6:4, 5

Like John 3:16, the above Scriptures are one of the most significant and important verses in the entire Bible, bar none! The Lord's name is very sacred, but many have no fear of the living God. (Since they have **no fear** of the living God, there are some who seem to *throw* His blessed and literal Name in HEB around like it is nothing.) Yes, and even those who know the Blessed Name, some speak the sacred Name with arrogance and not knowing they are acting like a fool.

Nevertheless, allow me to give a word to the *intellectuals*, "*the know it all*" and the so-called *theists*. We could never, and I mean **never**, know God unless He first communicated Himself to His creation. One might only conclude correctly there is indeed a Creation. As David said long ago,

> [4]What is man that You are mindful of him, or the son of man that
> You care for him? [5]You made him a little lower than the angels,[a] You
> crowned him with glory and honor. [6]You made him ruler of the works
> of Your hands; You have placed everything under his feet:
>
>   Psa. 8:4-6 (MSB)

> [a]Yes, the HEB is *Elohim* that refer to God. But wait, *Elohim* is used
> about 2300 times in the OT, and *Elohim* is used of *men* (*rulers* or
> *judges*), *pagan gods* (gods and goddesses), *demons*, and *holy angels*.
> The ENG Jewish Tanakh of 1917 uses the word *angel*, "GK, *aggelos*"
> for *Elohim* in Psalm 8:5. The Spirit of God uses "*aggelos*" in Heb. 2:5-9
> (which is a quote from GK OT). Friend, I would be careful if it was me;
> I would be careful in arguing against the Spirit of God.

Friend, as I have said, we can only know God because He has chosen to reveal Himself to mankind. If God tabernacled in flesh, which He did, [John 1:14; 1 Tim. 3:16] the Lord can certain safely give us the Bible without any difficulty. Listen, the Lord desires communion with His creation even fallen humanity if they will only repent and receive Jesus Christ as Lord and only Savior.

But as to the manifestations of God (God appearing to man), our Jewish brethren who know or ought to know the HEB Bible ought to know God has made about fifty *theophanies* as revealed in the HEB Scriptures. Hello! God appeared to Adam and Eve. Hello again! The Lord appear appeared to our father Abraham.[Gen. 12:7; 17:1; 18:1] The Messenger (Angel) of the Lord appeared to Moses, Joshua, to Manoah.[Exodus 3:2 Judges 6:12; 13:21, 2 Chron. 3:1] These were theophanies. Whether the phrase is "Angel (literally, Messenger) of the Lord," "the Angel of God," "His Angel," these are definitely the Lord Himself that made such appearances. Keep in mind the HEB word [*malak*] though translated "*angel*" actually means "*messenger*." So, the word HEB word *malak* applies to man, angel, and even to the Messiah.

Listen, "the Messenger" [*angel*] is not a spirit being (an angelic appearance). The meaning is unquestionable God manifesting Himself to humankind. For example,

> Then the angel [HEB *malak, the Messenger*] of the LORD appeared to him in a blazing fire from the midst of a bush; and he looked, and behold, the bush was burning with fire, yet the bush was not being consumed.
>
> Ex. 3:2

> Now when Joshua was near Jericho, he looked up and saw a man standing in front of him with a drawn sword in his hand. Joshua went up to him and asked, "Are you for us or for our enemies?" [14]"Neither," he replied, "but as [the] Commander[b] of the army of the LORD I have now come." Then Joshua fell facedown to the ground in reverence, and asked him, "What message does my Lord have for his servant?" [15]The Commander of the LORD's army replied, "Take off your sandals, for the place where you are standing is holy." And Joshua did so.
>
> Joshua 5:13-15 (NIV)

> [b]I place definite article "the" and rightly capitalize "Commander" because it refers to Christ. Actually, the YLT and LST translate the word Commander (HEB *sar*) rightly "Prince," which is the same word in HEB for Prince (Prince of Peace) Isa 9:6, which also means "Ruler."

The above references are example of the Messiah appearance. Keep in mind that the HEB "*malak*" means *messenger* not *angel an angelic holy spirit being*. Christ the Lord is **the Commander** or **the Ruler** of all things. Hence, Christ is **the Commander** of all things even the heavenly host of angels are His angels, He made them. JWs [Jehovah's Witnesses] ignorant and in darkness think this is Michael the archangel, but they are oblivious to who Christ the Lord really is: He is Almighty God, the Lord is blessed forever and ever. Amen!

Here is another kicker: the angel of the **Lord is worshipped as the LORD ALMIGHTY GOD**.Judges 6:12; 13:21 (Are you with me on the same page now?) The Messiah is attributed or declared as the Lord God.Isa. 9:6, 7; Micah 5:2 Even in Isa. 9:6, it can imply not just "mighty God" but "**Almighty God**." Even in the Psalm 2, David said,

> I will tell of the decree: The LORD said to me, "**YOU ARE MY SON**; today I have begotten^c you. ⁸ Ask of me, and I will make the nations your heritage, and the ends of the earth your possession. ⁹You shall break them with a rod of iron and dash them in pieces like a potter's vessel." ¹⁰Now therefore, O kings, be wise; **be warned**, O rulers of the earth. ¹¹**Serve the LORD with fear**, and rejoice with trembling. ¹²**KISS THE SON**, ^d lest he be angry, and you perish in the way, for his wrath is quickly kindled. **Blessed are all who take refuge in him.**
>
> (Psa. 2:7-12 ESV)

> ᶜNAS is giving the literal meaning, and the NSA is correct. Translation by some versions, "*I became your father*" ᵛ⁷, is too loose of a translation. Paul proves that Messiah is the eternal God by noting the phrase clearly that it is indeed a reference to the incarnation and His going to the cross, Acts 13:32-34.

> ᵈ"Kiss the Son:" [ᵛ¹²] is more than giving homage or even reverence. There is a sense of *submission* to a very powerful King and Ruler and even a sense of *fear*. Today, a kiss in Mideast today only implies a sense of respect, but the biblical meaning and connotation is much stronger.

I have labored to point these things out because God tabernacling in flesh ought to be the logical conclusion when studying the Scriptures. Besides, how else would an infinite God communicate to His finite, depraved, and wicked humanity unless He Himself visited mankind whom He made and whom He greatly loves?

A. The Word Tabernacles in human flesh

Those who are not open to the plain teaching of Scripture, they will surely do as they will. Regrettably, there is a price tag attached to any of our choices. (Sometimes the choice we make is irreversible.) Unfortunately, the decisions we make either by *choice* or by *default* (that make no decision) are unalterable once we cross over the threshold into eternity. So, friend, go ahead and foolishly smirk if you dare, but eternity is coming. Death does not have the last word; pay day is on the way with its reward for our decisions we make. Then, we shall see who has the last word. As I have said, keep in mind that once we crossover the threshold into eternity, there are two doors into eternity. Once the door slammed shut behind us, that door remained sealed shut. There is no turning back or reprieve. I wonder: who will be smiling them?

Many people do not get the point or message behind the purpose of the incarnation! Yes, the incarnation is infinitely incredible to contemplate for fallen and depraved humanity and especially those who imagine the universe just created itself. Friend, the incarnation is not incredibly difficult for the Lord our God to achieve since all His works are marvels, and yes, some of His works are indeed mysteries and baffling to mankind or angels. So, please get it right: **God loves you**! Let me say again, **GOD LOVES YOU**. The Lord wants you in His Kingdom, His Heaven. The *electionists allege* that the Lord has not given mankind the power to choose. Yes, true we are utterly wickedness before an infinite holy and righteous God. That is true! Nevertheless, He has given each of us the right to choose just as Joshua said long ago to Israel, "Choose this day whom you will serve –."[Joshua 24:15] Therefore, choose whom you will serve; I have chosen the Lord our God to serve for me and my family.

The apostle Paul is clear, "-the world did not know God through wisdom."[1 Cor. 1:21 ESV] Faith comes by hearing and heeding the Word of God.[Rom.10:17] Yes, we are utterly wicked and undone before the Lord, but praise the Lord, God in His infinite mercy and grace has opened the eyes by His mercy to everyone that will believe and receive Jesus Christ as Lord and Savior. The Lord has made a way back to Himself through cross of Christ. Man does not realize that he is alienated and separated from God due to his wicked sins and rebellion. Yes, humankind is in rebellion. The Good News is that God has made a way back to Himself through Jesus Christ.

As humans, we are spiritually blind as a bat concerning the things of God! Many people are attempting intellectually to reason their way into God's Kingdom. We cannot even comprehend many things in God's Word without the illumination and guidance of the Holy Spirit. I do not mean we cannot reason to know there is a God; we are too depraved and in rebellion to comprehend God's ways. As the apostle elegantly says,

> For the message [GK *logos*] of the cross is foolishness to those who are perishing, but to us who are being saved it is the power of God. [19]For it is written: "I will destroy the wisdom of the wise, And bring to nothing the understanding of the prudent." [20]Where *is* the wise? Where *is* the scribe? Where *is* the disputer of this age? Has not God made foolish the wisdom of this world? [21]For since, in the wisdom of God, the world through wisdom did not know God, it pleased God through the foolishness of the message preached to save those who believe. [22]For Jews request a sign, and Greeks seek after wisdom; [23]but we preach Christ crucified, to the Jews a stumbling block and to the Greeks [Gentiles] foolishness, [24]but to those who are called, both Jews and Greeks [Gentiles], Christ the power of God and the wisdom of God.　　　　(1 Cor. 1:18-24 NKJ)

> [d]The GK word "*message*" [NKJ] is "*logos*" [v18; same expression in John 1:1ff] not "*preaching*," [KJV]. "For the preaching of the cross is foolishness to those who perish; but unto us who are saved, it is the power of God."

If we truly desire to know God, we must come by faith to God through Jesus Christ. Without faith, that is faith in Christ, it impossible to please the Lord.[Heb. 11:6] Faith does not stand alone. Faith without the object of our faith, which is Christ the Lord, is no faith. In addition, faith is unless it is based upon obedience or action of either "WHAT GOD **SAYS**" or "WHAT GOD HAS **DONE**" is nothing more than a *credulous faith*, no faith at all.

Sorrowfully, we are void of real godly rational reasoning. Listen, reason ought to confirm genuine biblical faith and not discard reason. The problem is that humanity is too immersed and engulfed in his sin and enslaved to his depravity and wickedness of his mind to know or see the truth of God and His Word. Sadly, many believers and non-believers actually deny the biblical testimony that all humanity is indeed in bondage to sin and we are utterly depraved before the Lord our God. Friend, this is indeed the sad condition of everyone without Christ the Lord as their Redeemer.

The apostle Paul says,

> But God *commended* [GK *sunistemi, proved* or demonstrated] his love toward us, in that, while we were yet sinners, Christ died for us. [9] Much more then, being now **JUSTIFIED BY HIS BLOOD**, we shall be **SAVED FROM WRATH THROUGH HIM**. [10]For if, when we were enemies, we were **RECONCILED TO GOD BY THE DEATH OF HIS SON**, much

more, being reconciled, we shall **BE SAVED BY HIS LIFE**. [11]And not only *so*, but we also joy [*boastful or rejoiceful*] in God through our Lord Jesus Christ, by whom we have now received the atonement [GK katallage: *reconciliation*].

Rom. 5:8-11 (KJV)

Please listen to me! It is through the incarnation that God actually proved His infinite love to **ALL** **MANKIND**. Christ the Lord humbled Himself and voluntarily came into this world sacrificing Himself on the cross for our sins. This is the point of Paul's argument with the Jews at Antioch of Pisidia,

[28]And though they found no cause for death *in Him* [*Jesus*], they asked Pilate that He should be put to death. [29]Now when they had fulfilled all that was written concerning Him, they took *Him* down from the tree [*cross*] and laid *Him* in a tomb. [30]But [*the Triune*] God[e] raised Him from the dead. [31]He was seen [*in His resurrection*] for many days by those who came up with Him from Galilee to Jerusalem, who are His witnesses to the people [*of Israel*].

[32]And we declare to you glad tidings— that promise which was made to the fathers. [33]God has fulfilled this for us [*and*] their children, in that He has raised up Jesus [*from the dead*]. As it is also written in the second Psalm: `You are My Son, **TODAY I HAVE BEGOTTEN YOU.**` [34]**AND THAT HE RAISED HIM FROM THE DEAD** [e], no more to return to corruption, He has spoken thus: `I will give you the sure mercies of David.'

Acts 13:28-34 (NKJ)

"Therefore let it be known to you, brethren, that through this Man [*Christ Jesus the Lord*] is preached to you the forgiveness of sins; [39]and by Him everyone who believes is justified from all things from which you could not be justified by the law of Moses. [40]Beware therefore, lest what has been spoken in the prophets come upon you: [41]`Behold, you despisers, Marvel and perish [*e.g. in your sin*]! For I work a work in your days, A work which **YOU WILL BY NO MEANS BELIEVE,** [even] **THOUGH ONE WERE TO DECLARE IT TO YOU.**'" Acts 13:38-41 (NKJ)

[e]"God raised Him from the dead:" those who endorse *subordinationism* put forth false notion the Son and Holy Spirit is subordinate to the Father. Still even further, it is alleged that Father has different substance or essence of being from the Son or Holy Spirit. The Triune God were all integrally involved in Christ's resurrection. God is one and only one in essence of being.

41

Again, if you did not get it: the expression "'You are My Son, Today I have begotten You'" [Psa. 2:7] most definitely includes *the Messiah's birth to the cross and glorious resurrection.* Unfortunately, many miss this salient point completely. Even if Gabriel declared it, many are too spiritually blind to see this truth which is so explicitly declared.

Please listen to me, my brother, the Lord in His wonderful wisdom and greatness has reached out to all humanity in His infinite love and mercy to save us from the penalty of sin. The Son of God came into this world to save sinners. Again, as the apostle gives his own personal testimony, he said:

> I am grateful to the one who has strengthened me, Christ Jesus our Lord, because he considered me faithful in putting me into ministry [*service*], [13]even though I was formerly a blasphemer and a persecutor, and an arrogant man. But I was treated with mercy because I acted ignorantly in unbelief, [14]and our Lord's grace was abundant, bringing faith and love in Christ Jesus. [15]This saying is trustworthy and deserves full acceptance: "**CHRIST JESUS CAME INTO THE WORLD TO SAVE SINNERS**"– and I am the worst of them! [16]But here is why I was treated with mercy: so that in me as the worst [*of sinners*], Christ Jesus could **demonstrate his utmost patience, AS AN EXAMPLE FOR THOSE WHO ARE GOING TO BELIEVE IN HIM FOR ETERNAL LIFE.** [17]Now to the eternal king, immortal, invisible, the only God, be honor and glory forever and ever![e] Amen.   1 Tim. 1:12-17 (NET)

> [e]V17 is a doxology of praise by the apostle. The phrase "the only God" a reference to Christ the Lord. Those blind by Ecclesiastical Tradition and Semi-Arianism are blinded to the Biblical Truth.

It is not surprising for the apostle to declare one of the earliest Christian confessions of faith:

> By common confession, the mystery of godliness is great: God [f]appeared in the flesh, was vindicated by the Spirit, was seen by angels, was proclaimed among the nations [or *Gentiles*], was believed in throughout the world, was taken up in glory.   1 Tim. 3:16 (MSB)

> [f]Some scholars think the pronoun "**He** was manifest in the flesh" which is more acceptable. I wonder if maybe the truth "*God appeared in flesh*" is that it's too hot to handle? Ha, ha!

What the Hebrews' writer says is a little long and weighty but very necessary to note:

But there is a place where someone has testified: "What is mankind that you are mindful of them, a son of man that you care for him? [7] You made them [humanity] a little lower than the angels; you crowned them with glory and honor [8] and put everything under their feet." [from Psa. 8:5-8] In putting everything under them, God left nothing that is not subject to them. Yet at present we do not see everything subject [e.g., under humankind's dominion] to them.   (vv 6-8)

[9]But we do see Jesus, who was made [voluntarily condescended] lower than the angels for a little while, now crowned with glory and honor because he suffered death, **so that by the grace of God HE MIGHT <u>TASTE DEATH</u> <u>FOR</u> <u>EVERYONE</u>**. [10]In bringing many sons and daughters to glory [e.g.; Heaven], it was fitting that God, for whom and through whom everything exists, should make the pioneer [GK _archegos_, author NAS] of their salvation perfect through what he suffered.   (vv 9, 10)

[11]Both the one who makes people holy and those who are made holy are of the same family. So Jesus is not ashamed to call them brothers and sisters. [12]He says, "I will declare your name to my brothers and sisters; in the assembly I will sing your praises." [13]And again, "I will put my trust in him." And again he says, "Here am I, and the children God has given me."   (vv 11-13)

[14]Since the children have flesh and blood, he [Christ the Lord] too shared in their humanity so that by his death he might break the power of him who holds the power of death-- that is, the devil— [15]and free those who all their lives were held in slavery by their fear of death. [16]For surely it is not angels he [Christ the Lord] helps, but Abraham's descendants [e.g., a reference to all humanity].   (vv 14-16)

[17]For this reason he [Christ the Lord] had to be made [become] like them, **fully human in every way**, in order that he might become a merciful and faithful high priest in service to God, and that he might make atonement [GK _hilaskomai_, lit. _propitiation_] for the sins of the people. [18]Because he [Christ the Lord] himself suffered when he was tempted, he is able to help those who are being tempted.   Heb. 2:6-18 (NIV)

Now the hyper-dispensationalists allege that Hebrews is not writing to the church. I say, _hogwash_! Christ the Lord _would not be a priest if He was on earth_?[Heb. 8:4] So then, whose priest is our Lord if not for the body Christ, the church?

Therefore, the incarnation not only stands to reason; God tabernacling as fully human is the most logical in order to redeem sinful humanity for all those who truly trust in His blessed Name.[John 1:12] Praise the Lord!

B. We beheld the glory of the Word, Jesus

For the moment, let us focus on "beheld His glory,"[v 14 KJV] "we have seen his glory."[v14 ESV] (*Grace and truth* by Jesus Christ shall be discussed in the next chapter.) The thought of *"seeing Christ's glory"* is much more weigher than many of us may realize. The significance of the glory of Christ is beyond infinity to the mortal mind. This is no hyperbole or overstatement. The word "**glory**" is far more profound. Even the most brilliant human minds cannot grasp the depth and significance of the "glory" of God. His glory is even beyond the holy angels of God!

The apostle John says,

> And the Word became flesh, and dwelt among us, and **we saw** [look upon] **His glory**, glory as of the only begotten from the Father, full of grace and truth.   John 1:14

As the apostle John uses the word "glory" (GK *doxa,*[v 14]) in this particular text, the meaning is way beyond just the concept of "honor." This is true even though the word "glory" (*doxa*) can suggest this idea of simply *honor*. The word doxa has a wide range of connotative and denotative meaning which escapes many of us. Interestingly, the Bible Hub gives this general statement concerning the topic of *the glory of God*, which one particular aspect as it especially relates to nature of God.

"The "**Glory of God**" is a central theme throughout the Bible, representing the manifestation of God's presence, majesty, and holiness. It is a concept that encompasses both the visible and invisible attributes of God, reflecting His divine nature and the honor due to Him."[1]

This my friend the glory he mentioned in John 1:14 is known as *"the Shekinah glory."* The Shekinah glory is infinite light years beyond fallen humanity to ever grasp the most minute speck of understanding. My friend, again, this is no hyperbole, the glory of God is beyond our comprehension.

The NET rightly uses the connotative meaning rather using the denotative meaning, which is the HEB word *nathan*. The connotative used is to *"share."* Please note that the context in Isaiah clearly bears conclusively the connotative meaning as it relates to the nature of God.

> I am the LORD! That is my name! I will **NOT SHARE MY GLORY** [HEB nathan] with anyone else, or the praise due me with idols.   Isa. 42:8 (NET)

44

Yes, Christ the Lord *shares* in the glory within the blessed Trinity. Christ the Lord could only share in the "glory of God" if the Messiah Himself is indeed fully Eternal God. This is the very point that the apostle John is driving home. That is, to *look upon* Christ is to look upon the fullness of God. However, except during Christ's transfiguration [e.g. Matt. 17], our Lord's full glory was veiled from all of humanity.

Jesus declared very plainly to Philip who requested to reveal the Father to the apostles. Jesus said,

> Thomas said to Him, "Lord, we do not know where You are going, how do we know the way?" [6]Jesus said to him, "I am the way, and the truth, and the life; no one comes to the Father but through Me. [7]"If you had known Me, you would have known My Father also; from now on you know Him, and have seen Him." [8]Philip said to Him, "Lord, show us the Father, and it is enough for us." [9]Jesus said to him, "Have I been so long with you, and *yet* you have not come to know Me, Philip? **He who has seen Me has seen the Father**; how *can* you say, 'Show us the Father'? [10]"Do you not believe that **I am in the Father**, and **the Father is in Me**? The words that I say to you I do not speak on My own initiative, but the Father abiding in Me does His works. [11]"Believe Me that **I am in the Father** and **the Father is in Me**; otherwise believe because of the works themselves.   John 14:5-11

As we have noted before, Jesus **did** **not** mean the heresy of the "oneness doctrine" that denies biblical doctrine of the blessed Trinity. Jesus was very explicit as anyone reads the GK text:

GK:	Ego kai o' pater hen **esmen**
Transliteration:	I and the Father one **we are**
ENG	I and the Father **we are** one

The "**esmen**" means in GK "**we are**," even though it is not translated, this is unequivocally understood by translators.

The Father, the Son, and the Holy Spirit share in one essence of the being of God include the full glory of God. One God but in three distinct persons: The Father, the Son, and the Holy Spirit. Hallelujah and amen!

Therefore, Christ the Lord does not share part of the glory of God, He shares in the fullness and the glory of God incarnate.

> For in him dwelleth all the **FULLNESS OF THE GODHEAD** bodily.
>
> Col. 2:9 (KJV)

45

For in him **ALL THE FULLNESS OF GOD**[g] was pleased to dwell.

Col. 1:19 (ESV)

[g]The phrase *"the Father"* does not appear in any GK text. This is an unfortunate insertion. Again, this a reference to the Triune God and not just the Father God.

[1] God, formerly multifariously and abundantly having spoken to the fathers in [by] the prophets, [2] At these last days spake [spoken] to us in the Son, whom he set [established as]h heir of all things, by whom also he made the times [GK *aion*, ages, universe NIV]; [3] Who being the brightness of glory, and the figure of his foundation, and bearing all things by the word of his power, having made by himself the purification of our sins, he sat down on the right hand of the Majesty among the highest ones; [4] Being so much better than the angels, inasmuch as he has inherited a more distinguished name than they.   Heb. 1:1-4 (SLT)

[h]Note: the Trinity "set" or "established" the Son as Supreme heir of all things.

We must understand that Christ the Lord *cloaked*, *veiled*, or *shrouded* His glory during the earth ministry. This is very evidence when our Lord was on the mount of His transfiguration when Moses and Elijah appeared.

And he was transfigured before them. His face shone like the sun, and his clothes became white as light.   Matt. 17:2 (NET)

What does it mean when the belove apostle John stood in the presence of the **risen** and **glorified** Christ the Lord in Heaven and John falls dead like a dead man? (The meaning is clear: Christ was in His **fully glory**.) The resurrected Christ in His fully glory is lightyears beyond depraved man's understanding this truth.

And in the middle of the lampstands [a reference to the 7 churches] *I saw* one like a son of man, clothed in a robe reaching to the feet, and girded across His chest with a golden sash. [14]His head and His hair were white like white wool, like snow; and His eyes were like a flame of fire. [15]His feet *were* like burnished bronze [e.g., a highly refined metal or alloy, Friberg lex.], when it has been made to glow in a furnace, and His voice *was* like the sound of many waters [e.g., thundering very loud]. [16]In His right hand He held seven stars [7 Pastors], and out of His mouth came a sharp two-edged sword; and His face was like the sun shining in its strength [the full brilliance of the sun]. [17]**When I saw**

Him, I FELL AT HIS FEET LIKE A DEAD MAN. And He placed His right hand on me, saying, "Do not be afraid; I am the first and the last. Rev. 1:13-17

John says,

And the Word became flesh and dwelt among us. And **we beheld** [GK *theaomai, looked upon*] **His glory**, a glory as of an only begotten from *the* Father, full of grace and truth. John 1:14 (BLB)

John is describing the incredible *glory of God* which beamed from Christ Himself. If you think it's meaning is only "honor," then, that is on you my brother. However, standing in the presence of Christ the Lord's glory ought to be beyond comprehension of all those who know and love Him.

Conclusion

Even His name **JESUS (YEHOSHUA)**; means, **the LORD SAVES** or **THE LORD WILL SAVE**. It is not surprising that before the unbeliever is cast into an eternal Lake of Fire, the apostle Paul declares,

For this reason also, God highly exalted Him, and bestowed on Him the name which is above every name, [10]so that at the name of **JESUS** [*Yehoshua*] EVERY KNEE WILL BOW, of those who are in heaven and on earth and under the earth, [11]and that **every tongue will confess** that **Jesus Christ is Lord**, to the glory of God the Father. Phil. 2:9-11

Confess and receive Jesus right now to be your Lord and Savior. Praise God, Jesus will save you, and He will make you a citizen of Heaven **today**. John 1:12, 13; Rom.10:9-13 Wait until eternity's doors open for you, and you will indeed confess Yehoshua as Lord but your confession shall not be unto salvation but to your own condemnation to Hell without any mercy or retrieve.

As Jesus said:

This is why I told you that you would die in your sins. If you don't believe that **I Am**, you will die in your sins." John 8:24 (CEB)

Just as the Philippian jailer asked Paul and Salis how to be saved, it is also true for each of us today.

Then he [jailer] called for a light, and sprang in, and came trembling, and fell down before Paul and Silas, [30] And brought them out, and said, Sirs, what must I do to be saved? [31] And they said, Believe on the Lord Jesus Christ, and thou shalt be saved, and thy house. Acts 16:29-31 (KJV)

Hallelujah, as the angel announced to Joseph,

And she [your wife, Mary] will bring forth a Son, and you shall call His **name JESUS** [HEB, **YEHOSHUA**], **for He will save His people from their sins.**"
Matt. 1:21 (NKJ)

If you will genuinely trust and commit your life to Jesus as Lord and Savior, He will surely save you from your sins. Jesus in His love for you died on the cross for your sins and my sins. Friend, He will surely save you from your sins right now. Call upon Him!

Footnotes:

1. *The glory of God*, from Bible Hub, under topical search. (Available over the internet free.)

CHAPTER 4

Christ is the Revelator of God

John [the Baptist] testified about Him and cried out, saying, "This was He of whom I said, 'He who comes after me has a higher rank[a] than I, for He existed before me.'" For of His fullness we have all received, and grace upon grace. For the Law was given through Moses; grace and truth were realized[b] [GK *ginomai, came into* being] through Jesus Christ. No one has seen God at any time; the only begotten God who is in the bosom of the Father, He has explained *Him.*   John 1:15-18 (NAS)

[a]In the prologue of John Gospel, the Word (GK logos) is not only with God; the Logos was indeed the Eternal God Himself who lives forever and ever.

[b]Literally, "***came into being***:" the connotative meaning might suggest the idea "*realized*" [v17], but the more natural flow is *grace and truth came through Jesus Christ.* As given by CEB, "grace and truth came into being through Jesus Christ."

Introduction

Before we get too far into this chapter, allow me to clarify John the Baptist's statement concerning the Logos, Christ the Lord. John the Baptist declares the Word (Logos) existed before him:

GK:	hoti protos[b] mou en
Transliteration:	because before me [He] was
ENG	because He existed[b] before me

"*Protos*" means "*first*," but in this sense, the meaning is "*before me*" [*protos mou*]; that is, the Logos existed before John the Baptist. Keep in mind that John the Baptist was born before Jesus.[Luke 1:39-45] John the Baptist (like everyone else) was unaware of the Logos' full and complete identity. The Logos, Christ the Lord, existed from all eternity.[John 1:1-3]

> And thou, *Bethlehem*, house of *Ephratah*, art few in number to be *reckoned* among the thousands of Juda; *yet* out of thee shall one come forth to me, to be a ruler of Israel; and his goings forth were from the beginning, *even* **from eternity**.   Mic. 5:2 (LXE)

John the Baptist spoke by divine revelation since he did not know Jesus was the Messiah, the Eternal One-Himself.

The GK expression "*protos*" is very significant in reference to the Lord our God. The apostle John declares that the risen Christ the Lord is First: the Preeminent One,

> And when I saw Him, I fell at His feet as dead. But He laid His right hand on me, saying to me, "Do not be afraid; I am the "**First**" [GK *protos*] ^c and the Last. [18] "I *am* He who lives, and was dead, and behold, I am alive forevermore. Amen. And I have the keys of Hades and of Death.
>
>   (Rev. 1:17, 18 NKJ)

> ^cThis is in Rev. 2:8; 22:13. Also, this is particularly noted in Isaiah as the Suffering Servant.[Isa. 41:4; 44:6; 48:12]

This title (*the First and the Last*) is used of the God of Israel the Lord, the Eternal One.

> "Who has performed and accomplished *it,* Summoning the generations from the beginning? 'I, the LORD^d, am the <u>first</u>, and with the last. I am He.'"   Isa. 41:4

> ^dThis is the preincarnate Christ the Lord. (See Isa. 43:10, 14, 15; 45:21; 48:12.)

> "Thus says the LORD, the King of Israel, And his [*Israel's*] Redeemer, the LORD of hosts: `I *am* the **First** and I *am* the **Last**; Besides Me *there is* no God."   Isa. 44:6 (NKJ)

The phrase: "'I *am* the First and I *am* the Last; Besides Me *there is* no God'" refers to Almighty God. Christ the Lord is the Preeminent One, the

Eternal One, and from Everlasting to Everlasting. He is Almighty God and there is no other, the Triune God.

There are numerous heretics bombarding the person of Christ and His redeeming grace. Unfortunately, there are indeed a host of heresies and too numerous to recount in this study here. However, there are the heretics that attempt to slip through the pretense of orthodoxy. They may say, "Christ and the Holy Spirit were begotten of the Father," as noted earlier. The phrase "the First and the Last" obligates such heresy because Christ the Lord is from all eternity and without beginning or end.

In the same way, others allege that the Father has a different substance or essence of being than the Son and the Holy Spirit. Hence, there is the fracturing the oneness of God. Jesus declared that 'I and the Father **we are one**.'[John 10:30] The blessed Trinity are one in essence and being; there is no God but Lord.

Still other heretics attack Christ on the word "begotten" or "son" attempting to suggest that Christ has an *origin* or *beginning*. Christ is the *Source* of all creation; Christ is the Creator and Sustainer of all things. The apostle Paul is clear,

> [15]He [Christ] is the image of the invisible God, the firstborn [Preeminent One] of all creation.
>
> [16]For by him [Christ] all things were created, in heaven and on earth, visible and invisible, whether thrones or dominions or rulers or authorities-- all things were created through him and [created] for him.
>
> [17]And he [Christ] is before all things [eternal], and in him all things hold together [and maintained, sustained].
>
> [18]And he [Christ] is the head of [Supreme over] the body, the church. He is the beginning [GK arche, Source or Origin of all things], the firstborn from the dead [Sovereign], that in everything he might be preeminent.
>
> [19]For in him [Christ] all the fullness of God was pleased to dwell,
>
> [20]and through him to reconcile[e] to himself all things, whether on earth or in heaven, making peace by the blood of his cross. Col. 1:15-20 (ESV)
>
> [e]Note, "reconciled:" man is alienated from God due his sin. A person cannot be reconciled until he genuinely receives Christ and is born by the Spirit.[Rom. 8:9-11; Gal. 4:4-7]

Those blinded by power of darkness **cannot** see the truth of God's Word or grasp the awesomeness of Christ the Lord. For those whose eyes and hearts have been opened and illuminated by the Spirit, His truth has been made known to you. Get on your knees and praise the Lord for His very great mercy towards you. For King David said in Psalm 2,

> Kiss the Son, that He not be angry and you perish *on* the way, For His wrath may be kindled quickly. How blessed are all who take refuge in Him!
> Psa. 2:12

A. We have all received — grace upon grace.[V16]

The translation is indeed a little hard to put into ENG, but Young's Literal Translation by Robert Young of 1862 does an excellent job.

> And out of his [*Christ*] fulness did we all receive, and grace over-against grace.[f]
> John 1:16 (YLT)

> [f] "Grace for grace"[KJV] (GK "*charin anti charitos*"): to paraphrase it, perhaps, "*superabounding with grace and overflowing with even more grace.*" A difficult phrase.

This is as close as it get in literal translations. This is similar to what Paul declares in Romans,

> [18]So then, as through one offense [*of Adam*] the result was condemnation to all mankind, so also through one act of righteousness [*Jesus Christ*] the result was justification of life to all mankind. [19]For as through the one man's [*Adam's*] disobedience the many [*that is all*] were made sinners, so also through the obedience of the One [*Jesus Christ*] the many [*availability to all*] will be made righteous. [20]The Law came in so that the offense would increase; but where sin increased, **GRACE ABOUNDED** [g] [GK *huperperisseuo, superabound*] all the more, [21] so that, as sin reigned in death, so also **GRACE WOULD REIGN through righteousness to eternal life through Jesus Christ our Lord**.
> Rom. 5:18-21

> [g]The word "*abound*" has a prefix, "*hyper.*" The grace of Christ the Lord is continuing to "*overflow* or *superabound*" in His infinite grace to save even more and more sinners. Salvation is for everyone that will genuinely commit their life to Christ and put their complete trust in Him as Lord and Savior. Hallelujah!

Christ's grace is continuing to *superabound and overflow* to all mankind even though man is increasing to sin more and more. Yet, the apostle continues by saying,

What shall we say then? **Are we to continue in sin so that grace may increase?** [2]May it never be! How shall **we who died to sin** [*in Christ*] still live in it? [3]Or do you not know that all of us who have been baptized[h] [e.g., *engrafted by the Spirit*] into Christ Jesus [*we as believers*] **have been baptized** [*engrafted in Christ*] **into His death?** [4]Therefore **we have been buried with Him** through baptism [*engrafted in Christ*] into death, so that as Christ was raised from the dead through the glory of the Father, **so we too might walk in newness of life.** Rom. 6:1-4

[h]**"Baptism:"** Paul is **not** referring to water baptism. When we are genuinely saved in Christ by faith in Him, we are **engrafted** or **united** in Christ's death, burial, and resurrection by work of the Spirit. (Read carefully Rom. 6:5-11, 1 Cor. 12:13 and Col. 2:9-13.) This is the sole work of the Holy Spirit.[1 Cor. 12:13] Water baptism by immersion is portrait of our dying, burial, and resurrection in Christ. Water baptism was an OT practice by immersion, but NT water baptism is not a continuation under the Old Covenant. Baptism by immersion ought to be a **testimony of being in Christ** and **not** an entrance into Christ. Some only have "*a canned confession*" but void of genuine regeneration by the Holy Spirit.

Again, the apostle says,

And out of his [*Christ*] fullness did we all receive, and grace over-against grace. John 1:16 (YLT)

As we noted in Rom. 5:20 that grace of Christ the Lord *superabounds* to all of us as rebellious sinners as we even continue to sin more and more. This is because our Lord is seeking out sinners to save by His mighty grace. Hallelujah!

Electionists', their God is too small. The *electionists* allege that He is only electing to save a few. They allege that no one will come to the Gospel; so, God is electing a few to be saved since no one will come to Christ. Friend, this is blatant theological insertion of eisegesis. Upon this point, the *electionists'* are in serious exegetical error and theologically incorrect. The *electionists'* do injustice to the infinite mercy and beneficence of the Lord our God to the world. Simply stated, just one of greatest verses in the Bible obligates the electionists' hypothesis:

"For **GOD SO LOVED THE WORLD** that He gave His only begotten Son, that **WHOEVER BELIEVES** in Him should not perish but have everlasting life." John 3:16 (NKJ)

Yes, the grace of the Lord is superabounding to save more and more sinners. The apostle John says in his first letter,

> My dear children, I write this to you so that you will not sin. But if anybody does sin, we have an advocate with the Father-- Jesus Christ, the Righteous One. ² He is the atoning sacrifice [GK *hilasmos, propitiation*] for our sins, and not only for ours but also for the sins of the whole world.
>
> 1 John 2:1, 2 (NIV)

John the Baptist said by Spirit of God,

> The next day John saw Jesus coming toward him and said, "Look, the Lamb of God, **who TAKES AWAY THE SIN OF THE WORLD**!
>
> John 1:29

> For this is good and acceptable in the sight of God our *Savior,*[i] **⁴WHO WILL [*desires*] THAT ALL MEN *SHALL BE SAVED*,** and come *unto* the acknowledging of the *truth.* ⁵For there is one God, and one *Mediator between* God and man, which is the man Christ *Jesus,* **⁶WHO GAVE HIMSELF A *RANSOM* FOR ALL MEN,** to be that *testimony* in due time
>
> 1 Tim. 2:3-6 (GNV)

> ⁱNo words have been changed in the GNV; only the spelling has been updated to the present ENG.

> For it is for this we labor and strive, because we have fixed our hope on the living God, **WHO IS THE SAVIOR OF ALL MEN, ESPECIALLY OF BELIEVERS**.
>
> 1 Tim. 4:10

Salvation is indeed available for all mankind, though only the genuine believer will realize it. As I have said before, the election of God is an absolute paradox or a conundrum which neither men or angels can comprehend. It is incumbent that we as saints legitimately and faithfully seek to persuade everyone to come to Christ. The door of salvation is opened to everyone without exception.

As to the grace of God in Christ, the Bible is clear,

> **For the grace of God that brings SALVATION HAS APPEARED TO ALL MEN**, ¹²teaching us that, denying ungodliness and worldly lusts, we should live soberly, righteously, and godly in the present age, ¹³looking for the blessed hope and glorious appearing of our great God and Savior Jesus Christ, ¹⁴**who gave Himself for us, that He might redeem us from every lawless deed and purify for Himself *His* own**

special people, zealous for good works. [15]Speak these things, exhort, and rebuke with all authority. Let no one despise you.

Titus 2:11-15 (NKJ)

As the apostle Peter says in the close of his First Epistle,

- exhorting and declaring that this is the true grace of God. Stand firm in it. 1 Peter 5:12 (ESV)

B. The Law came by Moses, but grace and truth came by Jesus Christ,[v17]

Let us note this verse again as given by the Common ENG Bible,

As the Law was given through Moses, so **grace and truth came into being through Jesus Christ**. John 1:17 (CEB)

Christ Jesus the Lord is *dispenser* or the **Giver** of the grace and truth of God. Grace and truth of God is illuminated by work of the Holy Spirit. The doctrine of pluralism (the doctrine that says that there is no single absolute truth) has *blanketed the world*. Hence, everything is said to be relative, and everything is subject to change. That is, there is no absolute truths.

What contradiction! Here is Pluralism logic which diminishes their incongruent logic.

Everything is relative.
There are no absolutes.
Everything is relative since there are no absolutes.

Here is their fallacy in their syllogism or logic of "*pluralism*." If there are no absolutes in the doctrine of pluralism, how then can "Pluralism" declare _absolutely_ there are no such thing as absolutes? Therefore, pluralism is a contradiction, and pluralism is unable to stand to reason. Pluralism is strongly espoused in Western Philosophy.

God and His Word is in reality the only thing that is truly absolute. Only the Word of God surpasses in time and eternity. Mankind is totally *impotent* to grasp this simple truth: God and His Word is the only thing that is truly absolute. As I have said, mankind is like a young chick that just cracked its shell, and the young chick is unaware of dangers awaits it. If it were not for the grace of God, mankind would have fallen from the pages of history long ago. Man is upheld and sustained by the mercy and grace of God. The Lord gave this divine promise to Noah and his posterity, which is still true today,

"While the earth remains, Seedtime and harvest, Cold and heat, Summer and winter, And day and night Shall not cease." Gen. 8:22

The apostle Paul tells us that the goodness and longsuffering of the Lord ought to lead humankind to repentance.

> Or do you despise the riches of his [*God's*] kindness and forbearance and patience? Do you not realize that God's kindness is meant to lead you to repentance? ⁵But by your hard and impenitent heart you are storing up wrath for yourself on the day of wrath, when God's righteous judgment will be revealed. ⁶For he will repay according to each one's deeds ^[*behavior*]:
>
> Rom. 2:4-6 (NRS)

Isaiah said it well,

> The LORD God is waiting to show how kind he is and to have pity on you. The LORD always does right; he blesses those who trust him.
>
> Isa. 30:18 (CEB)

Moses was indeed one of the most humble men of God. Someone has rightly noted Moses' life went this way:

> ➢ For forty years Moses had thought to himself that *he was really somebody* being raise in the Pharaoh's house.

> ➢ Then, for the next forty years, Moses was placed on the backside of the desert, and *now he realized that he was a nobody.*

> ➢ Ah, but at eighty God showed him that for the next forty years *the Lord can use a nobody.*

Moses was given the Law to give to Israel. The Law is good, holy, and righteous. Though the Law is holy and good, the Law does not impute righteous. The Law only reveals or declares the true nature of all things. For instance, the Law declares the holiness and righteousness of the Lord our God. In the same way, the Law reveals the wickedness and sinfulness of humankind. Yet, the Law cannot give or impute righteousness. The Law makes known the holiness and righteousness of God. One might say that the Law is like a mirror: the Law reflecting the holy and righteous standards of God. But as mirror, the Law also reveals all of humanity under sin. Therefore, we are all guilty before the Lord, a holy and righteous God. As a righteous God, He shall surely judge sin and the sinner.

The apostle Paul declares,

> Yet we know that a person is not justified by works of the law but ^[*they are justified*] through faith in Jesus Christ, so we also have believed in Christ

Jesus, in order to be justified by faith in Christ and not by works of the law, because by works of the law no one will be justified.　　　(v16)

I have been crucified with Christ. It is no longer I who live, but Christ who lives in me. And the life I now live in the flesh I live by faith in the Son of God, who loved me and gave himself for me. I do not nullify the grace of God, for if righteousness were through the law, then Christ died for no purpose.　　　Gal. 2:16, 20, 21 (ESV)

So, we must understand that "**grace** and **truth** came into being through Jesus Christ."[John 1:17 CEB] The Lord tabernacles among humanity was indeed the personification or the embodiment of grace and truth. This is the point in the apostle John's prologue. But even more importantly, true grace and truth became fully realized through Jesus Christ.

The apostle John says that the Word came into this sinful world. He entered the world "full of grace and truth," .

And the Word was made flesh, and dwelt among us, (and we beheld his glory, the glory as of the only begotten of the Father,) **FULL OF GRACE** and **TRUTH**.　　　John 1:14 (KJV)

Grace and truth are realized in and through Jesus Christ. In Christ, there is available **grace** that reaches out even to the most defiled and profane person that is willing to genuinely repent, receive, and trust Him as Lord and only Savior. He will forgive you of all your sin. He will clean up from inside out. He will impute His righteousness to you. (You read me correctly, "Christ *will impute His righteousness to you.*") Yes, He will even make you a citizen of Heaven **today**. In addition, Jesus will empower you to live a godly life and have victory over sin and its power over your life today. This is all possible when you genuinely repent, and trust and commit your life to Him.

As to truth, this is one of very names or titles attributed to Christ the Lord. Since the Lord alone is absolute full of truth. It is impossible for the Lord to lie. [Titus 1:2] This is an absolute truth which pluralism can never comprehend. Jesus was very clear,

Jesus saith unto him, I am the way, the truth, and the life: no man cometh unto the Father, but by me.　　　John 14:6 (KJV)

Jesus is not one of the truths; my friend, Jesus is **the TRUTH**. The Bible declares,

In whom [*Christ Jesus*] are hidden **ALL** the **TREASURES** of **WISDOM** and **KNOWLEDGE**.　　　Col. 2:3

Grace and truth are available, but it is only available in Jesus Christ. Pluralism does not want to know the truth, since to them everything is relative and there is no absolute truth. Therefore, pluralism cannot bear the truth. As Jesus said,

> "If the world hates you, be aware that it hated me first. [19] If you belonged to the world, the world would love you as its own. However, because you do not belong to the world, but I chose you out of the world, for this reason the world hates you.　　　　　John 15:18, 19 (NET)

Listen, the grace and truth of Jesus Christ will save you (if you genuinely trust and receive Him). Ah, but Jesus' grace and truth will wonderfully transform you for the better in this life! Yes, Jesus will change your life for the better today. You must personally trust and receive Him and seek to walk in His will. He is the greatest Friend you will ever have in this life and in the life to come.

C. The only begotten — He has explained God, [v 18]

There are two very important points that must not be overlooked in John 1:18. The first, we noted earlier, but need to look at once more due to the extreme importance to the doctrine of Christ: the phrase *"the only begotten."* The second, there is the significance to the purpose behind the incarnation: *"He has declared Him [God]."* (Though the second aspect might be easily overlooked by some.)

1. "The only begotten —"

This phrase *'the only begotten'* as it relates to the Christ is **interwoven** with two very important thoughts. Some think *only begotten son* focuses on the uniqueness, BYZ GK *monogenēs huios*: translation, "one and only unique Son."

> *(a). This is connected with <u>the incarnation</u>. Some older GK texts read (GK <u>monogenēs theos</u>, only begotten **God** NAS): translation "only begotten God." I favor the NAS text here.*

> *(b).* Also equally important, 'the only begotten' is related to <u>the redemption for humankind</u>, which is indeed of extreme importance in the doctrine of the incarnation. Let us consider these two concepts. What sometimes is overlook is how the incarnation, "begotten" is interwoven with the doctrine of redemption.

2). "The only begotten"

David said by Spirit of God,

> "I will declare the decree: The LORD has said to Me, `You *are* My Son,
> Today **I have begotten You.**'   Psa. 2:7 (NKJ)

The context and the NT revelation conclusively reveals the emphasis is definitely that the Messiah (the Anointed One or the Christ) was prophesied as coming into the world to bring justice and godly rule, Psa. 2. Hidden in the mysteries of God, the Messiah also came as the **Redeemer** of mankind **through the cross.** Ah, but this mystery **(the Redemption through the cross)** was hidden within the blessed Trinity but concealed from angels and man through God's plan was clearly prophesied.

> Yet among the mature we do speak wisdom, though it is not a wisdom of this age or of the rulers of this age, who are doomed to perish. [7] But we speak **God's wisdom, secret** [a mystery] and **hidden** [GK *apokrupto, concealed*], which God decreed before the ages for our glory. [8]**None of the rulers** of this age understood this; for if they had [understood the cross], they would not have crucified the Lord of glory.   1 Cor. 2:6-8 (NRS)

2. *The interweaving with the incarnation*: there was the mystery of the cross.

Here are some main texts that are related to *the incarnation* - Psa. 2:7, Acts 13:33f, and Heb. 1:5;5:5. The emphasis of the prophetic Psalm 2:7 clearly points to the incarnation, and particularly, from **the *cradle* to *the* *cross*.**

"I will declare the decree: The LORD has said to Me, `You *are* My Son, Today I have begotten You. Psa. 2:7 (NKJ)	God has fulfilled this for us their children, in that He has raised up Jesus. As it is also written in the second Psalm: `You are My Son, Today I have begotten You.' Acts 13:33 (NKJ)
	For to which of the angels did He ever say: "You are My Son, Today I have begotten You "? And again: "I will be to Him a Father, And He shall be to Me a Son "? Heb. 1:5 NKJ
	So also Christ did not glorify Himself to become High Priest, but *it was* He who said to Him: "You are My Son, Today I have begotten You." Heb. 5:5 (NKJ)

There is nothing implying origin or beginning of the Christ. The Christ is forever.[John 12:34; Rom. 9:5; Heb. 13:8, 21] Christ the Lord is without beginning or end; He is eternal. The salient point here is that the word "begotten" is addressing the Christ coming into the world not origin. Hence, "begotten" has nothing to do with origin or having a beginning in time. This is by far one of the most important observations that must be <u>underscored</u> here. Again, there is nothing referring to Christ's origin or beginning. Cults and unbelievers have no concern for contextual exegesis or study of God's Word. (That is, let Scripture interpret Scripture.) They are only looking from the natural man, which eisegesis reading the texts. The unregenerate and immature are completely alienated and blinded from the truth Scripture is declaring.[2 Cor. 4:3f, Eph. 2:1-3]

a). The interweaving in the incarnation was redemption: - Christ came as the Lamb of God.

Christ the Lord is the One who bore our sins on the cross.[2 Cor. 5:21; 1 Peter 2:24] Christ came as the Lamb of God; He bore our sins on the cross. The blessed Triune God was all equally at work in the resurrection.[John 10:10f; Rom. 8:9-11; Gal.1:1] The Trinity of God's justice was satisfied at cross: sin and sinner's debt was paid in full. The redemption of man is fulfilled and became available to **all mankind** that **would repent**, **believe**, and **receive the Gospel**.[1Cor.15:3f]

Therefore, when one examines every reference to the word "only begotten" (in reference to Christ), we ought to understand that the phrase "*only begotten*" is interwoven into the doctrine of redemption:

> And the Word became flesh, and dwelt among us, and we saw His glory, glory as of the **ONLY BEGOTTEN from the Father**, full of grace and truth. John 1:14

> No one has seen God at any time; the **ONLY BEGOTTEN GOD** who is in the bosom of the Father, He has explained *Him*. John 1:18

> "For God so loved the world, that He gave His **ONLY BEGOTTEN SON**, that whoever believes in Him shall not perish, but have eternal life. John 3:16

> "He who believes in Him is not condemned; but he who does not believe is condemned already, because he has not believed in the name of the **ONLY BEGOTTEN SON OF GOD**." John 3:18 (NKJ)

> By this the love of God was manifested in us, that God has sent His **ONLY BEGOTTEN SON** into the world so that we might live through Him. 1 John 4:9

The previous verses should be quite obvious that the incarnation includes the plan of God for the redemption of mankind. This is the hidden mystery of God.[1 Cor. 2:6-8]

If there is any lingering doubt, let us note once again Paul's message to the Jews at Antioch in Pisidia.

> "And though they found no cause for death *in Him*, they asked Pilate that He should be put to death. [29]Now when they had fulfilled all that was written concerning Him, they took *Him* down from the tree [cross] and laid *Him* in a tomb. [30]But [Triune] God raised Him from the dead. [31]He was seen for many days by those who came up with Him from Galilee to Jerusalem, who are His witnesses to the people. [32]And we declare to you [the] glad tidings— that promise which was made to the fathers. [33]God has fulfilled this for us [and] their children, in that He has raised up Jesus. As it is also written in the second Psalm: `**You are My Son, Today I have BEGOTTEN YOU**.'" Acts 13:28-33 (NKJ)

> [36]"For David, after he had served his own generation by the will of God, fell asleep [e.g., his body die, but his soul went to Heaven], was buried with his fathers, and saw corruption [of his body]; [37]but He [Christ Jesus] whom [Triune] God raised up saw no corruption. [38]Therefore let it be known to you, brethren, that through this Man [Jesus] is preached to you the forgiveness of sins; [39]and by Him everyone who believes is justified from all things from which you could not be justified by the law of Moses." Acts 13:36-39 (NKJ)

I hope you can grasp the significance of the incarnation, God tabernacling Himself in flesh. The main purpose of the incarnation was to go to the cross for sinners, but the cross was concealed from mortal man and angels. (Yes, even Satan and the evil angels saw the cross a defeat.) Ah, but the cross was the Triumph of God. The victory was won at cross. Hallelujah!

> And having disarmed the powers and authorities, he made a public spectacle of them, triumphing over them by the cross. Col. 2:15 (NIV)

b). "—He *[Christ]* has declared *Him* [Triune God]," which is the last clause in.[v18]

Let us note again the complete verse 18.

> No one has seen God at any time. The **only begotten Son**, who is in the bosom of the Father, **He has declared *Him*.** John 1:18 (NKJ)

The word "declare"[v18] is the GK word *exegeomai*; it is the root word where we derive the word in English "exegesis." Exegesis meaning "to explain" or

61

"interpret."[1] The NAS is on target. The word *exegeomai* **implies** much more than "to declare God," or "to make God known." The prophets, the apostles, and the *ish Elohim* (the men of God) declared God and His Word (the Bible). Christ's incarnation was to "**explain**" or "clearly make God **understood**." (To understand or to be understood is the connotative meaning, but the denotative meaning would be "to explain.")

Tradition had so overridden or superseded the Scripture that the true meaning has become *obscured or eclipsed*. This is exactly what has happened to the Church: the Scripture has become *circumscribed* or *secondary to tradition or church doctrine and practices*.

Christ's incarnation included declaring the full clarity of God and His revelation to fallen humanity. The prophets and apostles declared the revelation of God. In the incarnation, Christ made God *fully* or *plainly* know.

Today, it is so *popular* and *less offensive* to use the generic, "*God*." The generic use of "*God*" allows fallen mankind to put in the meaning of the "god" of their wicked imagination. Rarely, do we ever hear the word "the Lord" even from the pulpit. Friend, this is no exaggeration; we rarely hear the name the Lord our God in sermon. After all, "We don't want to be offensive to world." How sorry is that? Well friend, I am here to tell you the Gospel is foolishness and offensive.

> For the preaching of the cross is to them that perish foolishness-
>
> 1 Cor. 1:18b (KJV)

> -[23]we preach Christ crucified, unto the Jews a stumblingblock, and unto the Greeks foolishness; [24] But unto them which are called, both Jews and Greeks, Christ the power of God, and the wisdom of God.
>
> 1 Cor. 1:23, 24 (KJV)

The woman at Jacob's well was quick to use the generic name "God." Jesus rejoined and sharply corrected her by says,

> "Sir," the woman said, "I can see [*perceive*] that you are a prophet. [20]Our ancestors worshiped on this mountain, but you Jews claim that the place where we must worship is in Jerusalem." [21]"Woman," Jesus replied, "believe me, a time is coming when you will worship the Father neither on this mountain nor in Jerusalem. [22]**You Samaritans WORSHIP WHAT YOU DO NOT KNOW** [GK *oida*, or *understand*]; we worship what we do know, for salvation is from the Jews. [23]Yet a time is coming and has now come when the true worshipers will worship the Father in the Spirit

and in truth, for they are the kind of worshipers the Father seeks. ²⁴God
is spirit, and his worshipers must worship in the Spirit and in truth."

John 4:19-24 (NIV)

Note again, Jesus said to the Samaritan woman, 'worship what you <u>do</u> <u>not</u>
<u>know</u>.' Two things to give close attention here. One, the Samaritans did not
know what they were worshipping though they "worship *a god*." Samaritans
were a religious mixture paganism and a little dab Judaism which they did not
understand or know. Two, Samaritans were *void of the revelation* and *knowledge of the true God* of Heaven, the Lord. Samaritans only accept the Five
books of Moses, the Torah.

The apostle Paul tells us plainly who the pagans are truly worshipping of
which many in the church still do not get the point here.

Nay, but that these things which the Gentiles sacrifice, they sacrifice to
*devils*ⁱ [GK *daimonion, demons*], and not *unto* God: and I would not that ye should
have fellowship with the *devils* [GK *daimonion, demons*].   1 Cor. 10:20 (GNV)

ⁱNo words have been changed in the GNV; only the spelling updated
and the words in brackets "[ ]" are for clarity. (Also see Lev.17:7;
Deut.32:17; 2 Cor.11:15; Psa. 106:37; Gal.4:8; Rev.9:20;13:4.)

I was aboard an Alaska cruise ship, and it was one evening for dinner.
There was a very well-to-do Russian woman sitting at our table. As we enjoyed
our meal together, she knowing I was a Pastor, said,

"Well, you know the difference between the Roman
Catholics and Russian Orthodox Church, don't you?"

At the moment, I thought to myself, "*No, but she is about
tell me.*"

She rejoined by saying, "Roman Catholics '**pray to
Mary**;' we only **pray through her!**"

Jesus told the Sadducees who only believe in five books of Moses (like the
Samaritans), but the Sadducees did not believe in life after death, [*Jesus said,*]
'You neither know the Scripture nor the power of God."ᴹᵃᵗᵗ· ²²:²⁹
As we alluded to the Pharisees, our Lord corrected them with Scripture,

And so you cancel the word of God in order to hand down your own
tradition. And this is only one example among many others."

Mark 7:13 (NLT)

63

There was a very unique encounter with intellectual religious leaders in Jerusalem by our Lord at the age of twelve. Jesus is twelve years old and perhaps this might have been His "bar mitzvah," though thirteen is the age many Jews set for the age. Any rate, we are given this amazing account,

> And when he was twelve years old, they went up according to custom. [43]And when the feast was ended, as they were returning, the boy Jesus stayed behind in Jerusalem. His parents did not know it, [44]but supposing him to be in the group they went a day's journey, but then they began to search for him among their relatives and acquaintances, [45]and when they did not find him, they returned to Jerusalem, searching for him. [46]**After three days they found him in the temple, sitting among the teachers, listening to them and asking them questions.** [47]**And all who heard him were AMAZED AT HIS UNDERSTANDING and HIS ANSWERS.** [48]And when his parents saw him, they were astonished. And his mother said to him, "Son, why have you treated us so? Behold, your father and I have been searching for you in great distress." [49]And he said to them, "Why were you looking for me? **DID YOU NOT KNOW THAT I MUST BE IN MY FATHER'S HOUSE?**" [50]And they did not understand the saying that he spoke to them.
>
> Luke 2:42-50 (ESV)

The whole point here is that in the incarnation of the Lord, Jesus will set the record straight. Jesus not only declared the Word of God, but He set the record straight. He explained God and that He is the Word.

Finally, the Pharisees sent a delegation to examine Jesus' teaching. This is result of their encounter with the Logos,

> The officers then came to the chief priests and Pharisees, and they said to them, "Why did you not bring Him?" The officers answered, "Never has a man spoken the way this man speaks."   John 7:45, 45, 46

Conclusion

I am hopeful that one thing is very clear, *the Prologue* or *the Introduction* [John 1:1-18] by the apostle John has helped to set the tone and whole purpose for his writing the Gospel of John. John is the plainest and clearest Gospel written for evangelism. Still, without the Prologue decisively in mind, the complete purpose for writing his Gospel may escape most of us who read the Gospel of John. (Sadly, many are too fixated as being verse originated rather being totally contextually originated.) As one person rightly observed: *a verse with the context is a pretext.* For John says,

> Now Jesus performed many other miraculous signs in the presence of the disciples, which are not recorded in this book [*the Gospel of John*]. But these [*signs*] are recorded so that you may believe that Jesus is the Christ, the Son of God, and that by believing you may have [*eternal*] life in his name.   John 20:30, 31 (NET)

Friend, I must warn you that if you reject the testimony of Scripture, you are rejecting the witness of God Himself.[1 John 5:10-13] To declare God is a liar (that is exactly what anyone is doing if they reject the witness of Scripture). Let me warn you that only a fool would make a mistake in calling God's Word a lie. This is the testimony from God: "in hope of eternal life which God, who cannot lie, promised before time began."[Titus 1:2 NKJ]

Therefore, as we proceed with the eight miraculous signs of our Lord, there is much more being declared than just the astonishment of miracles. Each miracle establishes the true identity of God tabernacling in full humanity. In addition, each miracle unveils something unique concerning Christ the Lord.

Hopefully, we shall discover some of the very unique elements in order to enrich our study, illuminate, and walk even more godly with our Lord in this world of sin and woe.

Footnotes:

1. "Declared" in John 1:18 NKJ: this is the GK "exegeomai." Friberg, Analytical GK Lex: (from Bible Works 10) "(1) as giving a description or detailed report *explain, report, describe* (Acts 10:8); (2) of God's self-revelation through Christ *reveal, make fully known* (John 1:18)."

Part Two

The Miraculous Signs of Jesus

The First Miraculous Miracle and Sign:
Jesus Transformed Water into Wine

Now on the third day there was a wedding at Cana in Galilee. Jesus' mother was there, [2]and Jesus and his disciples were also invited to the wedding. [3]When the wine ran out, Jesus' mother said to him, "They have no wine left." [4]Jesus replied, "Woman, why are you saying this to me? My time has not yet come." [5]His mother told the servants, "Whatever he tells you, do it." [6]Now there were six stone water jars there for Jewish ceremonial washing, each holding twenty or thirty gallons. [7]Jesus told the servants, "Fill the water jars with water." So they filled them up to the very top. [8]Then he told them, "Now draw some out and take it to the head steward," and they did. [9]When the head steward tasted the water that had been turned to wine, not knowing where it came from (though the servants who had drawn the water knew), he called the bridegroom [10]and said to him, "Everyone serves the good wine first, and then the cheaper wine when the guests are drunk. You have kept the good wine until now!" [11]Jesus did this as the first of his miraculous signs, in Cana of Galilee. In this way he revealed his glory, and his disciples believed in him.   John 2:1-11 (NET)

CHAPTER 5

"What [*is that*] to Me and to you, woman?"LSV

¹And [on] the third day a wedding happened in Cana of Galilee, and the mother of Jesus was there, ²and also Jesus was called, and His disciples, to the wedding; ³and wine having failed [*run out*], the mother of Jesus says to Him, "They have no wine"; ⁴ Jesus says to her, "What [is that] to Me and to you, woman? My hour is not yet come." ⁵His mother says to the servants, "Whatever He may say to you—do."   John 2:1-5 (LSV)

Introduction

One of the most preposterous notions by many religious groups is referring to "*Mary as the mother of God.*" Their misguided and erroneous doctrine is very zealously espoused by different religious groups. This doctrine is so zealously held in some areas of the world that the rejection of such doctrine, or even dare to laugh at some groups, might get you killed. (Friend, this is true, and this is not a joke.)

Many of these people are not ignorant. Some of these people are wealthy and fairly well educated. Still, unfortunately, the followers who endorse such false and misguided doctrine are blinded or seduced by demons. As you might recall the one Russian woman, well-to-do, remarked to me that Roman Catholics "pray to Mary;" but the Russian Orthodox woman said, "We only pray through her."

I had a brief discussion with three women (all with master's degrees or higher.) One woman said to me, "When I pray, I pray to Saint Jude, and I always get what I ask for-"

Another of the women remarked, "Amen."

The third woman shockingly said, "I'm mad at God."

My response was, "Ladies, I only bow my knees to Jesus; He is Lord over-all." Then, I said to the ladies, "When I pray to the Lord, His answer is not always *yes*. His answer is sometimes: '*yes,*' but He may also say, '*no*' or '*wait.*'" The didn't say anything. So, I continued, saying, "The Lord does this because He loves me." With that remark, the discussion ended, and I walked away.

Do you recall what the apostle Paul says concerning many Gentiles idolatry worship?

> Rather, that the things which the Gentiles sacrifice they **sacrifice to demons** and **not to God**, and I do not want you to have fellowship with demons. 1 Cor. 10:20 (NKJ)

So, when people bow their knee in worship to anything other than the Lord our God, "Who do you suppose they worship?" The danger today is people use the generic name for the Creator as simply, "God."

As I have said, many times, and I say again, *the road to Hell is paved with sincerity*. Doesn't anyone remember Joshua's final exhortation to Israel? He said,

> But if it seem not good[a] to you to serve the Lord, choose to yourselves this day whom ye will serve, whether the gods of your fathers that were on the other side of the river [*Euphrates*], or the gods of the Amorites, among whom ye dwell upon their land: but I and my house will serve the Lord, for he is holy. Joshua 24:15 (LXE)

> [a]The HEB word *raa* can mean "evil or bad," but the Septuagint (GK OT) uses "*apesko-*" meaning *acceptable* or *pleasing*.

I am sorry to say but when the door into eternity opens for many people, many people may discover that they have been worshipping demons. Yes, they were worshipping demons not the Lord our God who alone is blessed forever and ever! Remember, our Lord said,

> "Enter through the narrow gate; for the gate is wide and the way is broad that leads to destruction, and there are many who enter through it. For the gate is small and the way is narrow that leads to life, and there are few who find it." Matt. 7:13, 14

A. Jesus addresses Mary as "woman"

Please note the situation surrounding the event before noting the water being turned into wine. Note particularly how our Lord Jesus addresses Mary.

> Jesus said to her, "**Woman**, what does your concern have to do with
> Me? My hour has not yet come."   John 2:4 (NKJ)

Jesus did not address Mary as "mother" or even her given name, "Mary."
Mary was **not** Christ the Lord's mother! The Lord Christ is eternal, forever
and ever, Almighty God. Do you grasp what am saying? Mary was not Christ's
mother! Mary was only an instrument or the means our Lord used to enter the
world of humanity. This is the very event when the Jews said concerning the
Messiah: 'We have heard from the Law that the Christ remains forever.'[John
12:34 ESV] Yes, even though Mary and Joseph are referred to as Jesus' mother
and father.[Luke 2:48] Luke is recording the words of Mary, but careful, the words
are accurately recorded by Luke. Yet, Luke is not endorsing Mary's words as
divine revelation or inspiration.

Jesus said at twelve years old,

> And He [Jesus] said to them [Joseph and Mary], "Why is it that you were looking
> for Me? **Did you not know that I had to be in My Father's house?**"
> But they did not understand the statement which He had made to them.
>
>   Luke 2:49, 50

Joseph or Mary were **not** Christ's father and mother. As I have already
said, Mary was the means by which the Lord came into this world. (Mary **is
not mother of God!**) Furthermore, our Lord refers to God the Father in His
relationship within the blessed Trinity. Mary was only a channel or means God
Himself used to enter the world of humanity. Mary is not "the mother of God."
Such thinking is completely pagan idolatry. God forbid!

Even the word "_son_" (as it is used of Christ, holy angels, and redeemed
men, women, and children) does not mean being an offspring by God. Christ
the Lord, the Son of God, **is not** "_second generation_ god." To allege that the
Son of God is a so-called "_second generation_ god" is very _abhorrent_ and
depraved theology that has even been espoused by idolaters.

As I have already clarified, the holy angels and the redeemed are referred
to as "sons of God." However, the **holy angels** and **the redeemed** are **not** sons
of God by offsprings of God or as though they were generated by physical
birth. The expression "sons of God" is also used of **men**, **women** and **children**. This proves conclusively that the phrase "son of God" is referring to the
relationship with God. The expression "son of God" does not mean offsprings
by God. The meaning "_sons_" do **not mean being an offspring** when referring
to holy angels or the saved in Christ.[See Gal. 3:26-29.] Yes, in human relationships,
"_sons_" does mean offspring.

71

Many laugh when they are charged with worship Mary or praying through saints in their religious origination. Wait! It is more erroneous than praying through so-called canonized saints. First, everyone that is genuinely saved and born again in Christ is a saint. Hello! The word *saint* is derived from the word *"holy, consecrated, dedicated,* or just simply implies *set-part."* Hence, the genuine believer has been **set-part** by the Holy Spirit, and we are now citizens of Heaven.[Phi. 3:20] (A genuine Christian is not going to be a citizen of Heaven; **we are already now citizens of Heaven TODAY since we are in Christ.** Hallelujah!)

What is even more grotesque and unbelievable is what some of these wealthy religious originations falsely espouse. Such religious originations allege that their canonized saints did so many extraordinary good works that they immediately went directly to Heaven at death based upon their so-called *good works.* (Thus, declaring anyone can reach Heaven if their works are good enough.) Never mind that most people, includeing the most highest-ranking religious leaders, are suffering in their sins with erroneous doctrine of purgatory for eons and eons to atone for sins after water baptism. With such groups, Jesus did not die for all our sins. These false religious originations allege that people atone for our sins after water baptism. This is indeed another ecclesiastical fabrication.

So, these religious originations allege that their canonized saints did so much overabundance of good works that these saints' good works have been deposited in the bank in Heaven. Their so-called good works were deposited in the **Bank of Merit**. How sick is that? Their religious origination has authority over the **Bank of Merit**.

Wait, there is more! These same religious groups tell the people that if you paid enough money into their religious group (*"religious indulgences"*) that they can buy their way out of purgatory, and so, they can buy their way into Heaven. What a wicked lie! This is a lie right out of Hell. Listen to me, if you are not alarmed or greatly offended with such theology, shame on you. Friend, this kind of theology is not funny. Hear me, this is a **direct slander and a wicked insult at our Lord** and His merciful and gracious offering of Himself and **His completed redemption on Calvary**!

Friend, the Bible is clear, Jesus Christ "bore **ALL** our sins in His own body on the cross."[1 Peter 2:24] No human can atone for his/her sins and certainly not by works.[Eph. 2:8-10; Titus 3:3-7] Here is what the Word God declares about so-called good religious works,

> "For I through the law died to the law that I might live to God. [20]I have been crucified with Christ; it is no longer I who live, but Christ lives in me; and the *life* which I now live in the flesh I live by faith in the Son

of God, who loved me and gave Himself for me. [21]I do not set aside the grace of God; for if righteousness *comes* through the law, then Christ died in vain."   Gal. 2:19-21 (NKJ)

Therefore, please listen to me. Yes, Mary was specially chosen to be the vessel to bare the Lord Christ as He was to tabernacle (dwell) and live as a human being. Mary, however, is **NOT the mother of God**. Perish that thought forever! Mary was a sinner just like the rest of mankind. Mary said in her praise to the Lord for being selected to bare the Messiah,

> And Mary said: "My soul magnifies **THE LORD**, And **my spirit has rejoiced in GOD MY SAVIOR**."   Luke 1:46, 47 (NKJ)

Mary was a sinner just like all humanity. (Mary was **not** sinless.) Christ the Lord is the only sinless One. The Lord Jesus Christ is without sin. Hebrews cannot be any plainer when he says,

> But this man, because *he endures ever* [continues forever],[b] *has* a Priesthood, which cannot *pass* from one to another [inviolable, nontransferable]. [25]Wherefore, *he* is able also perfectly [completely] to *save* them that come *unto* God by him, seeing he *ever lives*, to make intercession for them. [26]For such *a* high Priest it became *us* to *have*, which is holy, *harmless, undefiled*, separate from sinners, and made *higher than* the *heavens*: [27]Which *needs* not daily as those Priests to offer *of* sacrifice, first for his *own sins*, and then for the peoples: for that did he once [He died once for sin], when he offered *of* himself. [28]For the Law *makes* men *high Priests*, which *have infirmities* [weakness]: but the word of the *oath* that was since the *Law*, *makes* the *Son*, who is consecrated for *evermore*. Heb. 7:24-28 (GNV)

> [b]There are no changes in wording in Geneva Bible. The spelling has been updated and words in brackets "[ ]" are used for clarity.

In the surrounding context, John's Gospel is clear that Mary and Joseph had other children.

> After this he went down to Capernaum, with his mother <u>and his brothers</u>[c] **AND** his <u>disciples</u>, and they stayed there for a few days.
>
> John 2:12 (ESV)

> [c]The meaning "*brothers*" [GK *adelphos*] cannot refer to His disciples" in this context. The word "disciples" is used in reference to the apostles. The word "brothers" is clearly Jesus' siblings in the family of Joseph and

Mary. Other similar texts include John 6:42; Matt. 12:46 and 13:55, Luke 8:19-21, and Mark 3:31-35.

In addition, Christ the Lord is indeed our Intercessor. This is no greater Intercessor than Christ Jesus the Lord!

> This is good and acceptable in the sight of God our Savior, [4]who desires all men to be saved and to come to the knowledge of the truth. [5]For there is **ONE GOD**, *and* **ONE MEDIATOR ALSO BETWEEN GOD AND MEN,** *THE* **MAN CHRIST JESUS,** [6]who gave Himself as a ransom for all, the testimony *given* at the proper time   1 Tim. 2:3-6

There is no other Intercessor as priest: Jesus our High Priest, Christ the Lord. (Yes, the Holy Spirit intercessor, but the Holy Spirit is not the High Priest for the New Covenant.) Yes, we also pray for one another as believers, but Jesus is the only High Priest for believers in the church. Nevertheless, Mary is **not** the mother of God. Equally, Mary is **not** an intermediator for believers. There are no so-called "canonized saints" in Heaven we pray to for aid. (Praying to saints is pagan idolatry.) Praying to Mary or praying to so-called "canonized saints" is idolatrous, [1] and this is praying to demons. Therefore, Christ the Lord is indeed the sole Intercessor as High Priest for the Redeemed.

B. "My hour has not yet come."[NIV]

Additionally, our Lord gives Mary a gentle but decisive rebuke, 'My hour has not yet come!' We do not know how much Mary or Joseph knew or understood concerning the Lord's God actual physical presence as the Messiah. (Certainly, the family members knew very little since none of his brothers believed in Him, [John 7:5].) Joseph and Mary did not understand or grasp that the child conceived by Mary was indeed God Himself. "God was revealed in the flesh."[1 Tim. 3:16 WEB] I am certain that Jesus' full identity was veiled by the Spirit of God from Joseph and Mary and the rest of humanity. (As noted above, none of Jesus' siblings knew who Jesus truly was.) So, we should be very careful to not add or imply more than what Scriptures declare. For instance, the Scriptures reveals that people have been visited by angels, and some have even hosted angels but unaware of the angel(s) true presence or identity. How much more when the Lord made theophanies or when He tabernacles in a human body?

The Lord appeared to Abraham and Sarah with angelic beings.[Gen. 18:1ff] Yet, I am doubtful Abraham and his wife fully realized this was Christ the Lord with several angels. It is certain then that Joseph and Mary may have had minute inklings of the coming Messiah, but in reality, Joseph and Mary didn't have in truth the faintest clue of Jesus' identity. So then, we ought to realize our Lord's comprehensive identity was *concealed* from every human being. Be assured that every angel, whether holy or evil, certainly knew Jesus is the Messiah. Upon God's appointed time, Christ the Lord did reveal more of Himself and His identity. Still, without the illumination or enlightenment from God and His Word, no human knew that Jesus was God Incarnate.

Sadly, there are things in the Bible saints in Christ do not really grasp today even though they earnestly study the Scriptures. *Please give me your attention here*! We are totally at the mercy of the Lord in our understanding and knowing of the Lord and His will for humankind. We are just at the kindergarten-knowledge of the Word of God. Even if anyone is able to quote the entire Bible "verbatim," still, they are lightyears from understanding the eternal Word of God. Peter even says of the angels, "These are things that even **the angels desire to look into**."[1 Peter 1:12b ISV] Keep in mind that the angels of God are far more advanced in the study of God's Word than mankind and have been give illumination. This means that angels are meticulously studying God Word with divine enlightenment.

Yes, our knowledge of God's Word is only at the kindergarten level. This is because we are totally dependent on illumination from the Spirit of God and rightly so. Simply put: we are too full of self and unable to be illuminated. *"Don't confuse me with facts, my mind is already made up!"* Our *culture, background*, our *associations, traditions, superstitions*, the *pagan world*, our own *experiences* and *perceptions*, and other things weigh heavily on each of us as influences. How sad is that? To top it off, we do not pay attention to God's Word even when reading the Word, and here is why. The reason we seem to give less attention to God's Word even when studying Scriptures is that our hearts have become too **_calloused_** or **_hardened_** by sin.[Heb. 3:7, 8, 15; 4:7] Friend, this is one of major reason for the need of on-going confession of sin in our daily lives and praying when studying the Word. (There is the continuing or on-going need for confession of sin and biblical repentance.) Well, let me ask you, "When is the last time you confessed your sins to the Lord?" Hello!

What I am trying to tell you is that in many instances we may be out of fellowship due to unconfessed sins and lack of repentance, and we do not even know it. Yet, I think we can be oblivious being out of fellowship with God.

> [6]If we say that we have fellowship with him while we are walking in darkness, **we lie** and do not do what is true; [7]but if we walk in the light as he himself is in the light, we have fellowship with one another, and the blood of Jesus his Son cleanses us from all sin. [8]If we say that we

75

> have no sin, we deceive ourselves, and **the truth is not in us**. [9]**If we
> confess our sins**, he who is faithful and just will forgive us our sins and
> cleanse us from all unrighteousness. [10]If we say that we have not sinned,
> **we make him a liar**, and his *Word* is not in us.   1 John 1:6-10 (NRS)

Even if the truth of God's Word would smack us in the face, we would
sometimes not grasp it. Take a moment and listen and think with me. When
we are reading the Bible, let's say for devotion, we often tend to *overread ourselves* or read ahead of ourselves. I mean we are already anticipating what is
coming ahead in our Scripture reading, and we are not staying with contextual
flow of our Bible reading. So, we are reading ahead of ourselves (*overread-
ing.*) So, how can we be open for any new insights by the Spirit of God? We are
not remaining focused on the immediate verse or central point. We cannot be
open to greater illumination because we think we already know what is coming. (This is coming close to showing contempt in our reading.) Many times,
even before we read the "*next phrase*" we may assume we already know the
very next clause. So, I asked you, "How can we gain new insights when we
already think, 'We know what is coming?'"

Let me illustrate my point. When we are listening in a conversation with a
person, do we realize that we might be anticipating their next words? So, where
are we in the conversation? Well, we are <u>not</u> listening and staying with the flow
of the conversation. True? We are actually anticipating their next words. In
fact, we may rudely interject or even interrupt and start talking. We interrupt
because we think that we already know where the other person is going in
conversation. We are jumping ahead in the conversation. We are acting like
an "**AI** [Artificial Intelligence] computerize machine" filling the blanks of the person's
conversation even before they are completely speaking. The result is that we
do not always completely hear one another or even hear them correctly. (Yes,
we are all guilty of "*jumping ahead in conversation.*") The exception is for
those who are hard of hearing or have a hearing impairment when we fail to
hear others when they are still talking.

So, the point is that in our Bible reading, we are *jumping ahead*. We are
not attempting to remain concentrated or totally focused with the flow of the
immediate context of text. So, how can we grow spiritually if we are often
anticipating what coming in reading or studying Scripture? We just say to our
inner-self: "I know, I know!" Fact is perhaps the Spirit of God is trying to tell
us, "**No!** You do not know." Hello!

We should not be surprised at our Lord's rebuke of Mary, 'My hour has not
yet come.' This was not the time for our Lord to reveal Himself to the nation

Israel and begin His ministry. Our Lord was methodically on target: "*His* face was set toward Jerusalem."[Luke 9:53] Still, our Lord is so overflowing in abundance of mercy and infinite grace. Nevertheless, our Lord intervenes by granting the request to Mary and on behalf of the wedding and the guests. What a merciful and gracious Lord we serve and His shepherding His redeemed. While the time for His manifestation was perhaps not yet, but glory to God, He intervenes because He is overflowing with mercy and grace. I ask you, "How amazing is that?"

This reminds me how many of us as Pastors and other Christian workers are so quick to give orders to our Lord. Oh, but yes, we certainly do! This is self-evident when we pray. Yet amazingly, many of us will not even lift a finger to follow His commands, His imperatives. "We want to do our own thing and do it our way." Perhaps we somehow assume that we are following His directives when we are surely not. Truth is that as to talking and seeking the Lord's plans, we are completely bankrupt.

I do not hear anyone say, "Lord, what would You have me to do today?" (Maybe you think you needn't bother to ask Him what is His will for you today?) Even when we *bother* to prayer, we are too full of "the *Give me*!" You might say that the churches are full of "**Give-mes**.'" "Lord I need this-" "Lord I want this." Who is the servant? Who is the Master? Well?

Here is another *kicker*! Even when the Lord answers our requests, "Are we like the ten lepers? Except for one leper, no one turns back and says, 'Thank You,' or 'Praise the Lord?'"[See Luke 17:11-17.] We are too much like a pig: once the belly is full, we just go and lie down. Okay, when the Lord answers our prayers, which He always does if we know Him. He answers our prayer- *yes*, *no*, or *wait*; right? Do we praise or thank Him for His answers? Who bothers to thank the Lord for His answers?

There is no record of Mary saying, "Praise God" or "Thank You Jesus." It is so quaint nowadays to just says, "*No problem*," "*No problemo*!" (However, "No problem," actually implies in Spanish, "You're welcome, glad to do it.") I do not hear people say, "Thank you," much anymore. Certainly, few of us are saying, "Thank You, Lord." Don't you think that we ought to give "thanks" to things the Lord granted to us? No! We do not even bother to say, "thank you" to people when they have done something for us. How much more then we ought to "thank the Lord" [Eph. 5:20; 1 Thess. 5:18] for His mighty mercy and grace?

What if prayer meetings were given over to just praise or thanks to God for all the answers to prayers in our daily lives. Well, would there be just silence in the church? Would prayer meetings just be very short? There is a hymn called "The Rocks Will Cry!"[2] We would do well if put into practice.

77

¹When Jesus went to Jerusalem town
The crowd rose up with a mighty sound.
They lifted their voices in one accord,
*   "Here comes the king, in the name of*
*   the Lord."*

²The Pharisees cried, "Master, do you
*   hear?*
The crowd is shouting that Jehovah is
*   here!*
Rebuke these people for their ignorance
*   now."*
But Jesus said, "No! (No!) If they hold
*   their peace*
Then the rocks'll cry out!
The rocks'll cry out!"

³If we do not sing, then the rocks'll cry out,
If we do not praise, then the mountains will
*   shout.*
The earth will shake; the trees will bow.
We can't be silent or the rocks'll cry out.

⁴Creation sings of the glory of God
The ocean thunders in wild applause.
The lily's sweet bloom and the sparrow's
*   song*
Join in the praise that goes on and on.

⁵His majesty speaks from the forest tall;
His splendor calls out in the waterfall.
"Behold His glory!" all of nature shouts.
And if we don't sing, (sing)
If we hold our peace then the rocks'll cry
*   out!*
The rocks'll cry out!

⁶If we do not sing, then the rocks'll cry out,
If we do not praise, then the mountains will
*   shout.*
The earth will shake; the trees will bow.
We can't be silent or the rocks'll cry out.

⁷If we do not sing, then the rocks'll cry out,
If we do not praise, then the mountains will
*   shout.*
The earth will shake; the trees will bow.
We can't be silent or the rocks'll cry out.

⁸We can't be silent,
We won't be silent.
We'll never be silent,
Or the rocks'll cry out.

Note: there is no numbering in the original song. Numbering is only to follow the actual sequence in the song.

What we must see is that the Lord out of mercy answers the request even though it was not His time to reveal Himself. But, like today, I rarely hear anyone say, "Give Thanks" whether His answer is "*yes, no,* or *wait*." Well, let me ask you point blank, "When was the last time you said, '*Thank You Lord*' or '*Praise the Lord for your answer?*'" As the pig that never says thanks, so, the saints never look up and just say, "Thank you. Lord."

Conclusion

Well, do you know that the **idolaters are offended** when they are charged with idolatrous worship or praying to Mary or praying so-called *canonized saints*? They say, "Why we do not worship Mary or the saints," as they laugh!

Who is going to be bold for the Lord and say, "Friend, I am sorry, but you are certainly worshipping Mary and the saints" when you pray to such so-called saints. Furthermore, "Friend, you are idolaters when praying to anyone except the Lord our God. Your actions are not funny to the Lord our God and His mighty angels." Friend, this should not be funny to any redeemed child of God in Christ.

Even to this very day many people are given over to being *sacramentalists* and *ritualists* or even unknowingly praying to demons. Little do they realize that they have actually given themselves to demons in their idolatrous worship.

What is so unconscionable is that some who do such practice give the impression that Mary or the saints are more merciful than that of our Lord. How misguided and sorrowful is that my friend? That is, indeed, very sad.

No doubt the *sacramentalists* and *ritualists* are offended when they are charged with being idolatrous worshippers. Well, we will surely either offend the Lord our God if we **do not speak out** in a godly manner; or we are going to offend idolaters who pray to so-called canonized saints. So, let me ask you once again, "Which one do you think is wiser not to offend?" If we hold our peace (remain silent) are we not being complicit?

Footnotes:

1. Idolatrous worship: is the worship of anything or anyone other the worship of the Lord our God. (This is the biblical meaning; this is not secular or worldly meaning.) We worship the Lord. We do not worship a generic Creator referred to as "<u>God</u>."[Joshua 24:15] Sadly, many are reducing the LORD and His blessed name to nothing more than to a pagan deity, a so-called "*god*." Thus, many are leaving it up to depraved and fallen humanity to envision or conceive of "a god" of His own wicked imagination.

2. The Rocks Will Cry, https://www.songlyrics.com/ron-hamilton-feat-shelly-hamilton/the-rocks-will-cry-out-lyrics.

CHAPTER 6

"Water made into wine"

Now there were six stone waterpots set there for the Jewish custom of purification, containing twenty or thirty gallons each. [7]Jesus said to them, "Fill the waterpots with water." So they filled them up to the brim. [8]And He said to them, "Draw *some* out now and take it to the headwaiter." So they took it *to him*. [9]When the headwaiter tasted the water which had become wine, and did not know where it came from (but the servants who had drawn the water knew), the headwaiter called the bridegroom, [10]and said to him, "Every man serves the good wine first, and when *the people* have drunk freely, *then he serves* the poorer *wine*; *but* you have kept the good wine until now." [11]This beginning of *His* signs Jesus did in Cana of Galilee, and manifested His glory, and His disciples believed in Him.   John 2:6-11

Introduction

The four Gospels share similar information of our Lord earthly ministry when we compare them. Yet, each Gospel writer brings his unique contribution and particular insight by the Spirit of God. Sometimes overlooked is that each author of the four Gospel has a very unique purpose in mind for writing. So, it is natural for the information to vary according the scribe's purpose or intention for writing.

As noted earlier, Luke says in his introduction to the Gospel of Luke,

Since many have undertaken to set down an orderly account of the events that **have been** [*prophetically*] **fulfilled** among us, [2]just as they were handed on to us by those who from the beginning were **eyewitnesses and**

servants of the WORD,[a] [3]I too decided, after investigating everything carefully from the very first, to write an orderly account for you, most excellent Theophilus, [4]so that you may know the truth concerning the things about which you have been instructed.   Luke 1:1-4 (NRS)

[a]Note: "**the Word**"[v2], there is a definite article "*the*" in the phrase "the word" in the GK text. This then seems clear to me that Luke is using apostle John's phrase for Christ, "the *Logos* or the *Word*." Therefore, Luke is not referring Scripture but the Word of God. Luke is referring Christ when he uses "the *Logos* or *Word*." So, the phrase "the Word" should be capitalized.

The expression "excellent Theophilus" is like a *cryptic name* for the person to whom Luke is writing. (Christians were already under persecution by Rome at time of Paul's imprisonment. So, Luke uses the cryptic name, Theophilus.) Luke writes to "Theophilus" (in Luke and Acts) for Paul's defense. Whether Theophilus was a defense attorney in Rome, I don't know. While it is evident that Luke's Gospel is similar to Matthew's and Mark's accounts, Luke's purpose for writing is distinctive and with a unique purpose in mind. Therefore, we should not be surprised at the unique distinctions and information founded in each of the four Gospels.

Here is another *tidbit* for your information. Matthew, Mark, and Luke are commonly known as the synoptic[1] Gospels. These three Gospel are known as *synoptic Gospels* because they often parallel and supplement each other. Also, these three Gospels seem to place their emphasis on the Northern ministry of Jesus, which is the Galilean and Perea areas.

John's Gospel places his emphasis on Jesus' Southern ministry, Jerusalem and Judea area. This might suggest that John is writing in particular to a zealous Jewish audience. The reason I say, a Jewish audience is because John's frequently uses the word "*sign(s)*" in his Gospel. Please note that though GK is literally "signs" (*semeion*), the KJV uses the word "miracles" rather than *signs*. (Many of the old ENG used the word miracles rather than sign.) Signs were for the Jews.[See John 2:11, 18; 4:48; 6:30; Matt. 23:38; 1 Cor. 1:22.]

The apostle John not only gives emphasis of signs by Jesus, but John's purpose for emphasizing signs was for evangelism of Jews in Judea area. On the other hand, Luke is writing to some Roman official, Theophilus, who I have said may have been Paul's defense attorney at Rome. John, in writing his Gospel with an evangelistic purpose, is very unique, but John's purpose for writing is unfortunately sometimes too minimized. For example, as we have noted earlier, John says,

Now Jesus did many other signs [*miraculous signs*] in the presence of the disciples, which are not written in this book; [31]but these [*miraculous signs*] are written so that you may believe that Jesus is the Christ, the Son of God, and that by believing you may have [*eternal*] life in his name.

John 20:30, 31 (ESV)

Additionally, many expositors seem to think that John's Gospel only discusses *seven miracles* or *signs*. Actually, there are eight and not just seven signs in John's Gospel. The most astounding miracle or sign is the eighth. The eighth sign is Jesus own intrinsic power and authority within Himself to **lay down His life** and **then He raised His dead physical body out from among the dead**. Note: Jesus said that He lays down His life.[John 10:17, 18] Again I say, our Lord had the intrinsic power and authority within Himself to raise His own body from the dead. Jesus raised His own body even after his body was in the state of decaying.

At the very outset of John's Gospel, John says,

The Jews then responded to him, **"What sign can you show us to prove your authority to do all this?"** [19]Jesus answered them, **"Destroy this temple, and I will raise it again in three days."** [20]They replied, "It has taken forty-six years to build this temple, and you are going to raise it in three days?" [21]But the temple he had spoken of was his body. [22]After he was raised from the dead, his disciples recalled what he had said. Then they believed the scripture and the words that Jesus had spoken. [23]Now while he was in Jerusalem at the Passover Festival, many people saw the signs he was performing and believed in his name. [24]But Jesus would not entrust himself to them, for he knew all people. [25]He did not need any testimony about mankind, for he knew what was in each person.

John 2:18-25 (NIV)

Jesus said concerning the eighth sign,

"For this reason the Father loves Me, because **I lay down My life so that I may take it again. No one has taken it away from Me**, but **I lay it down on My own initiative. I have authority to lay it down**, and **I have authority to take it up again.** This commandment **I received from My Father."**

John 10:17, 18

There are other Scriptures that testify that the resurrection of Jesus Christ is a definitely or conclusively a sign. For example, the resurrection as sign to the Jews.[See John 12:38-42.]

Finally, the reader needs to be very much aware of some key words in the Gospel of John. Here are some key words or phrases in John's Gospel: *sign*, *believe* (or trust), *life* (= eternal life), *light* and *darkness*, *abide*, *love*, and "**I AM.**"[see Exo. 3:13-15]

A. The Water is made into wine

The wedding at Cana of Galilee was no ordinary wedding. The wedding party provided a *head-servant* (a wedding party administrator or steward over the whole affair.) This was probably a fairly large celebration and very costly. There were apparently a host of *waiters*, *cooks*, and no doubt *many other workers*. (All of this cost a lot of money up-front to pay in advance.) The fact that they run out of wine might suggest that there was an overflowing of many guests, even more guests than what was expected. So, the family (or families) that hosted the wedding were probably influential and or financially well-to-do.

The human nature is the same today as then: when there are such large wedding of a lot people will show up (*uninvited*). Therefore, "Don't run out of wine!" Ha, ha!

What is interesting is that where the wedding occurred, there was likely a dug well (*wellspring*), from where they drew water. Because the family owned a well at his residence, this suggests to me, that again, the family had plenty of money. It is unlikely there was any flowing stream or river in that area. It is doubtful that the poor would have been able to afford a personal well is because wells were too costly. Many homes may have had cisterns to hold rainwater. Water may have been in short supply in some areas or during certain seasons or when there is a long and serious drought.

At any rate, the apostle John says,

> Now there were **six stone waterpots** set there for the **Jewish** custom of **purification**, containing twenty or thirty gallons each.　　　John 2:6

These large **stone jars** were for Jewish purification and ceremonial cleansing under the Law plus added cleansing customs or tradition of the elders. By the way, *stone jars* as opposed to *clay jars* were a lot more costly to own; plus, there were six large stone jars, which was very costly. Keep in mind the stone jars were empty and needed to be filled up once again. (The *empty* stone jars suggest again the wedding was perhaps overcrowded. It was certain that the host must have been fairly wealthy.

> Now the Pharisees and some of the experts in the law who came from Jerusalem gathered around him. ²And they saw that some of Jesus'

disciples ate their bread with unclean hands, that is, unwashed [religious ceremonial unwashed hands]. 3(For the Pharisees and all the Jews do not eat unless they **perform a ritual washing**, holding fast to the tradition of the elders. 4And when they come from the marketplace, they do not eat unless they [ceremonially] wash. They hold fast to many other traditions: the washing [GK baptismos, baptize by immersion] of cups, pots, kettles, and dining **couches.**a) 5The Pharisees and the experts in the law asked him, "Why do your disciples not live according to the tradition of the elders, but eat with unwashedb [ceremonial washed] hands?" 6He said to them, "Isaiah prophesied correctly about you hypocrites, as it is written: 'This people honors me with their lips, but their heart is far from me. 7They worship me in vain, teaching as doctrine the commandments of men.'

Mark 7:1-7 (NET)

a**Couches** (GK _kline_, mean _bed, couches,_ KJV _tables or bed_) is not in earlier GK MSS; it is an insertion.

bThe Pharisees are not referring good hygiene. Pharisees had established a ceremonial washing involving even holding your hand at a particular angle for religious purification.

Apparently, these large stone jars were used for purification rites as note above, but the stone jars where now empty due to the large crowd. Thus, we read,

Jesus said to them, "Fill the waterpots [the stone jars] with water." So they filled them [jars] up to the brim."

John 2:7

These stone jars held twenty to thirty gallons of water. Where could the servants immediately have access to get such large amount of water at moment notice? The servants would not have had such immediate access to so much water without a fairly sizeable well at the residence of the wedding. As already noted above, to have one's own well was costly, this demonstrates the family was wealthy hosting the wedding and perhaps somewhat influential.

Here comes the amazing command,

And He said to them, "Draw _some_ [from the large stone jars] out now and take it to the headwaiter."

John 2:8

The head steward is busy managing the wedding feast and taking care of all the dinner guests. He is totally unaware where things came from at this large wedding. The waiters are probably stunned at Jesus command, '_Draw some water out_ [from the stone jars]?' Then Jesus says, '_Now take it to the headwaiter._'

What? The servants might have thought to themselves: 'Take the water from the stone jars and put it into pitchers; okay, but this doesn't make sense.' Friend, this would have made **no sense** then to waiters or servants, and it would not make any sense to us today either. Ah, but this is the power and *wisdom* of the Lord our God. Hallelujah!

With all the *hustle and bustle* and all the *people milling around*, the head steward or others at wedding are not going to say, "Hey, where did you get the wine." People just think, keep pouring and keep on serving the wine. Ha, ha! Thus, we read,

> When the headwaiter tasted the water which had become wine, and did not know where it came from (but the servants [*multiple servants*] who had drawn the water knew), the headwaiter called the bridegroom, [10]and said to him, "Every man serves the good wine first, and when *the people* have drunk freely, *then he serves* the poorer *wine*; *but* you have kept the good wine until now."   John 2:9, 10

The head steward's reprimands the bridegroom for keeping the best wine until the end. Holding the best wine until last was *insulting* and *offensive*. The bridegroom is stunned by steward's remarks, but the bridegroom probably has no clue what the steward is jabbering about. Was the bridegroom *"three sheets to the wind?"*[2] Who knows?

We know from the evidence in the Scripture that the wine Jesus miraculously made probably had a *buzz* to it, which is the characteristic of excellent and superb wine and accentuating the taste buds I would imagine. This is no trick or just making grape juice. There is nothing fake by our Lord. He performs genuine and authentic miracles.

So, watch-out that you do not charge our Lord with intoxicating people. Only a fool would dare entertain such ignorant notions. The Bible speaks out against drunkenness. However, our Lord's critics charge Him as being, 'The Son of Man has come eating and drinking, and you say, "Behold, a gluttonous man and a drunkard [KJV, *winebibber*], a friend of tax collectors and sinners!"'[Luke 7:34]

Nowadays, the *soothsayers*, so-called *miracle-workers*, and *charlatans* might put forth the notion that "If you have enough faith, you can change water into wine." What fools!

> You turn things upside down, as if the potter were thought to be like the clay! Shall what is formed say to the one who formed it, "You did not make me"? Can the pot say to the potter, "You know nothing"?
>
> Isa. 29:16 (NIV)

Jesus said,

> "Truly, truly, I say to you, he who believes in Me, the works that I do,
> he will do also; and greater *works* than these he will do; because I go to
> the Father." John 14:12

What blind ignorance today. This is shear madness. No one, and I mean **NO ONE** can out do greater miracles than the Creator and Sustainer of all things, Christ the Lord.[Col.1:16f] Who has the power to lay down his life and actually die and His body is in the process of decomposing, and then, three days later raise Himself from the dead There is **NO ONE** else that can do that but the Lord Himself. Our Lord alone has the intrinsic power and authority. Yet, over six hundred million professing Christians in the world have fallen prey to the Charismatics and Pentecostals delusion. Yes, and I do mean spiritual delusion. Such teachers allege, '— greater *works* than these he will do.' Some people must in truth be *brain dead*!

This is Christ the Lord who spoke the universe into being and maintaining it. As Job says, 'He spreads out the northern skies over empty space; he suspends the earth over nothing.'[Job 26:7 NIV] Hebrews says,

> By faith we understand that the universe [GK *aion, universe* or *ages*] was formed
> at God's command, so that what is seen was not made out of what was
> visible. Heb. 11:3 (NIV)

Friend, Jesus turned the water into wine just by having the **thought** to change the water into wine. He did not speak a word. He did not wave His hand or say any so-called *magical words*. He did not pray. He simply **"willed it**, and so, hallelujah, it was done."

Like Peter who stepped out on roaring sea of Galilee at night. **Jesus willed it**, and hallelujah, Peter walked on water. Listen carefully to me: Peter did not walk on the roaring sea because he had so-called "sufficient faith." Erase such carnal thoughts from your mind forever. Peter walked on water **at the command of Jesus**. Mock Peter if you want because he took his eyes off Jesus and began to sink. However, I am reminded, there were still eleven others who remained in the boat. Got you!

Here is another kicker: this was **not** the time for our Lord to begin His ministry and especially with miraculous signs. So, this marvelous sign and miracle was hide from people. This miracle was made or performed *incognito*. Except for the apostles and the servant**s** serving at the wedding, no one actually knew or was aware of the marvelous miracle. What an amazing and wonderful merciful Lord we serve. This was not the exact time for Jesus to begin doing signs or miracles. Nevertheless, Jesus mercifully preformed a sign, but He did it *incognito*.

B. The wine is real not counterfeit

This miracle is where the water is changed into actual wine. There is nothing fake concerning our Lord. The miracle was the genuine thing. The wine was no doubt the most excellent and of highest quality. The head steward knew that the wine brought to him (by the servants carrying the wine which our Lord transformed from water into wine) was of most excellent quality.

> When the master [*head steward*] of the feast had tasted the water that was made wine, and did not know where it came from (but the servants who had drawn the water knew), the master of the feast called the bridegroom. ¹⁰And he said to him, "Every man at the beginning sets out the good [*excellent or superior*] wine, and when the *guests* have well drunk, then the inferior [*less expensive wine*, NLT]. You have kept the good [*excellent or superior*] wine until now!" John 2:9, 10 (NKJ)

> The word "good" is the GK word "*kalos*" which implies *the highest standard* or *the finest quality*, and hence, the inference is "*excellent* or *superior quality*" and not just generally good.

Some seek to playdown the high quality of the wine our Lord miraculously transformed from water. I say, "Shame on you." First, as I have said, there is nothing *fake* or *fraudulent* concerning our Lord's miracles. The churches are overloaded and flooded with charlatans that deceive the millions or millions. Our Lord is no liar or con-man. Whatever He does is holy, righteous, genuine, and true.

Yes, the world is full of alcoholics, other stimuli, or mind-altering substances. Thus, they abuse themselves or abuse others. However, this does not mean those who drink wine are any greater sinners. No one is sinning just because they drink some kind of alcohol. God forbid for anyone to think of such a thing. However, drunkenness is indeed wrong, and it can destroy one's life, career, and even destroy one's family. Anything addictive, dependence, obsession, or compulsion can wreck a life.

Are we to say that those who overeat or gore themselves or have a disorder of bulimarexia or anorexia, that those who sell food are at fault? No! Those who over-drink or drink an excess of wine that our Lord miraculously transformed, that our Lord is at fault? Never! Such people are abusing themselves, and they are held accountable. (Some will still foolishly charge our Lord like Pharisees of being: 'Look at him! A glutton and a drunkard, a friend of tax collectors and sinners!'$^{Luke\ 7:34\ ESV}$) However, anyone selling alcohol to some-one already highly intoxicated for example in a bar or restaurant today would definitely be held accountable in many courts today. This is especially true if there was any very serious accident of people or property. However, anyone charging our Lord a fault for making excellent quality wine are in grave error. I have already said, the religious leaders of His days made such wicked charges against our Lord. Jesus said,

> ^{31}"To what can I compare the people of this generation?" Jesus asked. "How can I describe them? ^{32}They are like children playing a game in the public square. They complain to their friends, 'We played wedding songs, and you didn't dance, so we played funeral songs, and you didn't weep.' ^{33}For John the Baptist didn't spend his time eating bread or drinking wine, and you say, 'He's possessed by a demon.' ^{34}The Son of Man, on the other hand, feasts and drinks, and you say, 'He's a glutton and a drunkard, and a friend of tax collectors and other sinners!' ^{35}But wisdom is shown to be right by the lives of those who follow it."
>
> Luke 7:31-35 (NLT)

The point here is that the fault-finders are overrun by foolish, unjust charges, or criticisms. It does not matter what one does or even doesn't do; the fault-finders will find fault where there is no fault.

Job describes his three friends as miserable comforters.$^{Job\ 16:2}$ Here Job's reply to his fault-finding friends.

> "Anyone who withholds kindness from a friend forsakes the fear of the Almighty. ^{15}But my brothers are as undependable as intermittent streams, as the streams that overflow."   Job 6:14 (NIV)

> "Truly then you are the people with whom wisdom itself will die [*with you.*]!"   Job 12:2

> How then will you comfort me with empty nothings? There is nothing left of your answers but falsehood."   Job 21:34 (ESV)

Others attempt to excuse our Lord actions as I have said by *minimizing* the mighty miracle or by saying the wine was *not real* or it was grape juice. Friend, the miracle was genuine wine, and as I have said, the wine was excellent quality and far superior to other wines.

> And he called the people to him again and said to them, After He called the crowd to Him again, He *began* saying to them, "Listen to Me, all of

you, and understand: [15]there is nothing outside the man which can defile him if it goes into him; but the things which proceed out of the man are what defile the man. [16][*"If anyone has ears to hear, let him hear."*] [d] [17]When he had left the crowd *and* entered the house, His disciples questioned Him about the parable. [18]And He said to them, "Are you so lacking in understanding also? Do you not understand that whatever goes into the man from outside cannot defile him, [19]because it does not go into his heart, but into his stomach, and is eliminated?" (*Thus He declared all foods clean.*) [20]And He was saying, "That which proceeds out of the man, that is what defiles the man. [21]"For from within, out of the heart of men, proceed the evil thoughts, fornications, thefts, murders, adulteries, [22]deeds of coveting *and* wickedness, *as well as* deceit, sensuality, envy, slander, pride *and* foolishness. [23]"All these evil things proceed from within and defile the man."   Mark 7:14-23

[d]Verse 16 is not found in older MSS.

The human heart is full of *unethical practices* or *cultural traditions influences*. We bring all this excess baggage into our Christian Faith. Then, we have the gall to call "our *excess baggage*" biblical Christianity. The saints are incapable of separating tradition (especially with traditions of our own culture) as if it were Scripture. I am not saying it is okay to drink wine, and neither am I saying it is okay to use real wine in the Communion. Let each one be persuaded in his own mind.[Rom. 14:5]

The sign (miracle) Jesus transformed water into wine was real and genuine wine. We do not need to make excuses for our Lord. We had better do as Paul says as given by Worsley translation,

> God forbid: yea, let God be *acknowledged* true, though every man *be* a liar; as it is written, That thou mightest be justified in thy words, and mightest overcome, when thou judgest.   Rom. 3:4 (WNT)

Conclusion

Listen, Mary (who was a channel or means for our Lord entering this world) had no authority or particular influence on our Lord then nor now as some idolatrous worshippers seem to suggest. Yes, I am sorry some are offended in what is said here, but we shall either offend the Lord or man. So, which do you suggest we not offend?

Mary did not persuade Jesus what to do. Jesus simply said, 'Woman, what have I to do with thee? Mine hour is not yet come.'[John 2:4 KJV] Yes, our Lord did the marvelous sign or miracle as Mary informed the Lord, but He Himself already knew the wine ran out. He certainly knew what He planned to do. Nevertheless, our Lord did so out of His infinite mercy and grace for the wedding. Yet, the miracle was done "*incognito.*" The miracle was performed *but unknown to most everyone* because as Jesus said, 'mine hour is not yet come.' (No one was aware of the sign or miracle other than the disciples and the servants who drew the water made into wine.)

The professing churches have become so corrupt that the saints cannot separate truth from error in some cases. How sad is that? There is no call for "repentance What, no one sins anyone? No one says, "Thank you anyone." It is, "No problem." Who bothers to says, "Praise the Lord?" when God says, "No," to our prayer requests. If you do, people might think you fell and hit your head on a rock.

Those who **claim** "the gift of healing" had better keep in mind.^{Matt. 7:21-23} Otherwise, they will be found to be a lying charlatan and even outside the Faith. Such so-called "miracle workers" may be found to be a delusional or even worse, a liar! The Lord our God is indeed infinite in mercy and grace when we walk with Him according to His Word and will. Let us also keep in mind that the Lord is indeed a holy and righteous God; nevertheless, He will indeed judge sin. Let us remind ourselves once again as the Hebrew writer warns,

> Anyone who has set aside the law of Moses **DIES WITHOUT MERCY** on the evidence of two or three witnesses. [29]How **much worse punishment**, do you think, will be deserved by the one who has **TRAMPLED UNDERFOOT THE SON OF GOD**, and has **PROFANED THE BLOOD** of the covenant by which he was sanctified, and has **OUTRAGED THE SPIRIT OF GRACE**? [30]For we know him who said, **"Vengeance is mine; I will repay."** And again, **"THE LORD WILL JUDGE HIS PEOPLE."** [31]It is a **fearful thing to fall into the hands of the living God**.   Heb. 10:28-31 (ESV)

Footnotes:

1. Synoptic Gospels: the word "synoptic" means "*to see together*." That is, the synoptic Gospels look at some of the similar events. The synoptic Gospels, as I said that the *events are similar* but *not always noting the same detail* and *giving a different perspective from author's point and purpose*. That is, each of the synoptic Gospels give their unique reason and style for writing as guided by the Holy Spirit. Unfortunately, some critics miss this very important point in the uniqueness behind the various authors and the Spirit of God uses.

2. "Four sheets to the wind" is an idiom meaning someone is extremely drunk; it originates from sailing terminology where "sheets" refer to ropes controlling the sails, and having multiple sheets loose in the wind signifies a lack of control, similar to being heavily intoxicated. (From Google search)

Second Miraculous Miracle and Sign:
Jesus Heals a Nobleman's Son

Then he came again to Cana in Galilee where he had changed the water into wine. Now there was a royal official whose son lay ill in Capernaum. [47]When he heard that Jesus had come from Judea to Galilee, he went and begged him to come down and heal his son, for he was at the point of death. [48]Then Jesus said to him, "Unless you see signs and wonders you will not believe." [49]The official said to him, "Sir, come down before my little boy dies." [50]Jesus said to him, "Go; your son will live." The man believed the word that Jesus spoke to him and started on his way. [51]As he was going down, his slaves met him and told him that his child was alive. [52]So he asked them the hour when he began to recover, and they said to him, "Yesterday at one in the afternoon the fever left him." [53]The father realized that this was the hour when Jesus had said to him, "Your son will live." So he himself believed, along with his whole household. [54]Now this was the second sign that Jesus did after coming from Judea to Galilee.   John 4:46-54 (NRS)

CHAPTER 7

The healing of
the nobleman's son

Therefore He came again to Cana of Galilee where He had made the water wine. And there was a royal official whose son was sick at Capernaum. [47] When he heard that Jesus had come out of Judea into Galilee, he went to Him and was imploring *Him* to come down and heal his son; for he was at the point of death. [48] So Jesus said to him, "Unless you *people* see signs and wonders, you *simply* will not believe." [49] The royal official said to Him, "Sir, come down before my child dies."

John 4:46-49

Introduction

John does not identify the person who came to Jesus for the healing of his son. Some expositors suggest that the man was of royalty. Thus, implying someone related to the King Herod Antipas. Herod Antipas ruled Galilee and Perea and was appointed by Rome. Herod Antipas was of the line Herod the Great who built the temple in Jerusalem during the NT times.

This inference would imply that the royalty was likely a Gentile. While the meaning could refer to *royal* or *noble* (GK *basiliko*), I think this is less likely the case here. The meaning is more like an official very close to the royal family. However, he was probably only a nobleman employed by Herod. Yet, he was a high ranking official in service.

If the nobleman was not a royal officer (of Herod's family), then this suggests that he was likely a Jew and not a Gentle. The fact that Jesus remarks of requiring "signs," reinforces the likelihood that the person was a Jew and certainly not a Gentile.

> Then Jesus said to him, "Unless you see signs and wonders you will not believe."   John 4:48 (NRS)

There was an incident when a Gentile did seek out Jesus for healing, and our Lord mercifully healed a demon-possessed Canaanite woman's daughter. "Now the woman was a Gentile, of the Syrophoenician race."[Mark 7:26] Yet, Jesus is very explicit that He was only sent to Israel.

> [22]And behold, a Canaanite woman from that region came out and was crying, "Have mercy on me, O Lord, Son of David; my daughter is severely oppressed by a demon." [23]But he did not answer her a word. And his disciples came and begged him, saying, "Send her away, for she is crying out after us." [24]He answered, "I was sent only to the lost sheep of the house of Israel." [25]But she came and knelt before him, saying, "Lord, help me." [26]And he answered, "It is not right to take the children's bread and throw it to the dogs." [27]She said, "Yes, Lord, yet even the dogs eat the crumbs that fall from their masters' table." [28]Then Jesus answered her, "O woman, great is your faith! Be it done for you as you desire." And her daughter was healed instantly.
>
> Matt. 15:22-28 (ESV)

Therefore, the noblemen was likely only an employee in the house of Herod. The nobleman was no doubt very well paid and wealthy enough to own many servants and some may have been slaves.

I think it is uncommon for a Gentile to be seeking out Jesus in the beginning of His ministry since He was unknown by general public. Although, Gentiles heard of Jesus as He was approaching the Passion Week (the week before going to the cross[John 12:21]). Who would know of Jesus' power to heal in His early ministry? So, I think that very few would be aware Jesus and His healing. I am certain few people would have knowledge of Jesus as the Messiah in His early ministry. The first record miracle (the water in to wine) was probably preformed *incognito*. Our Lord never traveled over one hundred miles. His ministry was primarily to Israel.[Matt. 15:24; Rom. 15:8] So, the nobleman was most probably a Jew and of Hebrew descent.

A. A noble's son was very ill

The sequence here comes after our Lord's mighty results of His evangelism in the Samaria area [John 4]. The evangelism occurred due to Jesus' *preaching* and *teaching* there. There were no *signs and wonders* expected or required among the Samaritans. Samaritans were less connected with the strict demands and rules of Judaism. For example, the Pharisees anticipated and expected signs from Jesus. As Nicodemus said, 'Rabbi, **we know** that You have come from God *as* a teacher; for no one can do *these signs* that You do unless God is with him.' [John 3:2] The Samaritans were convinced of Jesus being the Messiah based upon clear teaching.

> They [*Samaritans*] said to the woman, "We no longer believe just because of what you said; now **we have heard for ourselves**, and **we know that this man really is the Savior** of the world." John 4:42 (NIV)

The Samaritans were a mixture from the ten northern tribes of Israel who intermarried with pagan Gentiles. The mixture of the nations was due the deportation of other nations into the ten northern tribes of Israel. Israel (the ten tribes) fell into captivity about 722 or 721 BC. So, the people of Samaria's roots were from the family of Jacob. Therefore, the Samaritans had the right to hear from Israel's Messiah.

This event with the nobleman and his very sick son is probably early on the ministry of our Lord. Our Lord is mostly unknown by the overall population among the Jews. So, I think it is reasonable to ask, "How did the nobleman know about Jesus and His miracle-power?" "How did the nobleman even gain an interest in seeking out Jesus to heal his son?" "What transpired in the life of the nobleman to have any hope of healing of his very ill son who may have had a serious illness due to a high fever?"[John 4:52] "Where did the nobleman hear about Jesus?"

Well, I would suppose the miracle of the "water in wine" spread very rapidly because of the servants even though the sign was what I would call an *incognito miracle*. That is, the miracle of water into wine though hidden from the general public's knowledge, the news leaked out. Likely, some other servant or servants heard about the amazing miracle. (Servants would talk among themselves.) So, the miracle of the water into wine spread like a *blazing fire*. Perhaps there were some people that actually served at the wedding that were somehow present in or near the home of the nobleman. Who would have keep quiet of such a miracle that transformed *water into wine* in front of their very eyes? This might be similar to how Naaman hears the miracles of Elisha. This situation is similar to Naaman the leper.

> Now Naaman, commander of the army of the king of Syria, was a great and honorable man in the eyes of his master, because by him the LORD had given victory to Syria. He was also a mighty man of valor, *but* a leper. ²And the Syrians had gone out on raids, and had brought back

captive a young girl from the land of Israel. She waited on Naaman's wife. [3]Then she said to her mistress, "**If only my master *were* with the prophet**[a] **who *is* in Samaria! For he would heal him of his leprosy.**" [4]And *Naaman* went in and told his master, saying, "Thus and thus said the girl who *is* from the land of Israel." [5]Then the king of Syria said, "Go now, and I will send a letter to the king of Israel." So he departed and took with him ten talents of silver, six thousand *shekels* of gold[b], and ten changes of clothing.   2 Kings 5:1-5 (NKJ)

[a]Elisha heard of Naaman's visit,[2 Kings 5:8ff] and Elisha initiated to help Naaman.

[b]Some suggest the value of the gold into today's market that this is about six million dollars in U.S. today.

News of an incredible miracle of "water made into wine" was *incognito*; still, the marvelous miracle cannot be kept hidde or silent. The nobleman was probably greatly distressed and *nearly out of his mind* with what to do for his son that was so sick. I think it is possible that someone, like one of the nobleman's servants advised him to see Jesus. "Jesus?" "Who is Jesus?" He may have thought to himself.

Maybe all the servant(s) of the nobleman could say, "Jesus is indeed a *real* and *genuine* prophet of God." In desperation, the nobleman immediate sought out "JESUS!"

In a similar way, the apostles could not heal a man's son that was apparently demon possessed, even though they were given the authority to heal through Jesus' Name. The disciples were unable to heal the boy that was demon possessed. The man with the demon possessed boy told Jesus, 'I asked your disciples to drive out the spirit, but they could not.'[Mark 9:18 NIV] In desperation, the father of the boy said to Jesus, 'but if thou canst do anything, have compassion on us, and help us.'[Mark 9:22 KJV] So, Jesus cast out the demon from the body.

The nobleman was at his *"wits end,"*[1] and the nobleman likely felt helpless and didn't know what to do concerning the raging fever in his son. Therefore, it is likely someone gave him the suggestion to seek out Jesus. Wow, how applicable this is today.

I recall sharing the Gospel to a native American who was the "medicine-man" in Anadarko, Oklahoma. This occurred at midnight in his home. (Yeah, it was midnight.) He told me that he married a white girl, which was a "no, no" as chief medicine-man to his tribe. I asked him, "Isn't your *god* strong enough?" Well, he became angry, but I told him the Lord is able to bring his wife back to him and even his car she drove off with at the time. The Lord is able to bring both back."

The medicine-man said, he would like to have both his wife and car back. The medicine-man said, "If God brought back just his car, he would believe that Jesus is indeed Lord."

So, I told the medicine-man, "I will pray, but it is left in the hands and will of the Lord our God for the *yes* or *no*." While the medicine-man said he would like to have his wife and car, he would like to at least have his car. Ha, ha! However, if the Lord brings her back or the car, he promised to consider Jesus and receive Him as his Lord and Savior.

Well, eighteen months later, I am back again in Anadarko. People are telling me, "The medicine is telling people to 'Try Jesus.'" They couldn't believe it. The people told me his wife ran off with the car, but she returned to him with even the car.

The nobleman for whatever reason sought out Jesus. Friend, how is it that we wait until we come to *the bottom of the barrel* before we begin to look up? I hate to say it, but many of our prayers are *empty* or even *bankrupt*. Do you know that prayer is the most powerful arsenal in the life of a believer?

B. Unless you see signs and wonders you will not believe

Some of the new versions read,

> "So Jesus said to him, "Unless you *people* see signs and wonders, you *simply* will not believe."" John 4:48

The GNV, KJV, ASV, NRS, and ESV omit the word "*people*." However, the meaning is not changed whether the word "*people*" is added or omitted. The "you" [in v48] is plural implying "you *people*." Our Lord is referring particular to "the nobleman and his delegation that is with him. As Jews, they are rightly seeking signs of a genuine prophet. Regardless of which way the sentence is translated, the statement is directed at the nobleman and his delegation, who were indeed Hebrews and Jews. Therefore, the man was definitely an Israelite. This suggests why the phrase is used, 'Unless you *people* see signs and wonders, you *simply* will not believe.'

The statement is a soft but gentle rebuke. Jesus' rebuke is one of mercy toward the nobleman. However, some think Jesus' rebuke is a strong rebuke, and while the statement can mean a sharp rebuke, I think Jesus statement is given with a "*sigh*" followed by the statement, 'Unless you see signs and wonders you will not believe!' [ESV]

Jews sought signs as credentials or proofs of a prophet of God.[1 Cor. 1:22] This is what a faithful Israelite ought to do in testing of a genuine prophet of the Lord.(See Deut. 13:1f; 18:15ff.) (See the following verses: Acts 2:22, 43; 4:30; 5:12; Rom. 15:19; 2 Cor. 12:12.2) So, it is probable that the nobleman was requesting proof of Jesus being a prophet. A true prophet exhibits signs as a true prophet of Israel.[Deut. 18:15ff] There is nothing in the text suggesting that the nobleman requested a sign, but still, please note particularly the last sentence in the Scripture below.

> Jesus said to him, "Go your way; your son lives." So **the man believed the word that Jesus spoke** to him, and he went his way. [51]And as he was now going down, his servants met him and told *him*, saying, **"Your son lives!"** [52]Then he inquired of them the hour when he got better. And they said to him, **"Yesterday at the seventh hour** [1 PM] the fever left him." [53]So the father knew that *it was* at the **same hour** in which Jesus said to him, **"Your son lives."** And **he himself believed**, and **his whole household.** [54]This again *is* **the second sign**[b] Jesus did when He had come out of Judea into Galilee.   John 4:50-54 (NKJ)

> [b]The GNV and KJV uses the word *"miracle,"* but the GK word is *"semeion,"* sign.

How the sign relates to the nobleman's son is not explicit in the text, but it may be that "a sign" was requested by the father. Jesus is clear in his statement to the nobleman,

> So Jesus said to him, "Unless you see signs and wonders you will not believe."   John 4:48 (ESV)

Nowadays, many churches and electronic ministries are deceiving countless millions and millions of people by using fake miracles or signs. These are indeed charlatans, counterfeiters of ministers, with fake and lying miracle workers. Jesus warns of such times as are today.

> And many false prophets will arise and lead many astray.
>
>   Matt. 24:11 (ESV)

> For false christs and false prophets will arise and perform great signs and wonders, so as to lead astray, if possible, even the elect.
>
>   Matt. 24:24 (ESV)

> "Beware of false prophets, who come to you in sheep's clothing but inwardly are ravenous wolves."   Matt. 7:15 (ESV)

Here is another *kicker*. These charlatans today tell people, "If you have enough faith, God will heal you." What a preposterous and blatant lie. Furthermore, as I have already pointed out many times, these false prophets and false teachers lie and allege that they will *even* do **greater miracles than Jesus**. (Do you see that? They will do greater miracles than the Creator Himself.) This is utter madness, beyond insane; it is unbelievable. These evil *practitioners* claim **greater miracles** today than Christ, the Creator and Sustainer of all things. How sick is that? Who can out do the Creator Himself? Yet, millions upon millions are being leads into Hell by their false and evil teaching and practices!

Yes, these charlatans are void of enlightenment in God's Word. These so-called healers are *bold-faced liars*; and some are so blinded by the evil one that they believe their wicked lies themselves. Millions of the very chronically ill in the so-called "Healing Services" are quickly and quietly ushered out the door. Yes, the chronically ill are whisk away (instantly, ushering them out through the *side-door*.) The desperately ill are put out side-door and dumped on a *side-street like a sack of trash*. Why are the chronically ill so quickly pushed or goaded out the side-door? First, these liars do not want anyone to know some of their wicked acts, whisking away the chronically ill. This is because these are lying *con men and women* milking people of their hard-earned money. They do not want to be found out that they are ready forgers of fake healing and liars of the worst sort. They have no fear of the living God.

They hook people like a sideshow in a carnival. '*If you have an enough faith, you will be healed.*' These charlatans are **not** servants of Christ. They are servants of the evil one.

The apostle John is clear,

> Now this is the confidence that we have in Him, that **IF WE ASK ANYTHING <u>ACCORDING</u> <u>TO</u> <u>HIS</u> <u>WILL</u>**, He hears us. [15] And if we know that He hears us, whatever we ask, we know that we have the petitions that we have asked of Him. 1 John 5:14, 15 (NKJ)

These charlatans lie by telling people that it is God will to always be free of any sickness, even free of any toothaches. Even worse, you can prosper financially if you have enough faith. Ah, but you have to give financially to the charlatan first to get your healing or get your healing or abundancy of money. These lying *Prosperity Gospel* con-men and con-women spring open their lying "Gospel" like a *Pandora's Box*. These con-men and con-women gained popularity in the 1950s when they spread their evil lies over TV, though they had been doing it for years in their so-called "tent meetings." Now, it is estimated there over six hundred million Pentecostals and Charismatics in nearly every major denomination in the world which are espousing such erroneous doctrines.

Finally, there are many men of God who know these so-called "healers" are fakers and liars. Yet, many men of God are without spiritual backbone and say, "Now, now, let us be positive towards our brethren." No, let us not be silent for glory and praise of our Lord. These false prophets in sheep's clothing; it is our spiritual right and God given duty to firmly rebuke such spiritual madness and lying charlatans. Aren't there any men of God spiritual enough to stand up and shout against these lying con men and women? Glory to the Lord our God forever and ever. Yes, let us rebuke such lying con-men and con-women that are turning the grace of God into a side-show.

Conclusion

Again, our blessed Lord warns us of these days. **Where are the godly men of war**? Aren't there any men willing to stand up for the truth of the Gospel? No wonder the churches are in many places in darkness. There are no *Ish Elohim* (men of God.) It is like in Ezekiel's day when the Lord told the prophet Ezekiel that the Lord sought for a man, "*Ish Elohim*," but He could not find even one man with spiritual backbone to stand in the gap, Ezek. 22:30. (The HEB "*ish*" refers to man; "*ish*" does not refer to men and women.) Who will stand and rebuke such liars? Will you stand up for Jesus? Well, my friend, some has rightly said, "If you do not stand for truth, then you are likely to fall for anything."

Friend, the Day of Reckoning is coming. Jesus warns,

> "Not everyone who says to me, 'Lord, Lord,' will enter the kingdom of heaven, but only the one who does the will of my Father who is in heaven. 22Many will say to me on that day, 'Lord, Lord, did we not prophesy in your name and in your name drive out demons and in your name **perform many miracles**?' 23Then I will tell them plainly, 'I never knew you. Away from me, you evildoers!'   Matt. 7:21-23 (NIV)

Friend, I am warning you. You had better decide which side of the fence you are on. Are you on the side of the false prophet? Well, Balaam remained on the side of the false prophet, and even though he said, 'Let *me* die the death of righteous,'[Num. 23:12] he perished in his sin of wickedness. Even so, in like manner, many fake healers and their workers shall perish in Hell like the false prophet Balaam, the followers of the evil one and his lies.

Jesus is clear there are no sidelines with Him.

> The one who is not with Me is against Me; and the one who does not gather with Me scatters. Luke 11:23

Listen, be very careful that you do not try to remain on the sidelines or straddle the fence with Jesus. You do not want to wake up in outer darkness, that is Hell. The risen Lord Jesus Christ gave a stern warning to the Church of Thyatira, which certainly applies to our day,

> **I am the one who searches MINDS and HEARTS, and I will give to each of you as your works deserve**. Rev. 2:22 (NRS)

Footnote:

1. *Wits end*: Also, "at wits end." Completely puzzled and perplexed, not knowing what to do. For example, *I've tried every possible source without success, and now I'm at my wit's end*. This idiom, which uses *wit* in the sense of 'mental faculties,' appeared in *Piers Ploughman* (c. 1377)." https://www.dictionary.com/browse/at-ones-wits-end

2. Scripture references are from the Pulpit Commentary on John 2:48 from Bible Hub.

CHAPTER 8

"Your son lives"

"Sir," the official said to him, "come down before my child dies."
[50]Jesus told him, "Go home; your son will live." The man believed the
word that Jesus spoke to him, and set off for home. [51]While he was on
his way down, his slaves met him and told him that his son was going to
live. [52]So he asked them the time when his condition began to improve,
and they told him, "Yesterday at one o'clock in the afternoon the fever
left him."   (John 4:49 NET)

Introduction

Sadly, there are many denominations and churches in spiritual shambles.
The reasons for the deterioration among many churches are too numerous to
recount here. But, just so you know here are a few reasons for the worsening,
the churches are overrun by "*spiritual quacks*." A spiritual quack is spiritually
bankrupt. He/she is without biblically maturity, void of any sound biblical
theology and unversed and untrained in Scripture. He/she is bogus: they are
spiritually blind leading the spiritually blind with little or no life of Christ in
them. They are "- twice dead, plucked up by the roots."[Jude 1:12 KJV]

Certainly, immortality is running rampant, and there is endless corruption
that plagues the churches, especially in many electronic churches. The pulpit
is silent in summing people to repent or giving a call to come to Christ or else
perish in their sins. There is no call for a revival or spiritual renewal. So, there
is no spiritual awakening. Sermons have become lectures or a little more than
a *chit chat*. There is no power in the pulpit coming from the Spirit of God. The
pulpit is lifeless!

Yes, in addition, there are also nowadays the so-called "*experientialists* [based on feeling] *groups*" and or "*sensualists* [carnal] *groups*, that appeal to senses of the natural man." Sorrowfully, many of the followers are often young college students who were caught up with an emotional frenzy but remaining *spiritually brain dead*! Listen, the Lord wants our "**minds** and **wills**" not our emotions running out of control. Our emotions are connected to our old nature. Yes, you read me correctly; our emotional are connected to our old nature. As saints in Christ, we are *expected* to walk in our new nature in Christ.

> [1]I entreat (exhort, call from close beside) you therefore, brothers, through the compassions (pity) [*mercies*] of God, to present (stand close beside) your bodies a living sacrifice, holy, well-pleasing, which is your reasonable sacred service. [2]And do not be conformed to (identified with the outward mold /form/expression) [*of*] this age, but rather be transformed (transformed after being with) by the renewing (completing the process of making fresh/new) of your thinking (mind, reasoning), for your proving what is the will of God- the good (intrinsically good), and acceptable (well-pleasing), and perfect (full-grown, consummated).
>
> Rom. 12:1, 2 (LET)

Again, Paul says,

> So I'm telling you this, and I insist on it in the Lord: you **shouldn't** live your life like the Gentiles [*the pagan world*] anymore. They base their lives on **pointless thinking**, [18]and they are in the **dark in their reasoning**. They are **disconnected** [GK *apallotrioo, alienated, cut off*] **from God's life** because of their ignorance and their closed [*callused*] hearts. [19]They are **people who lack all sense** of right and wrong, and who have turned themselves over to **doing whatever feels good** and to practicing every sort of corruption along with greed. [20]But you didn't learn that sort of thing from Christ. [21]Since you really listened to him and you were taught how the truth is in Jesus, [22]change the former way of life that was part of the person you once were, corrupted by deceitful desires. [23]**Instead, RENEW THE THINKING IN YOUR MIND BY THE SPIRIT** [24]and **clothe yourself with the new person** [*new nature*] created according to God's image in justice and true holiness.
>
> Eph. 4:17-24 (CEB)

So, what does all this mean? Many saints; (if indeed they are genuinely saved in Christ), they are **void** of any "**SPIRITUAL DISCERNMENT**." Those with spiritual discernment are not being *caught up* by such foolishness. They know better.

Spiritual godliness **is not** based upon the sensual appeal or driven by emotion of the old nature. Spiritual godliness is as the apostle says,

> I will pray with the spirit, but I will **pray with the mind** also; I will sing with the spirit, but **I will sing with the mind** also.   1 Cor. 14:15

Paul is simply saying that he will excise his **SPIRITUAL DISCERNMENT** in whatever he says or does, he does for the glory and praise for Christ.[Col. 3:17, 23] This my friend is the spiritual discernment that is sadly missing among the saints today.

A. The nobleman was distressed and hopeless

I do not know if you have ever experienced being distressed, distraught, or feeling hopeless? It is a frightening feeling. It is no stretch of the imagination to say the nobleman was very distraught and perhaps feeling overwhelmed with worry. Jesus was his last hope for his son that was on *brink of dying*. This was a very desperate situation for the nobleman. The father cried out to Jesus,

> The nobleman saith unto him, Sir, come down ere [*before*] my child die.
>
> John 4:49 (KJV)

'Jesus please come right now, or else I am afraid my son will die.' (The delegation accompanying the nobleman must echo very loudly the same sentiment.) This is the plea of a very distraught parent. The father was frantic.

Our Lord knew before the arrival of the nobleman and his group with him that the nobleman was coming. Jesus knew that the man would be *panic stricken*. Our Lord was already fully anticipating the man's arrival who was beside-himself. The nobleman was perhaps nearly *out of his mind* and *sick from worry*. The nobleman's family and servants had spent some sleepless nights together concerning the child. If you are a compassionate and loving parent, well, you know just exactly what I mean.

The urgency was immediate! Perhaps the man imagined that, *there was no time to waste*. Jesus was his last hope he may have thought to himself. The nobleman must have grappled with his emotions to hold back his tears with his blurry eyes. When we are almost in tears, it is hard to put things into words. We are just all choked up inside, and we are simply emotional wrecks. Friend, this is the state the nobleman found himself in now before our Lord.

> So he came again to Cana in Galilee, where he had made the water wine. And at Capernaum there was an official [*nobleman*] whose son was ill. [47]When this man heard that Jesus had come from Judea to Galilee, he went to him and asked him to come down and heal his son, for he was

at the point of death. ⁴⁸So Jesus said to him, "Unless you see signs and wonders you will not believe." ⁴⁹The official [*nobleman*] said to him, "Sir, come down before my child dies." ⁵⁰Jesus said to him, "Go; your son will live." The man believed the word that Jesus spoke to him and went on his way. ⁵¹As he was going down, his servants met him and told him that his son was recovering. ⁵²So he asked them the hour when he began to get better, and they said to him, "Yesterday at the seventh hour the fever left him." John 4:46-52 (ESV)

The man was totally panic stricken and running on pure nerves and sick of worry. Stunned by Jesus' words, 'Go; your son lives.' The nobleman by faith began his journey home with his servants; but like any of us, he no doubt was trembling and anxious with a lot of nervous fear. (If you have ever been in a similar situation, you know exactly what I mean.)

How easy it is to find fault with the nobleman. Wait: put yourself in his place, believe me, you will be struggling with your faith. So, friend, do not judge the man. As a nobleman he had plenty of money and power, but all his money and power were useless now. Listen, the nobleman had been riding an emotional roller coaster with his very ill son. Let me tell you his ride was not pleasant; it had been simply one large nightmare. Believe me, his nightmare was very frightening. He was dreadfully fearful that he was going lose his son to the grim reaper. He had felt so helpless.

The words keep ringing in his mind, 'Go; your son lives.' Nevertheless, the man obeyed Jesus words, and he turned back with hope. In amazement, the nobleman believed the words of Jesus, even though he did not know truly who Jesus was. The nobleman must have struggled inside himself.

Like I said earlier, this is like the man who had a demon possessed son, but none of the apostles were able to deliver his son.^{Mark 9:17f} Jesus assures the father of the demon possessed son, 'All things are possible when one believes,' ^{Mark 9:23}. Then, the father of demon possessed son cried out loud to Jesus,

> Immediately the boy's father **cried out** and said, "**I DO BELIEVE; HELP MY UNBELIEF!**" Mark 9:24

Perhaps, in the same way, the nobleman was struggling within him, '*I do believe; help my unbelief.*' In the same way, the nobleman believed Jesus' words, and he turned back in **obedience of faith**. Wow! Do you think you would have immediately turned back in faith and obedience? Listen, the nobleman **did not** ask any questions. Hallelujah! The father did exactly what Jesus instructed him to do. Do you think you would be able to do that, turn back towards home in obedient faith to Jesus' words? Come on, be honest with yourself.

Hoping against hope the father in desperation sought out the Lord Jesus, even though the nobleman **did not** fully **know** this is indeed the Lord of glory. Then, once the nobleman found Jesus, he pleaded his case. Amazingly, he turned back towards home in obedient faith. Yes, he started back to his acutely ill son. What awesome faith the nobleman shows.

> "Go home; your son will live."   John 4:50 (NET)

B. There is genuine hope in Jesus the Lord today

You can say what you want, but the nobleman fixed his hope on Jesus' words, 'Go home; your son will live.' The father didn't even flinch. Wow, what faith! We don't read anywhere that the father said, "Jesus, are You sure my boy is healed?" The nobleman turned back believing Jesus' words of comfort, 'Go home; your son will live.' What incredible and amazing faith the father exhibited in the words of Jesus! Well, let me ask you, "Are you walking with that same faith of the nobleman?" Or "do you have some lingering doubts?" James says,

> "For as the body apart from [the] spirit is dead, so also the faith apart from works is dead."[a]   James 2:26 (LSV)

> [a]The point here by James is if we have genuine biblical faith, then genuine faith ought to be exhibited in action.

The nobleman didn't just believe. Look at it carefully: the man believed Jesus. Then, the man demonstrates his genuine faith in Jesus' word, 'You shall live.' The nobleman believed and he immediately turned **in action-faith** heading back home with his delegation that accompanied him. The point here is that faith without faith in action or obedience is no faith at all. It is a dead faith. Genuine faith in Christ is measurable through "*faith in action.*"

Friend, the grim reaper is coming for everyone at death; there is no evading or bypassing death. Unless you are truly saved, you cannot escape Hell. If you are truly born from above by the Holy Spirit, then, are you at peace with God? So, if you are alive in Christ Jesus right now, you already have citizenship in Heaven today, [Phi.1:21-23; 3:20f; 2 Cor. 5:8]. Hallelujah! Jesus gave us these assuring words,

> [1]"Let not your heart be troubled; you believe in God, believe also in Me.
> [2]In My Father's house are many mansions; if *it were* not *so,* I would have told you. I go to prepare a place for you. [3]And if I go and prepare

> a place for you, I will come again and receive you to Myself; that where
> I am, *there* you may be also. John 14:1-3 (NKJ)

When you truly know Jesus as your Lord and Savior, your assurance is certain. As the Hebrews writer says,

> Therefore, since we are surrounded by such a great cloud of witnesses, let us throw off everything that hinders and the sin that so easily entangles [*us*]. And let us run with perseverance the race marked out for us, [2]**FIXING OUR EYES ON JESUS**, the pioneer [GK *archegos, author NAS*] and perfecter [GK *teleiotes, completer*] of faith. For the joy set before him he endured the cross, scorning its shame, and sat down at the right hand of the throne of God. Heb. 12:1, 2 (NIV)

The problem is that many us are coming up short on faith coupled with a lack of action and obedience. Please listen carefully: **faith is not a leap into the unknown**. Such actions before the Lord are credulous actions, and such actions are not biblical faith. Biblical faith is based upon **what God SAYS** in His Word, and **what God has already DONE**. This is not faith like the false prophets of the "Name it and Claim it" or "Prosperity Gospel" preach or espouse. They are full of lies *from the get-go*.

Our Lord conquered death and the grave, and He is alive forever more. Jesus' promises are sure and gloriously sealed with His word and the Holy Spirit. As the Hebrews writer says these encouraging words,

> Because God wanted to make the unchanging nature of his purpose very clear to the heirs of what was **promised**, he confirmed it with **an oath**. [18]God did this so that, by two unchangeable things [*He gave His **promise** and swear with an **oath***] in which it is impossible for God to lie, we who have fled to take hold of the hope set before us may be greatly encouraged. [19]We have this hope as an anchor for the soul, **firm** and **secure**. It enters the inner sanctuary behind the curtain [e.g., *holy of holies in Heaven*], [20]where our forerunner, Jesus, has entered on our behalf. He has become a high priest forever, in the order of Melchizedek. Heb. 6:17-20 (NIV)

I think it is easy to beat up on ourselves because we may feel a little short on faith. When we read about God's promise to Abraham in having a son by his wife Sarah (both stricken by age), we see they may have doubted. Abraham and Sarah both laughed at the Lord promise of having as son Yes, we would say that were a little short on faith. Ah, but praise God, the Lord saw their hearts (which we are unable see and He can see our hearts as well.) Thus, the Bible says of Abraham and Sarah,

¹⁶Therefore *it is* of faith, that *it might be* by grace; to the end the promise might be sure to all the seed; not to that only which is of the law, but to that also which is of the faith of Abraham; who is the father of us all, ¹⁷(As it is written, I have made thee a father of many nations,) before him whom he believed, *even* God, who quickeneth [*gives life to*] the dead, and *calls* those things which be not as though they were. ¹⁸**Who against hope believed in hope**, that he might become the father of many nations; according to that which was spoken, So shall thy seed be. ¹⁹And being **NOT WEAK IN FAITH**, he considered not his own body now dead, when he was about *a* hundred years old, neither yet the deadness of Sara's womb: ²⁰**He STAGGERED NOT AT THE PROMISE OF GOD** through unbelief; but was **STRONG IN FAITH**, giving glory to God; ²¹And being fully persuaded that, what he had promised, he was able also to perform.   Rom. 4:16-21 (KJV)

So, when we think of the nobleman, he put all his trust in the words of Jesus, 'Go home; your son will live.' The father never wavered. He was strong in his faith and trusting in the words of Jesus. Where is such faith today in the churches?

The nobleman didn't see any miracles or signs. He did not see or even know of Jesus' power and authority. He simply placed his trust in Jesus' words, 'Go home; your son will live.' Hallelujah!

This is an astonishing and amazing miracle or sign. Think about it. Jesus **did not pray**, as far as we know. He didn't lift up his hands as though to **lifted His hands to Heaven**. Jesus didn't say, **"It is done; your son is healed now."** Our Lord did not say anything to the distraught father but, 'Go home; your son will live.'

Like the marvelous miracle of turning the water into wine, our Lord said nothing but simply **will it so**. Hallelujah, what a Savior. Before Jesus even spoke the word to the nobleman, He had already healed the boy. Glory to God. Yes, get it right: the boy was already healed before He spoke to the father and his servants with him.

Do you know what is so amazing as well? The man immediately believed Jesus.

⁵⁰Jesus told him, "Go home; your son will live." The **man believed the word that Jesus** spoke to him, **and set off for home**. ⁵¹While he was on his way down, his slaves met him and told him that his son was going to live. ⁵²So he asked them the time when his condition began to improve, and they told him, "Yesterday at one o'clock in the afternoon the fever

left him." [53]Then the father realized that it was the very time Jesus had said to him, "Your son will live," and **he himself believed along with his entire household.** [54]Jesus did this as his second miraculous sign when he returned from Judea to Galilee.   John 4:50-54 (NET)

Friend, I am here to tell you that *there is genuine hope in Jesus the Lord* **TODAY**. These are promises from God who cannot lie![Titus 1:2]

Conclusion

Friend, Jesus laid down His life on the cross for sinners. No one could take Jesus' life. He laid down His life on the cross for our sins. Oh, yes He did, and friend, Jesus is coming back just like He said He would. You had better be ready because if you only have a profession of faith and not a genuine possession of saving faith in Christ Jesus as Lord and Savior, you shall surely perish in your sins in Hell.

Also, what is coming upon this world after the rapture of the church is the greatest nightmare this old world has ever seen. There are inklings that might suggest we are very close to that hour. Are you ready?

Our situation, regardless of our wickedness and profane condition, if you seek Jesus out with your whole heart, He will save you from your sins.[Rom. 10:9-13] Yes, He will be there when you need Him. **"He is an on-time God."** Did you get it? **HE IS AN ON-TIME GOD!** He will be there when you need Him. However, you cannot walk with the world and walk with Jesus at same time. God's Word gives us this injunction,

[15]Do not love the world nor the things in the world. If anyone loves the world, the love of the Father is not in him. [16]For all that is in the world, the lust of the flesh and the lust of the eyes and the boastful pride of life, is not from the Father, but is from the world. [17]The world is passing away, and *also* its lusts; but the one who does the will of God lives forever.   1 John 2:15-17

Third miraculous miracle and sign
Jesus Heals a Paralytic of Thirty-Eight Years

Now there is in Jerusalem by the sheep *gate* a pool, which is called in Hebrew Bethesda, having five porticoes. ³In these lay a multitude of those who were sick, blind, lame, and withered [e.g., *paralyzed*], *waiting for the moving of the waters;* [⁴for an angel of the Lord went down at certain seasons into the pool and stirred up the water; whoever then [*was*] first, after the stirring up of the water, stepped in was made well from whatever disease with which he was afflicted.ᵃ] ⁵A man was [*the paralytic*] there who had been ill for thirty-eight years. ⁶When Jesus saw him lying *there*, and knew that he had already been a long time *in that condition*, He said to him, "Do you wish [or *want*] to get well?" ⁷The sick [*the paralytic*] man answered Him, "Sir, I have no man to put me into the pool when the water is stirred up, but while I am coming, another steps down before me." ⁸Jesus said to him, "Get up, pick up your pallet and walk." ⁹Immediately the man became well, and picked up his pallet and *began* to walk. Now it was the Sabbath on that day.   John 5:2-9

ᵃVerse 4 is not found in many older GK text. Though verse 4 appears in NAS of 1995, the text does not appear in NSA of 2020. Unfortunately, it is unlikely to be in other older GK texts.

(Brackets "[ ]" are used to alert the reader that the sentence is probably not in the original GK text.)

CHAPTER 9

Jesus seeks out a paralytic to heal

Now a man was there who had been disabled invalid [*the paralytic*] ª for thirty-eight years. ⁶When Jesus saw him lying there and when he realized [*knew*] that the man had been disabledª [*the paralytic*] a long time already, he said to him, "Do you want to become well?" ⁷The sick man answered him, "Sir, I have no one to put me into the pool when the water is stirred up. While I am trying to get into the water, someone else goes down there before me." ⁸Jesus said to him, "Stand up! Pick up your mat and walk." ⁹Immediately the man was healed, and he picked up his mat and started walking. (Now that day was a Sabbath.)   John 5:5-9 (NET)

ªThe GK word "*astheneo*" for "*disabled*" [NET] just implies some type of *sickness* or *ill*. The context suggest he was unable walk which suggest he was a *paralytic*. From context, I think "*paralytic*" (connotative meaning) is more suitable, and the denotative meaning is less preferred than *disabled* or *infirmity* or *sick*.

Introduction

This is one of the most unique and unusual miracles, and unless we give close attention to apostle John's overall purpose for writing *all these signs*, it is likely we will miss the significance and the intention by John. That is, without seeing all the miracles tied together, the purpose of these miracles may indeed be elusive to us. This sign might leave some of us scratching our heads. (We may be wondering what does this all means.)

111

The location or place for the miracle oddly occurs in a place called in Hebrew Bethesda. The word Bethesda is made up two words in HEB, "*beth*" (*house*) and "*hesda*" (*mercy* or *grace*). Hence, meaning "*house of mercy*" or "*house of grace.*"[1]

Additionally, this miracle or sign occurs on the Sabbath. Jesus performing the miracle on the Sabbath was strictly forbidden by the ruling religious leaders. Anything that appeared as work on the Sabbath had sudden and grave consequences for anyone violating the Sabbath.

For instance, an Israelite was gathering wood on the Sabbath during wilderness wanderings. The man who violated this ordinance of the Mosaic Law paid the ultimate price for violation of the Mosaic Law. (Sincerity is not in question; the issue is strict obedience was required by all under the Mosaic Law at that time.)

> Now while the sons of Israel were in the wilderness, they found a man gathering wood on the sabbath day. [33]Those who found him gathering wood brought him to Moses and Aaron and to all the congregation; [34]and they put him in custody because it had not been declared what should be done to him. [35]Then the LORD said to Moses, "The man shall surely be put to death; all the congregation shall stone him with stones outside the camp." [36]So all the congregation brought him outside the camp and stoned him to death with stones, just as the LORD had commanded Moses.   Num. 15:32-36

Therefore, the ruling religious leaders at Bethesda saw the healing on the Sabbath as a very a serious violation of Mosaic Law. I doubt many of us today can grasp the seriousness of the offense among the religious leaders who were attempting to be obedient to the Mosaic Law.

I am fearful that many of us today cannot understand the reaction of the ruling religious leaders in Jesus' day. It was a horrific crime to violate the Law. As we shall discover more amazingly, Jesus clearly identifies and reveals Himself to the paralytic man whom He heals. Our Lord plainly identifies Himself, but still, our Lord's true identity eluded many unbelievers then as well as today. This is because they either do not believe the Scriptures or they remain spiritually blind to the truth of God's Word.

This is one unique sign by Jesus. The surrounding events are puzzling to many people; so, please stay alert as I attempt to explain and unravel this mystery.

A. Sought out by mercy

The name "Bethesda" (*house of mercy* or *house of grace*) gives us a hint into the amazing miracle. People believed that whoever stepped into the pool first after the *alleged* stirring or swirling "*by angels*" would be healed. (I warn you, take care how you read this account of the paralytic). Our Lord does not give any credence or endorsement to the tradition which is alleged in [John 5:4]. The stirring of a pool of water by a holy angel was to be from God. The people here imagined that an angel stirs the waters of the pool for healing. There is not one Scripture in the Bible that endorses such *taunting* by God or His holy angels.[1 Cor. 10:12,13; James1:13] (If you do endorse [John 5:4] as authentic or genuine Scripture, that is on you!)

Let us be careful reading and interjecting our opinions into the Bible. It is likely that tradition (or even *superstition*) gave the notion that an angel stirred the water. It is certain the Romanist and other ritualists that give rise to endorsing such actions. (Only Roman Catholicism and other ritualists give heed to such notions.) Such tempting is not by the God of the Bible. The Lord tests us, but **He does not tempt us**.[1 Cor. 10:12, 13; James 1:2-4, 12] Ironically, the very word for "*tempt*" or "*test*," whether HEB or GK, can be translated either way, tempting or testing. The translation of whether the meaning is "*tempt*" or "*test*" is determined by the context. I warning you again: you had better be careful you do not charge the Lord of tempting anyone!

The power and authority do not rest in so-called "*magical potions, magical words*, or *magical powers.*" Healing by God is solely by His sovereign *will* and *plan.*[1 John 5:14, 15]

The Bible gives us the true overall account of what transpired including traditional practices, but this does not mean that because it is recorded in the Bible that the Bible is endorsing or approving of the tradition(s) as authentic. In the same way, we need to be careful that we do not give way to intuitive feelings or traditions or ignorant superstitions that have no biblical bases. The Bible is accurately recording the information, but the Bible is not endorsing the tradition or foolish superstitions of manmade religions.

The charlatans of today supposed healing is based upon the man's quantity or magnitude of a person's faith to believe that God will heal him. That is, God will heal anyone if he/she has enough faith, and this is not true. This is beyond ignorance; this is indeed a lie! No one can manipulate the Lord regardless how zealous or unyielding their faith is in God. This is a lie right out of Hell.

The paralytic's hope was vanquished or erased to ever walk again. This man's illness was more than being "*ill, invalid, disabled* or having an *infir-*

mity;" he was indeed a "*paralytic*." The paralytic man had been paralyzed (or unable to walk) for thirty-eight years. His only *thread of hope* he "thought to himself" might be if he was fortunate enough to be placed in the pool in Bethesda, *the place of mercy*, when the *water was allegedly stirred by an angel*. He was hanging his hope on the thread or strand of tradition and superstition. He certainly wasn't placing much hope in God's Word. This is certainly typical of many religious people today. Yes, they are trusting more in religious tradition, religious fetishism, or so-called sacred shrines, rather than trusting the Lord. Others, though they do not place any hope in religious shrines, they put hope in *being lucky* or wearing some kind of *good luck charm*. The atheist places his hope in "*being lucky.*"

The Church of Rome declares an angel carried the "Pontius Pilate staircase" from Jerusalem to Rome. Dr. Martin Luther during reformation was doing penance on that supposed staircase when the verse in Rom. 1:17 struck home with him. Luther immediately went to his superior, and he asked him: "Sir what does it mean, 'The just shall live by faith.'"[Rom. 1:17 (KJV)] Luther's superior said to him, "It means exactly what it says!" The rest is history my friend.

NET is more descriptive of Bethesda. We read,

> Now there is in Jerusalem by the Sheep Gate a pool called Bethzatha in Aramaic, which has five covered walkways. A great number of sick, blind, lame, and paralyzed people were lying in these walkways.

John 5:2, 3 (NET)

There were (five porches, KJV) which were five walkways to the pool. There were possibly hundreds of hundreds of people gathered in these five walkways to the pool. These were desperate people willing to do almost anything to be the first to step into the pool immediately after what they thought was the miraculous stirring of the water by angels. (For they must have thought the stirring of the waters was a *sign* of God to be healed.)

This is much like today were con-artists yell at hopeless and desperately ill people: "I do not heal anyone; God heals. Ah, but if you have enough faith, God will heal you of all your diseases." Then, they are told: "- but you have to give generously to the Lord (*that means to me first*); so, demonstrate your faith in God by giving generously (*to me*)." These are liars telling people that you can manipulate God. What a deceiving lie.

Listen, my friend, what we receive, we receive by His mercy and grace. (This is Paul's point in 2 Cor. 4:7; he is implying it all by grace.) First, it is **not** God's will to heal all our diseases. This is a lie right out of Hell. Listen, the greatest healing (which charlatans and fake healers overlook) is Jesus saves us from all our sins. The healing of sin is forever! The Lord gives eternal life in Heaven with Him to all those that trust in Him as Lord and Savior. What greater gift is there if it is not eternal life by faith in Christ? Hence, Jesus said, those who genuinely trust in Him as Lord and Savior shall **never die**.[John 8:47, 51; 11:26] Hello! Are you with me? This is why we can say absolutely certainty from God's Word, "absent from the body and to be at home with the Lord." [2 Cor. 5:8] Hallelujah!

Secondly, biblically, we need to lineup our prayers with will of God since the death rate is the same among healers and non-healers. As John says,

> And this is the confidence that we have in him, that, if we ask any thing according to his will, he heareth us: And if we know that he hear us, whatsoever we ask, we know that we have the petitions that we desired of him.   1 John 5:14, 15 (KJV)

The charlatan healers know they are frauds except for naive and credulous that are being led astray. The great apostle, a man of full of faith and fervent and earnest man of prayer prayed for healing of his affliction three times that the risen Lord Jesus would cure him of his infirmary. The Lord of Heaven answered him,

> And he said unto me, My grace is sufficient for thee: for **MY STRENGTH IS MADE PERFECT IN WEAKNESS**. Most gladly therefore will I rather glory [boast] in my infirmities, that the power of Christ may rest upon me.   2 Cor. 12:9 (KJV)

The apostle Paul told Pastor Timothy, "I left Trophimus sick at Miletus."[2 Tim. 4:20] Similarly, Paul instructed Pastor Timothy with his frequent illness,

> Don't continue drinking only water, but use a little wine because of your stomach and your frequent illnesses.   1 Tim. 5:23 (CSB)

The biggest lie today is no one need be sick or poor. How is it people given into such "*malarkey*."[2] One might say that the false healers are "full of *malarkey*." Well, it sounds better than saying they are full of something else.

Well, it is certain that this paralytic was destitute, hopeless, and no place to turn like so many others like him. It is certain that he felt he had nowhere to turn. He was lost in an endless sea with a host of others in the same situation: hopeless and filled with despair.

B. Healed by grace

As the Scriptures give us information concerning the healing of the paralytic, I am using a newer translation to help clarity the text.

Now a man was there who had been disabled [a paralytic] for thirty-eight years. ⁶When Jesus saw him lying there and when he realized [GK *ginosko*, also knew or perceived] that the man had been disabled [a paralytic] a long time already, he said to him, "Do you want to become well?" ⁷The sick [the paralytic] man answered him, "Sir, I have no one to put me into the pool when the water is stirred up. While I am trying to get into the water, someone else goes down there before me." ⁸Jesus said to him, "Stand up! Pick up your mat and walk." ⁹Immediately the man was healed, and he picked up his mat and started walking. (Now that day was a Sabbath.) ¹⁰So the Jewish leaders said to the man who had been healed, "It is the Sabbath, and you are not permitted to carry your mat." ¹¹But he answered them, "The man who made me well [cured] said to me, 'Pick up your mat and walk.'"

John 5:2-11 (NET)

This is a portrait of the infinite mercy and grace of God. Amazingly, the place where the paralytic is healed is called Bethesda or Bethzatha, meaning *"the house of mercy."* The language of HEB and ARA are very similar, but the spelling in ENG will vary. Scholars differ on the actual ENG translation.

There is also the healing of similar paralytic in the Gospels account, but this is a different healing account. There is a little similarity between the account in Matt. 9:1-8 along with the other two synoptic Gospels. The event in John's Gospel is not the same as in the other three synoptic Gospels. Therefore, there is no need for comparison in these similar events since the accounts are separate and distinct.

The circumstances surrounding this healing in John's account and the reaction the religious leaders are difficult to fully grasp today. The subculture is very strict, and it is in a time when violation within that Jewish culture one might have to pay with their life. So, this event in Jerusalem at that time would be arduous or difficult for many people to fully understand today.

Furthermore, there were a great number of slaves and poor people throughout all of the Roman world. Besides, there were some people chronically ill in many of these metropolitan areas due to disease and many other problems. This was especially true in large cities or metropolitan areas like Jerusalem and other populated areas. The poor and very ill had to locate themselves where there were a lot of wealthy people and money so they could beg for a living. This is still very true in many third-world countries today. Sadly, many Christian leaders in these third-world countries are somewhat callused to the plight of the poor. The economy is seriously depressed, giving little hope to the poor and chronically ill.

Unless you have traveled to such area in the world, it is difficult to fully understand the situation. Begging is a necessary means as a way of life especially when people are chronically ill, disabled and unable to work. The unemployment might be as high as 85% in some places today. Add to this, there are war torn areas of the world, and some countries in political upheaval. There are dictators and tyrants ruling giving the common people little hope.

Here in the Scripture text, we see our Lord visiting some of the poorest people in the area. The Sheep's Gate was also very near the large *market place*. The market place was where people with money purchased food, and perhaps clothing, bedding, and other things. So, there were many people coming and going at Sheep's Gate and especially some wealthy people. The Sheep's Gate was somewhat adjacent to Bethesda. So, many hopeless people there were ill and destitute. The poor and chronically ill were forced to beg in order to survive. Living was no doubt a day by day struggle.

Out of the multitudes of hundreds and hundreds of people lying in these five covered walkways,[John 5:2 NET] Jesus sought out this man who has been paralyzed for thirty-eight years. The Scripture tells us,

> Now a man was there who had been disabled [*paralytic*] for thirty-eight years. When Jesus saw him lying there and when he realized [*knew*] that the man had been disabled [*paralytic*] a long time already, he said to him, "Do you want to become well?" John 5:5, 6 (NET)

There was nothing that the paralyzed said or did to draw Jesus' attention. The situation suggest that the paralytic was **not** expecting anyone to visit him. So, he had no awareness of who Jesus truly was. The paralytic was not expecting to be made whole. Jesus asked the paralytic, 'Do you want to become well [*whole*; e.g. *healed*]?' Jesus' question was one of compassion and mercy. There was nothing critical in Jesus' question. The text makes this known from the man's response to Jesus, which was equally congenial.

> "Sir, I have no one to put me into the pool when the water is stirred up. While I am trying to get into the water, someone else goes down there before me." John 5:7 (NET)

The paralytic did not manifest or exhibit any faith on his part. (If you say that the paralytic had faith to be healed, then, you are liar!) Jesus' questioned him, 'Do you want to become well?' The paralytic just says, "*Someone else gets into the water before me.*" So, there is nothing that suggested or implied the paralytic exhibited any faith or any thought of being healed.

117

Out of multitudes of people lying chronically ill in these "five covered walkways,"[5:2 NET] the paralytic was sought out by the *mercy and grace* of the Lord Jesus. The man did not seek Jesus. Friend, Jesus sought out the paralytic by our Lord's *mercy and grace*. The paralytic did not even imagine that a mighty miracle was about occur. What a marvelous picture of the grace and mercy of God seeking out sinners to save. Hallelujah and glory God forever and ever.

The charlatans and fake miracle workers want to tell you that the paralytic initiated the action and the faith. The man was paralyzed, and his hope was in tradition and superstition. This is certainly a picture of many *religious shrines* today and so-called *religious relics* all over the world. In reality, this poor man had no hope of ever walking. We only know he has been paralyzed for thirty-eight years. The paralytic man was totally helpless and void of any hope.

Then, our Lord Jesus who is infinite in mercy and grace looked at the paralytic and said,

> "**Stand up**! **Pick up your mat** and **walk**." **Immediately** [*instantly*] the man was healed, and he picked up his mat and started walking. (Now that day was a Sabbath.)   John 5:8, 9 (NET)

Jesus gives the paralytic three directives or three distinction commands. Amazing! "**Stand up**!" The man had been paralytic for thirty-eight years; so, how could he ever stand up? He couldn't with own will and power. He was paralyzed in his legs. Yet, though he could not stand, he did the impossible. The man was able to stand because Jesus instantly healed him and gave him the will and power to stand up.

Listen to me, the man's legs were dead! Jesus gave life and power to his legs, and now the paralytic's legs were immediately healed and his legs had life in them. More importantly, at Jesus' command, he was well and he was instantly standing. Jesus spoke with the absolute authority and ultimate power: **Stand up**, and through **the authority** and **the power** of Christ the Lord, the paralytic amazingly stood on his feet. He did not stand on his intrinsic faith or will. He arose and stood at the command and will of Christ Jesus.

The man must have been amazed at himself. "Yes, I am standing; "I cannot believe it," he thought to himself. "Hallelujah." Then, amazingly, Jesus said to him: "Now, **pick up your bed**." "Wow! I did it; I picked up my bed." (He must have thought to himself.) Then, Jesus told him, "**walk**." He could not walk because all his muscles in his legs had been virtually dead for thirty-eight years. Listen! Do understand, the muscles in his legs were completely dead. There was no life in his legs. So then, how in the world could a paralyzed man stand on his own? Ah, but Christ the Creator, Maker, and Sustainer instantly *re-created the man's muscles and gave life to his dead legs.* Yes, Christ *gave life to the man's dead muscles and legs, and our Lord gave the man the will power to walk* even though he had never been able to for thirty-eight years. (Friend, this is medically impossible.) What an amazing instantaneous miraculous sign of the Savior. Glory to God!

There is absolutely no faith exhibit here by the paralytic. The man was paralyzed, totally impotent. The language Jesus used here is an *imperative* in one command but three distinct actions: 'I say you **arise** [*paralytic and*] **pick up your bed** and **walk**.'

The *authority* and the *power* came from the command of Jesus. In Jesus' command, life came to the paralytic's legs and muscles. This man's legs were **dead**. The man was **helpless** as a paralytic. Christ even gave the paralytic will and power to obey His command. The man could do nothing on his own. Like Peter who walked on water at the command of Jesus,[Matt. 14:22-33] the paralytic walked at the command of Jesus.

> Jesus said to him, "**RISE, TAKE UP YOUR BED** and **WALK**." And **immediately the man was made well, took up his bed, and walked**.
>
> John 5:8, 9a (NKJ)

The paralytic was like Lazarus who was dead. The dead cannot to anything. There is no life within the dead body. In the same way, the paralytic's legs had no life; he could not stand even if had faith, he could never stand.

Listen! Get it right. The man was completely healed and given the will to obey Jesus' command first, and then came: "**RISE, TAKE UP YOUR BED** and **WALK**." Our Lord completely healed the paralytic before He gave the command to "rise, take up your bed, and walk."

Friend, I say again, this is a portrait of grace and mercy of the Lord Jesus. (The paralytic did nothing; he became a recipient of the marvelous mercy and grace of the Lord Jesus.) Jesus in His wonderful mercy and grace sought out the paralytic. The paralytic did nothing, and he warranted nothing since he was in same situation as *hundreds of hundreds* of other people at Bethesda.

Well, let me tell you that the *electionists* have it all wrong. God is not just willing to save a few. Friend, he is willing and eager to save all who will genuinely call the Lord Jesus: He will save everyone that genuinely calls upon Him.

> **For whosoever shall call** upon the name of the Lord **shall be saved**.
>
> Rom. 10:13 (KJV)

> "**Believe in the Lord Jesus, and you will be saved**, you and your household." Acts 16:31

> But **as many as received Him**, to them **He gave the right to become children of God**, to those who believe in His name: who were born, not of blood, nor of the will of the flesh, nor of the will of man, but of God. John 1:12, 13 (NKJ)

Salvation is a legitimate offer to everyone. Come and receive Him right now.[John 1:12, 13] Yes, regardless of how wicked you have been or how wicked you are right now, Jesus Christ the Lord will save you from all our sin. He will forgive you of all your sins, and God promises, 'I will remember their sins no more.'[Jer. 1:34; Heb. 8:12;10:17] Jesus will clean you up from the inside out. Listen, after you genuinely trust and receive Jesus as Lord and Savior, be faithful in *reading* God's Word the Bible, *praying* to the Lord throughout your day, and seeking His will as you *share* the Gospel with others. Most of all, be very faithfully *attending* a sound Bible church and *participating* in worship and service to Christ Jesus the Lord.

Conclusion

Please listen! **Salvation is all** by mercy and grace of the Lord Jesus Christ. The Lord Jesus' salvation is available to everyone. We cannot earn our way to Heaven. Salvation is by His mercy and grace. The redemption in Christ is a free gift of God.[Rom. 6:23; Eph.2:8-10; Titus 3:3-7] Friend, we cannot manipulate God by having sufficient faith. Our Lord is Sovereign over all creation. He is Sovereign over our lives. (Friend, Christ is sovereign over your life whether you believe or not.) The *electionists* have one thing correct: the Lord is Sovereign over all His universe and all that is in it. Ah, but the electionists are theologically *dead wrong about salvation. The Lord is not willing that any should perish; He wants everyone to repentance and come to the know of the truth.*[John 3:16-18; 1 Tim. 2:2-6; 2 Peter 3:9]

Like the paralytic man that was impotent to deliver himself of his slow death of his chronic illness, Jesus will save you from you sin and clean you up from inside out. (Sickness and pain in this life will cease when He calls us home to Heaven.[Rev. 21:4]) But, you need to call out to Jesus right now to save you, and the wonderful good news is He will save you if you call upon Jesus as Lord and Savior. His promise is genuine and real, but you must call upon Him right now. Here again is God's promise to you:

> Because if you **confess with your mouth that Jesus is Lord** and **believe in your heart** that **God raised him from the dead**, you will be saved.

[10]For **with the heart one believes** and thus has righteousness and **with the mouth one confesses and thus has salvation**. [11]For the scripture says, "Everyone who believes in him will not be put to shame." [12]For there is no distinction between the Jew and the Greek, for the same Lord is Lord of all, who **richly blesses all** who call on him. [13]**For everyone who calls on the name of the Lord will be saved**.

Rom. 10:9-13 (NET)

Friend, will you call upon the Lord Jesus to save you right now? He is waiting on you to call upon Him right now.

Footnotes:

1. "Bethesda:" is HEB, and the word is made up of two word, "*beth*" meaning "*house*" and "*hesda*" *mercy* or "*grace*." Although, there are others that suggest the word can mean "house of disgrace." Still others suggest that the implication is "flowing water." The meaning is likely "house of mercy." Information provided is from Google.

2. "Malarkey:" the root word meaning "foolish talk," but the actual origin of the word is unknown. In other words, what they are saying is "*none sense*."

CHAPTER 10

Who are You Jesus?

For this reason therefore the Jews were seeking all the more to kill Him [Jesus], because He not only was breaking the Sabbath, but also was calling God His own Father, making Himself equal with God. [19]Therefore Jesus answered and was saying to them, "Truly, truly, I say to you, the Son can do nothing of Himself, unless it is something He sees the Father doing; for whatever the Father does, these things the Son also does in like manner. [20]"For the Father loves the Son, and shows Him all things that He Himself is doing; and the Father[a] will show Him greater works than these, so that you will marvel. [21]"For just as the Father raises the dead and gives them life, even so the Son also gives life to whom He wishes. [22]"For not even the Father judges anyone, but He has given all judgment to the Son, [23]so that all will honor the Son even as they honor the Father. He who does not honor the Son does not honor the Father who sent Him. [24]"Truly, truly, I say to you, he who hears My word, and believes Him who sent Me, has eternal life, and does not come into judgment, but has passed out of death into life.   John 5:18-24

[a] The phrase "the Father" does not appear a second time in the GK text, v 20. The NAS uses the italic to alert the reader that it is an insertion, though the inference is indeed implied.

Introduction

There are many, many people today who allege to believe in Jesus. I think it is wonderful there are so many people professing to believe in Jesus. The problem that is troubling and sorrowful is that there is no unified biblical view concerning Jesus. So, many only profess to know Jesus, but they do not truly know Him since they have a different view of Jesus than that which the Bible declares concerning Him. We need to know and understand what the Bible declares who Jesus actually is. We should not be interested in gathering peoples' impression of Jesus. We should rather be concerned knowing with certainty what Bible definitely declares who Jesus really is.

In the same way, there were many opinions about Jesus during His ministry to Israel. Our Lord asked this very question to His apostles, and here is their response.

> Now when Jesus came into the district of Caesarea Philippi, He was asking His disciples, "Who do people say that the Son of Man is?" [14]And they said, "Some *say* John the Baptist; and others, Elijah; but still others, Jeremiah, or one of the prophets." [15]He said to them, "But who do you say that I am?" [16]Simon Peter answered, "**YOU ARE THE CHRIST, THE SON OF THE LIVING GOD.**" [17]And Jesus said to him, "Blessed are you, Simon Barjona [ARA, son of Jonah], because flesh and blood did not reveal *this* to you, but My Father who is in heaven."
>
> Matt. 16:13-18

Similarly today, Jesus is just a religious guru according to Hinduism and Buddhism. To many unbelieving Jews, Jesus is just an itinerant Rabbi (teacher) and a deceiver. Yet, there are many Jews that believe that Yehoshua [Jesus] lived and taught the Mosaic Law correctly without acknowledging Him as the Messiah but still hold Him in esteem. (Jews have their problem with Paul since he declares a person imputed righteous through faith in Jesus.) Within Islam, Jesus is regarded a Prophet who ascended to Heaven but He never died on the cross and arose again. Others today characterize Jesus as some fundamentalist preacher. There are also a host of other interpretations concerning Jesus. Some imagine Jesus is a high spiritual being, but to them, He is not the Creator rather He is a created being.

Allow me to paraphrase Paul's words to the Corinth Church[1 Cor. 2:14]:

> *The one with only the lower nature (the unregenerate nature) does not receive the things of the Spirit of God. For they are nonsense to him. He is incapable of knowing the things of God. This is because the things of God must be discerned by Holy Spirit of God.*
>
> 1 Cor. 2:14 (Paraphrased)

The reason for the natural man's (the unsaved) inability to understand the things of God is because the Holy Spirit must illuminate the person mind.

Then, the person must be willing to receive the thing made known to him by the Spirit. As Jesus said concerning Peter,

> "You are blessed, Simon son of Jonah, because flesh and blood did not reveal this to you, but my Father in heaven!"   Matt. 16:17 (NET)

Some are unable to receive the enlightenment from God for many reasons.

1. Some are not open to truth; their mind is already made up and closed.

2. They are blinded by the world, or the carnal mind, or misled by evil spirits.

3. They may be so entangled by the cults and false religions that the truth eludes them.

4. They are shrouded by their own maze of doctrine, ecclesiastical traditions, or superstitions.

5. Still others remain too indecisive to make up their minds.

6. Decision or no decision, the person remains lost in sin and alienated from God, headed for Hell.

The Ethiopian eunuch had an ear to hear the truth when he was reading Isaiah. Philip asked him if he understood what he was reading. The Ethiopian said, 'How can I, except some man should guide me?'[Acts 8:28 (KJV)] Only if a person is willing to be guided, he may be open to God's Word.

Therefore, there are at least two salient things that must not be overlooked in the healing of the paralytic. What was the Lord's purpose for healing on the Sabbath? Second, who is Jesus declaring Himself to be? These two questions are interconnected with the healing of the paralytic.

A. Jesus heals on a Sabbath

The Jewish leaders were very troubled by the healing of the paralytic on the Sabbath. The Jewish leaders were troubled because the healing of paralytic was on the Sabath which thought to be a violation of the Mosaic Law. Also, the man was carrying his bed on the Sabbath based upon Jesus' instructions. To religious leaders, these two actions were seen as a deliberate violation of the Law of Moses. While many minimize carrying a bed on the Sabbath, let us not forget the man gathering wood on the Sabbath was ordered by God to be stoned.[Num. 15:32-36] The violation or disobedience to the Mosaic Law was a very serious offense. Hebrews says,

> Anyone who has violated the law of Moses dies without mercy "on the
> testimony of two or three witnesses." Heb. 10:28 (NRS)

So, the offense is very serious under the Law. Therefore, the Scripture declares,

> For this reason the Jews persecuted Jesus, and sought to kill Him,
> because He had done these things on the Sabbath. John 5:15 (NKJ)

The method or punishment of violating the Law was immediate stoning the violator. Yet, the Mosaic Law allowed for exceptions, which many religious leaders conveniently overlooked. (Like many today, they see the *letter* or denotative meaning of the text, but they cannot seem to grasp the connotative meaning or capture the *spirit* of the text.) For instance,

> "If you encounter your enemy's ox or donkey wandering off, you must
> by all means return it to him. If you see the donkey of someone who
> hates you fallen under its load, you must not ignore him, but be sure to
> help him with it." Exodus 23:4, 5 (NET)

This means that you are to even aid an animal under distress that fell in a hole or was overloaded with a burden even on the Sabbath. God is merciful and the saints are expected to also be merciful since God is merciful. We are to be merciful to man or beast. The point here is if we are to be merciful to animals, how much more are to be merciful to fellow man, woman, or child? Jesus sites this biblical principle,

> And he said unto them, What man shall there be among you, that shall
> have one sheep, and if it fall into a pit on the sabbath day, will he not lay
> hold on it, and lift *it* out? How much then is a man better than a sheep?
> Wherefore it is lawful to do well [GK *kaloos*,b e.g., *honorably good*] on the sabbath
> days. Matt. 12:11, 12 (KJV)

> bI use a double "*oo*" to let the reader know that the GK word *kaloos* is
> with the GK letter, "omega;" this is not "omicron;" In ENG, the letters
> are indistinguishable.

The point here is we are to be merciful even to the dumb animals burdened down, trapped, or entangled and in a hopeless way. How much more a man burdened and paralyzed on the Sabbath? Still, the Pharisees were blinded by the *Elders' theological tradition and superstition.* In the same way, sadly, many people are blinded to the truth of their own making. How sad is that my friend?

More importantly, Yehoshua is our Creator and Sustainer of all things.[John 1:1-3] Yehoshua has the innate authority over all the laws, even the Mosaic Law since He is the one who first established the Law. Yet, our Lord did not override or violate one point in the Law of Moses. He fulfilled it to the letter. Nevertheless, the *spirit* or *principle* of the Law is equally important.

> At that time Jesus went through the grainfields on the Sabbath. And His disciples were hungry, and began to pluck heads of grain and to eat. [2]And when the Pharisees saw *it*, they said to Him, "Look, Your disciples are doing what is not lawful to do on the Sabbath!" [3]But He said to them, "Have you not read what David did when he was hungry, he and those who were with him: [4]"how he entered the house of God and ate the showbread [*bread of the Presence* or *consecrated bread*] which was not lawful for him to eat, nor for those who were with him, but only for the priests? [5]"Or have you not read in the law that on the Sabbath the priests in the temple profane the Sabbath, and are blameless [*guiltless*]? [6]"Yet I say to you that in this place there is *One* **greater than the temple**. [7]"But if you had known what *this* means, `**I DESIRE MERCY AND NOT SACRIFICE**,' you would not have condemned the guiltless. [8]"For the **SON OF MAN IS LORD EVEN OF THE SABBATH**.
>
> Matt. 12:1-8 (NKJ)

Jesus is Lord over the Sabbath because our Lord is the One that established the Sabbath for man. As our Lord said,

> "The Sabbath was created for humans; humans weren't created for the Sabbath.
>
> Mark 2:27 (CEB)

With [Mark 2:27], many Christian religious leaders still do not get Jesus' point. Some decades ago, the Russians set a city on 10-day work period. (At the end of each ten days, the people were given a day off to rest.) It is reported that nearly the whole town went "nuts." Well, maybe could it be there is more involved in the statement, *And God rested on the Seventh day?*[Gen. 2:3; Ex. 34:21]

There are many such principles latent in Scripture, but unfortunately such principles are overlooked or dismissed. The reason for being overlooked or dismissed is simply because they are looked at the Scripture strictly as legal insight, the letter, or denotative sense. Thus, some are unable grasp the *connotative* or *spirit of the text*. Pay attention! This is not just seeking spiritual application of Scripture. There is the proper appropriation of the text. By *appropriation, I mean in the most positive sense*; that is, Scripture is properly used for godly walk and victory in Christ. This is the point of Jesus' teaching of the

Mosaic Law. It is one thing to understand the denotative meaning, but it is also important to grasp the spirit of the text or connotative implication.

The Pharisees could readily understand the *letter of the Law,* but the religious leaders did not grasp the *inherent spirit and principle within the Law.* The Law was given as freedom, but it was not intended to restrict life but to give life.

Jesus describes this principle this way,

> "The thief comes only to steal and kill and destroy; I came that they may have life, and have *it* abundantly. I am the good shepherd; the good shepherd lays down His life for the sheep." John 10:10, 11

> If therefore the Son shall make you free, ye shall be free indeed.
> John 8:36 (ASV)

> For sin will have no dominion over you, since you are not under law but under grace. [15] What then? Are we to sin because we are not under law but under grace? By no means! Rom. 6:14, 15 (ESV)

B. Jesus declares Himself to be equal with God

This next truth many are unable to grasp the real intended meaning to Jesus' actual identity. Many miss the meaning given by our Lord due the *carnal and corrupt minds, world's perceptions* and *concepts,* and the *demonic blindnesses* and *interferences.* Humankind has struck out: one, two, and three. We have all struck out before a holy and righteous God who will judge sin and the sinner. The Lord shall surely judge sin and the sinner, which includes everyone without exception outside Christ's redemption! The Good News is that Christ Jesus died on behalf of the believer and his sin on the cross. There is no condemnation in Christ.[John 5:24; Rom. 8:1]

Our text says,

> But Jesus answered them, "My Father is still working, and I also am working." For this reason the Jews were seeking all the more to kill him, because he was not only **breaking the sabbath**, but was also calling God his own Father, thereby **making himself equal to God**.
> John 5:17, 18 (NRS)

The naïve, immature, secular-minded, unregenerate, the cult, liberal, and atheist miss the meaning as noted above. That is, the immature and the natural man is without illumination and understanding of the revelation of God. We

127

are **not** to read into Scripture our personal opinions, which is *eisegesis*. It is incumbent or necessary that we read out of the text of Scripture the intended meaning, which is to *exegete*. We must read out of the text the inherent meaning by scribe of Scripture.

For an example of eisegesis (e.g., wrongly reading out Scripture), Jesus refers to God as the Father, and He says,

> But He answered them, "My Father is working until now, and I Myself
> am working."   John 5:17

Thus, defective error or eisegesis would allege that Christ the Son is a second generation "*god.*" In other words, they would interpret the text as a *natural man* without consulting and basing their interpretation from the harmonizing the revelation of Scripture and illumination by the Holy Spirit.

Even the Jews that did not believe in Jesus as the Messiah knew that the Messiah or Christ of Scripture is Himself eternal or lives forever, as we have noted earlier,

> "And I, if I am lifted up from the earth,ᶜ will draw all men to Myself."
> [33]But He was saying this to indicate the kind of death by which He was
> to die. [34] The crowd then answered Him, "We have heard out of the Law
> that the Christ is to remain forever; and how can You say, 'The Son of
> Man must be lifted up'? Who is this Son of Man?"   John 12:32-34

> ᶜ"And I, if I am lifted up from the earth, will draw all men to Myself.'ᵛ³²
> Jesus' statement looks to and beyond the cross to His rightful honor
> and glorification. Christ will draw people to Himself by the Holy Spirit.

The Messiah (the Anointed One or Holy One) is also addressed as "Father" because the Christ is the Creator of all things, but the Messiah is not God the Father.

> For unto us a Child is born, Unto us a Son is given; And the government
> will be upon His shoulder. And His name will be called **Wonderful**,
> **Counselor, Mighty God,**ᵈ **Everlasting Father, Prince of Peace**. Of
> the increase of *His* government and peace *There will be* no end, Upon
> the throne of David and over His kingdom, To order it and establish it
> with judgment and justice From that time forward, even forever. The
> zeal of the LORD of hosts will perform this.   Isa. 9:6, 7 (NKJ)

> ᵈThe HEB can mean "**Mighty** or **Almighty God**." The Messiah is
> "**Everlasting Father**" since the Christ is the Creator of all thing: the
> Messiah is the Father of Creation. But I say again, the Messiah is **not**

God the Father. Messiah the **Prince of Peace**; Prince, hence implying the Messiah is the King and Sovereign Ruler.

Again,

> In the beginning was the Word, and the Word was with God, and the Word was fully God. ² The Word was with God in the beginning. ³ All things were created by him, and apart from him not one thing was created that has been created.   John 1:1-3 (NET)

> For by Him all things were created, *both* in the heavens and on earth, visible and invisible, whether thrones or dominions or rulers or authorities-- all things have been created through Him and for Him. He is before all things, and in Him all things hold together [*and sustains*].
> Col. 1:16, 17

> In the past [*the Triune*] God spoke to our ancestors through the prophets at many times and in various ways, ²but in these last days he has spoken to us by his Son, whom he appointed [*established*] heir of all things, and through whom also he made the universe [GK *aion,* or *ages*]. ³The Son is the radiance of God's glory and the exact representation of his being, sustaining all things by his powerful word. After he had provided purification for sins, he sat down at the right hand of the Majesty in heaven.
> Heb. 1:1-3 (NIV)

To keep mind, the unique and separate distinction within the blessed Trinity of God, Jesus said literally,

> "I and my Father, **We are One.**ᵉ"   John 10:30 (ABPE)

> ᵉAs I have said, this is the literal translation. Though the verse is understood as "We are One," it is generally not translated by most translators.

Therefore, the Scripture interprets Scripture! We do not bring our natural and unregenerate minds to override Scripture's explicit meaning. Scripture stands inherently upon its own intrinsic authority. Scripture interprets Scripture! We do not let tradition, church history, church dogma, or superstition, or other outside sources to superimpose or determine the meaning of the Word of God. The Bible stands as its own inherent authority.

Therefore, get it right! We do not say, "I feel the Bible is saying this-" **WRONG**! Feeling has nothing to with interpreting the Bible. The Bible must stand on its own inherent authority. Again, **the Scripture interprets Scripture**!

Conclusion

Therefore, when Jesus refers to God as His Father; the text is very explicit and leaving no doubt

> But He answered them, "My Father is working until now, and I Myself am working." For this reason therefore the Jews were seeking all the more to kill Him, because He not only was **breaking the Sabbath**, but also was **calling God His own Father, MAKING HIMSELF EQUAL WITH GOD**. John 5:17, 18

Friend, we cannot override the inherent and plain declaration of Scripture. Christ is fully and completely Eternal God. Yet, in His infinite mercy and grace He pitched His tent of flesh. His very being took on also a fully human nature but without diminishing, compromising, or effecting His eternal nature as God or His human nature as man. Truly the Eternal God and full humanity in one person is Jesus Christ the Lord.

> And the Word was made flesh, and dwelt among us, (and we beheld his glory, the glory as of the only begotten of the Father,) full of grace and truth. John 1:14 (KJV)

> By common confession, the mystery of godliness is great: God appeared in the flesh, was vindicated by the Spirit, was seen by angels, was proclaimed among the nations, was believed in throughout the world, was taken up in glory. 1 Tim. 3:16 (MSB)

It matters not whether one believes Christ Jesus is God incarnate or not. The truth stands, and stand it will because the declaration comes from God who cannot lie, [Titus 1:2]. Christ Jesus the Lord is indeed Almighty God. Therefore, anyone that denies the truth of Scripture and refuses to repent and receive Jesus as the Lord and Savior shall indeed perish forever in Hell. Believe and receive Jesus Christ right now. He died on the cross for your sins, and He arose again the third day. He is coming for His church. Receive Him right now,

> But as many as received him, to them gave he [the] power to become the sons [GK teknon, children] of God, *even* to them that believe on his name: Which were born, not of blood, nor of the will of the flesh, nor of the will of man, but of God. John 1:12, 13 (KJV)

The Fourth miraculous miracle and sign
Jesus Feeds 30,000 with 2 Fishes and 5 Barley-cakes

After this Jesus went away to the other side of the Sea of Galilee (also called the Sea of Tiberias). ²A large crowd was following him because they were **observing the miraculous signs** he was performing on the sick. ³So Jesus went on up the mountainside and sat down there with his disciples. ⁴(Now the Jewish feast of the Passover was near.) ⁵Then Jesus, when he looked up and saw that a large crowd was coming to him, said to Philip, "Where can we buy bread so that these people may eat?" ⁶(Now Jesus said this to test him, for he knew what he was going to do.) ⁷Philip replied, "Two hundred silver coins worth of bread would not be enough for them, for each one to get a little." ⁸One of Jesus' disciples, Andrew, Simon Peter's brother, said to him, ⁹"Here is a boy who has five barley loaves and two fish, but what good are these for so many people?" ¹⁰Jesus said, "Have the people sit down." (Now there was a lot of grass in that place.) So the men sat down, about five thousand [men] in number. ¹¹Then Jesus took the loaves, and when he had given thanks, he distributed the bread to those who were seated. He then did the same with the fish, as much as they wanted [to eat]. ¹²When they were all satisfied [full], Jesus said to his disciples, "Gather up the broken pieces that are left over, so that nothing is wasted." ¹³So they gathered them up and filled twelve baskets with broken pieces from the five barley loaves left over by the people who had eaten. ¹⁴Now when the people saw the miraculous sign that Jesus performed, they began to say to one another, "This is certainly the Prophet who is to come into the world."

John 6:1-14 (NET)

CHAPTER 11

Jesus feeds 5,000 men plus women and children

[10]Then Jesus said, "Make the people sit down." Now there was much grass in the place. So the men sat down, in number about five thousand. [11]And Jesus took the loaves, and when He had given thanks He distributed *them* to the disciples, and the disciples to those sitting down; and likewise of the fish, as much as they wanted. [12]So when they were filled, He said to His disciples, "Gather up the fragments that remain, so that nothing is lost." [13]Therefore they gathered *them* up, and filled twelve baskets with the fragments of the five barley loaves which were left over by those who had eaten.   John 6:10-13 (NKJ)

Introduction

Please note: John says that Jesus **did other signs** or miracles, and due to the many signs, the people were following our Lord.

A large crowd followed Him, because they **saw the signs** which He was performing **on those who were sick**.   John 6:2

The Jews then said to Him, "What sign do You show us as your authority for doing these things?" [19]Jesus answered them, "Destroy this temple, and in three days I will raise it up." [20]The Jews then said, "It took forty-six years to build this temple, and will You raise it up in three days?" [21]But He was speaking of the temple of His body.

> Now when He was in Jerusalem at the Passover, during the feast, many **believed in His name, <u>observing His signs</u>** which He was doing.
>
> John 2:18-21, 23

> For this reason also the people went and met Him, because they heard that He had **performed this sign**.
>
> John 12:18

> Now Jesus **performed many other miraculous signs** in the presence of the disciples, which are not recorded in this book. [31]But these [*signs*] are recorded so that you may believe that Jesus is the Christ, the Son of God, and that by believing you may have [*eternal*] life in his name.
>
> John 20:30 (NET)

As it has been noted, the apostle John selected eight signs or miracles to establish conclusively that Yehoshua is the Holy One, the Messiah and the Anointed One by the Triune God as the Redeemer of the world.

It is obvious that the charlatans and counterfeiters of the faith are unable preform such awesome miraculous miracles. Still, these impostors are foolish and blindly ignorant to actually imagine that they can do greater miracles than Jesus, the Creator Himself. Our Lord said,

> Very truly, I tell you, the one who believes in me will also do the works that I do and, in fact, will do greater works than these, because I am going to the Father.
>
> John 14:12 (NRS)

Anyone who professes to do greater miracles than the Creator Himself is either a fool or a liar. No one can do greater miracles than Christ the Lord, the Designer, Creator, and Sustainer of all life. As Hebrews says concerning Christ the Lord,

> For he is The Brilliance of his glory, The Image of his Being, and upholds all things by the power of his word; and he in his Essential Being has accomplished the purification of our sins, and he sat down at the right hand of the Majesty on high.
>
> Heb. 1:3 (ABPE)

The feeding five thousand men plus all the women and children is an incredible miracle, and it baffles the mind. (The number of people present was staggering upwards of 20,000 to 30,000 conservatively speaking.) The miracle of feeding such large crowd is so amazing. The distributing of the five barley-cakes and the two fishes so rapidly and swiftly and carried out with precision is indeed mystifying.

133

In the first miracles, Jesus immediately **at will** changes the water and its **chemistry into a wonderfully** gourmet or most excellent **wine**. The second miraculously sign Jesus heals the nobleman's son immediately **at will** without saying or doing anything. The third miracle is instantaneously **giving life to the DEAD LEGS** of a man paralyzed thirty-eight years. Then paralyzed man's **DEAD LEGS** were immediate given life and power to instantly stand and walk. Awesome indeed! The man was at once granted the **power to not only to stand up** but even **walk**. He even carried his own mat. Who can do such miracles but God Himself?

A. Feeding of an incredibly large multitude

Drawing such a crowd, especially in a desolate or uninhabited area of 20,000 to 30,000 people in that day is indeed astonishing. This was no ordinary gathering. These were people drawn by the Spirit of the living God. Glory to God. The people saw His mighty signs.

John the Baptist said well,

> He must increase, but I *must* decrease.   John 3:30 (KJV)

The NET rightly translated it this way,

> "He must become more important while I become less important."

> John 3:30 (NET)

It is certain those following the "Prosperity Doctrine" haven't a clue as to what the John Baptist meant. They are not drawing people to Jesus to be redeemed and transformed by the grace of God. The Name and Claim it or the Preachers of the Prosperity Gospel are drawing people to themselves to fleece them of their money. After all, they are claiming greater miracles than Jesus. Some are even claiming to be "*a god*." These false teachers are following the lie of the devil: '*ye shall be as gods, knowing good and evil,*' Gen.3:5. This is a lie right out of Hell.

Friend, we are to lift up Jesus and not to lift up ourselves, our church, or our doctrine. As Jesus Himself said, 'I, if I be lifted up from the earth, will draw all *men* unto me,' John 12:32. Yes, yes, Jesus is referring to the cross and His resurrection and glorification, but there an important spiritual application. Today, more than ever, *the saints need to be lifting up Jesus as Lord more in our lives and in our preaching*! Let no one be desirous to hear others say to us, "What wonderful sermon." Let us exalt our Lord, and let us hear the people say, "*What a wonderful Savior we have*." Amen? The apostle Paul said,

> Wherefore God also hath highly exalted him, and given him a name which is above every name: That at the name of Jesus [**YEHOSHUA**] every knee should bow, of *things* in heaven, and *things* in earth, and *things* under the earth; And *that* every tongue should confess that **JESUS CHRIST** *IS* **LORD**, to the glory of God the Father.
>
> Phil. 2:9-11 (KJV)

Interestingly, "Herod Antipas built *the city of* Tiberias in the Herodian Tetrarchy of Galilee and Perea."[1] Here is the amazing miracle on shores of Tiberias Sea, the Galilean Sea. (Actually, the water is fresh water and not salt water, and it is the largest lake in Israel.)

> Jesus then took the loaves, and having given thanks, He distributed to those who were seated; likewise also of the fish as much as they wanted. When they were filled [*completely full*], He said to His disciples, "Gather up the leftover fragments so that nothing will be lost."   John 6:11, 12

Perhaps it had been a long day for the apostles and certainly with all the people who sat during Jesus teaching them. Our Lord was no doubt exhausted, very weary, and worn-out, but as the loving, faithful, and caring Shepherd, He pushes His human body to the maximum endurance. What physical condition and stamina He exhibited.

The time frame was probably approaching evening. The apostles were apparently bewailed, frazzled, and not knowing what to do with such a large crowd. The disciples said to Him,

> "Send the crowd away, that they may go into the surrounding villages and countryside and find lodging and get something to eat; for here we are in a desolate place."   Luke 9:12

Ah, but the Great Shepherd of the sheep saw all the people coming to Him, and the Scripture says,

> When Jesus went ashore, He saw a large crowd, and **He felt compassion** for them because **they were like sheep without a shepherd**.
>
> Mark 6:34

Can you imagine 20 or 30 thousand sheep all in one place. But there was no food to feed the sheep? Can you also imagine what it was like at feeding time for the sheep but with nothing to feed them? But these were people (not sheep) with their families, and this means there were lots of children. No doubt some children were crying out to their dad or mom, "I am hungry." Now, what are you going to do? The apostles may have thought, "Jesus send the people away to care for themselves, or else, who knows what this crowd will do if they get out of control." Yes, it was evening time, and with such large crowd, there might be rumbling throughout the massive multitude.

Jesus knew well ahead of time what He would do, but He wanted to put the apostles to a test by asking them,

> [4]Now the Passover, the feast of the Jews, was near. [5]Therefore Jesus, lifting up His eyes and seeing that a large crowd was coming to Him, [Jesus] said to Philip, "Where are we to buy bread, so that these may eat?" [6]This He was saying to test him, for He Himself knew what He was intending to do. [7]Philip answered Him, "Two hundred denarii[a] worth of bread is not sufficient for them, for everyone to receive a little."
>
> John 6:4-7

> [a]A denarii is a day's wages for a general laborer then. So, this is over six and half months' pay. But as Philip said, it is like a *drop in the bucket*; it is insufficient to do anything. The crowd was too numerous.

The apostles hearing Jesus tell them, '-They do not need to go away; you give them *something* to eat!'[Matt.14:16] Maybe the disciples thought to themselves, "*Is Jesus so exhausted that He is 'beside Himself?'*" The disciples may have thought to themselves: "Is Jesus out of His mind; we cannot feed all these people." Amazed, they are wondering, "How can we feed such a great multitude?"

Many of us are *a day late and a dollar short*. Meaning that many of us miss out on the opportunity the Lord may provide, but instead, we do nothing. Jesus is **an on-time God**, and praise the Lord: He is in control. Jesus is there before the crisis hits. He already knows when and where the crisis is in our life long before the crisis arrives.

If our Lord knows when each of our crises is coming, He is ready and able to see us through it. Amen! And God's Word instructs us to pray.[Phi.4:4-6]

The apostles were stunned! The apostles were indeed overwhelmed with such a very large multitude! Who wouldn't be overwhelmed by such a large crowd? The disciples did not know what to do with such large crowd but to dismiss the 20 to 30 thousand men, women, and children. Maybe their thought was, "Let them *sink* or *swim* or every man for himself." Thus, the disciples imply *it is all on them*. Let us remember, when such an enormous crowd initially gathered, our Lord had compassion upon them because Scripture declares,

> When Jesus went ashore, He saw a large crowd, and He felt compassion
> for them because they were like sheep without a shepherd.   Mark 6:34

The Lord is very keenly well-organized, a master of self-discipline, and He is unceasingly methodical and very meticulous to detail. The Bible says,

> And He said to His disciples, "Have them sit down *to eat* in groups of
> about fifty each."   Luke 9:14

In rows of 50 or 100,[Mark 9:40] this suggests each apostle was responsible for fifteen to thirty or even upwards of twenty-five to fifty rows depending on the size of each group sitting down. It is likely that the miracle occurs in the front of the eyes of everyone as the food is passed along. (People are observing this marvelous miracle with their own eyes.) That is, the miracle occurred as the small cakes of bread were passed along so ever quickly within each of the groups of 100s or 50s. The same occurred when the fishes were rapidly passed along within the ranks of 100 or 50. For we read,

> And He took the five loaves and the two fish, and looking up toward
> heaven, He blessed *the food* and broke the loaves and He kept giving
> *them* to the disciples to set before them; and He divided up the two fish
> among them all.   Mark 6:41

We do not know exactly how the marvelous sign or miracle occurred, but it is likely that the apostles handed the food to each group, and each group passed the food, and behold, the incredible miracle occurs before the peoples' very eyes. Amazingly, Jesus

> — **broke the loaves** and **He KEPT GIVING *THEM* to the disciples**
> to set before them; and **He DIVIDED UP THE TWO FISH among**
> **them all**.   Mark 6:41

This astonishing miracle occurs in plain sight of most everyone. Listen, there was no way anyone could deny this miraculous sign. Keep in mind that the people took whatever they wanted, and they were all full, *completely satisfied*. Hallelujah; what a Savior.

> And **when everyone was full**, He said to His disciples, "Gather the
> pieces that are left over, so that nothing will be wasted."
>   John 6:12 (MSB)

B. Everyone was satisfied; they gather 12 baskets full

This miracle is similar to where the Lord fed Israel in the wilderness for forty years with manna. (Six hundred thousand men came out of Egypt, which suggest nearly two and a half million total number.) Interestingly, the HEB word "man hu" for manna means, "**what is this**?" However, some theorize the word is ARA meaning, "to allot" or "to give."

Here is the account of the manna that God provided.

> [13b]— in the morning there was a layer of dew around the camp. [14]When the layer of dew evaporated, behold, on the surface of the wilderness there was a fine flake-like thing, fine as the frost on the ground. [15]When the sons of Israel saw *it,* they said to one another, "**What is it**?" For they did not know what it was. And Moses said to them, "It is the bread which the LORD has given you to eat. [16]This is what the LORD has commanded: 'Everyone gather as much as he will eat; you shall take an omer[b] apiece [each one] according to the number of people each of you has in his tent.'" [17]The sons of Israel did so, and *some* gathered much and *some* little. [18]When they measured it by the omer, the one who had gathered much did not have too much, and the one who had gathered little did not have too little; everyone gathered as much as he would eat.
>
> (Exodus 16:1-18)

> [b] An omer is nearly 2.2 liters or 2.3 quarts according to Google's AI.

Please note again the Scripture declares,

> When they measured with an omer, the one who gathered much had nothing left over, and the one who gathered little lacked nothing; each one had gathered what he could eat.   Exodus 16:18 (NET)

So, you do not miss the obscure truth here, let us not be like the lying and false *Prosperity Doctrinaires*. The apostle Paul applies this principle to our faithfulness in our stewardship of the genuine work of the Lord. (The Scripture text is slightly long, but it is very important to note.) So, pay attention! Paul says as he applies this principle to our financial giving to the Lord,

> My point is this: The person who sows sparingly [in his offering] will also reap sparingly, and the person who sows generously [in his offering] will also reap generously. [7]Each one of you should give just as he has decided in his heart, not reluctantly or under compulsion, because God loves a cheerful giver. [8]And God is able to make all grace overflow to you so that because you have enough of everything in every way at all times, you will overflow in every good work.
>
> [9]Just as it is written, "He has scattered widely [generously], he has given to the poor; his righteousness remains forever." [10]Now God who provides

seed for the sower and bread for food will provide and multiply your supply of seed and will cause the harvest of your righteousness to grow. [11]You will be enriched in every way so that you may be generous on every occasion, which is producing through us thanksgiving to God, [12]because the service of this ministry is not only providing for the needs of the saints but is also overflowing with many thanks to God. [13]Through the evidence of this service they will glorify God because of your obedience to your confession in the gospel of Christ and the generosity of your sharing with them and with everyone. [14]And in their prayers on your behalf they long for you because of the extraordinary grace God has shown to you. [15]Thanks be to God for his indescribable gift! 2 Cor. 9:6-15 (NET)

Paul is saying **YOU CANNOT OUT GIVE THE LORD**. The blessings from God whether they come in this present life in some respects or if the reward by His grace comes in Heaven, the Lord will give it back many times over. However, the overflowing grace of God and His giving back may not be evident in our lifetime. The problem is that many of us do not believe it; many do not give generously. We do not believe His Word. (The charlatans falsely use such verse(s) to fill the pockets.)

Still, such lack of giving on our part is a shameful faith. (We give in **three ways**:

- ✓ **We give with our TIME-**

- ✓ **We give with our abilities/RESOURCES-**

- ✓ **We give with our FINANCES-**

If we believe God's Word, then the saints would overflow in their giving. We giving of our *time*, *abilities* or *resources*, and *finances*. However, for the charlatans and con men and women who use the above verses to exploit the saints' payday is coming for them in full measure without mercy!

Our Lord reminds us where to wisely invest,

[19]Lay not up for yourselves treasures upon earth, where moth and rust doth corrupt, and where thieves break through and steal: [20]But lay up for yourselves treasures in heaven, where neither moth nor rust doth corrupt, and where thieves do not break through nor steal: [21]For where your treasure is, there will your heart be also. Matt. 6:19-21 (KJV)

Again, our Lord said,

'Give, and it shall be given to you; good measure, pressed, and shaken, and running over, they shall give into your bosom; for with that measure with which ye measure, it shall be measured to you again.'

Luke 6:38 (YLT)

The quacks, the charlatans, the lying and cheating false prophets distort the above Scriptures to their own destruction. The truth is that God is faithful, and He will care for His genuine redeemed. But we may not see the fruit or reward in this life. However, the promises of God are true, and we have this assurance from God who cannot lie, [Titus 1:2].

For no matter how many promises God has made, they are [*all*] **"Yes"** in Christ. And so through him the **"Amen"** is spoken by us to the glory of God.   2 Cor. 1:20 (NIV)

The Lord in feeding the great multitude did not allow any leftover food to be wasted. Please note the wonderful miracles once again. Jesus ordered the disciples,

[39]And He commanded them all to sit down by groups on the green grass. [40]They sat down in **groups** of **hundreds** and of **fifties**. [41]And He took the five loaves and the two fish, and looking up toward heaven, He blessed *the food* and broke the loaves and **He KEPT GIVING** *them* **to the disciples** to set before them; and He **divided up the two fish among them all**. [42]They **all ate and were satisfied,**[c] [43]and they picked up twelve full baskets of the broken pieces, and also of the fish. [44]There were five thousand men who ate the loaves.   Mark 6:39-44

[c]GK *chortazo*, the KJV is preferred, *"filled"* or *"full."*

Some might ask, "Where did they get twelve baskets?" I do not know, but with such a large crowd, some people were no doubt carrying baskets. This is much like a large group today. What did they do with twelve baskets of leftovers? I do not know, but there were surely some large families that would have been ecstatic to have the leftovers, *I kid you not*. Only if you came from a poor or large family, many others would not bother to take the leftovers. Still, those who had a large family or extended family, they would have been more than glad to have the leftovers for their family. Those with large families would be eager to have the leftovers!

By the days end, everyone is fed and ready to return home. Our Lord was no doubt completely exhausted. This is likely a typical day in our Lod's ministry, very long hours. This where we tend to forget or overlook Jesus' humanity at work. Yet, He remained fully God and man in one person. Please note also, His day was not half done. True! The Lord taught the large crowd, and no doubt, He gave instructions and sent apostles on their way. Our Lord then dismissed the great multitude, as I said, He probably also taught the people with final exhortation. Our Lord may have answered many questions by the people and by the apostles concerning the 20 to 30 thousand. What a grueling day that must have been for our Lord who was probably in top physical and mental conditioning.

After our Lord sends the disciples away in their boat, Jesus took the task of blessing and dismissing the large crowd. (Sadly, whoever blesses his people with proper invocation, benediction, or blessing anymore?) Did you know that the psalmist suggest that the animals of the world give thanks to God?(See Psa. 148:7-10.) Isaiah says,

> The ox knew his possessor [its owner], and the ass his lord's stall: Israel
> knew not; my people understood not.   Isa. 1:3 (SLT)

What would Isaiah say about the church today?

Now, Jesus walked to the top of the mountain to pray. What a glorious example of godliness and spiritually well-disciplined. Many of us would simply crash in bed (or wherever we could crash) and without a whimper of prayer or giving thanks. However, our Lord shows by example and a principle that few of us exhibit in leadership in the church. Jesus not only gave thanks to Father and prayed for those who genuinely believed, but our Lord also certainly prayed for His own temptations and was seeking directions and guidance for the coming days. The people were going to try and force Jesus to be King. But Jesus submits His will to the Father's and Holy Spirit's leading.

You may remember, Hebrews says concerning Jesus' ministries and now a high priest of God in the order of Melchizedek,

> So also Christ did not glorify Himself to become High Priest, but *it was* He who said to Him: "You are My Son, Today I have begotten You."d
> 6As *He* also says in another *place*: "You *are* a priest forever According to the order of Melchizedek".

> 7who, in the days of His flesh, when He had offered up prayers and supplications, with vehement cries and tears to Him who was able to save Him from death, and was heard because of His godly fear, 8though He was a Son, *yet* He learned obedience by the things which He suffered. 9And having been perfected, He became the author of eternal salvation to all who obey Him,   Heb. 5:5-9 (NKJ)

141

ᵈNote: some translate "begotten you" as "I became your Father." The literal and preferred translation is, 'You are my Son, today I have **begotten you**.' This is a quote from Psa. 2:7. Paul sees Psa. 2 as fulfillment of Scripture.[Acts 13:33ff]

Let us note the grueling ministry our Lord maintained. His schedule and daily ministry are astonishing. There are few in the ministry today who have such grueling and demanding ministry like our Lord. (Jesus did more in the ministry in one week than many do in a year or more.) Do not cop out and say, "Jesus had such grueling schedule be because He was God." Such answers are following the evil doctrine of Docetism, which minimized the humanity our Lord. Jesus work was long and hard labor, and exhausting as a human.

Sadly, it is rare to find any Pastor or Christian worker even devoting just a full day (eight hours for five days) including going door to door evangelizing throughout the community of the church of the saints. At best, there is nothing but a dribble, few hours out of the entire week. Then, they wonder, "Why don't I have more people?" Some, believe it or not, do absolutely nothing. There is no vision, planning, or unity of direction. In the community of church, some people do not even know the church exist.

The church does not bother to put up multiple signs with the **church's name**, times of services, or when some will be present, especially the Pastor. How do they expect people will come to the church? May they want to follow the electionist's pattern and do nothing! It is for sure they are not following Jesus' pattern of hard work or His mandate: 'Follow me, and I will make you **fishers of men**.' [Matt. 4:19 KJV] Maybe their desire is getting people in their church rather getting them into the Kingdom of God.

Conclusion

When anyone is challenged to follow our Lord's godly example, they cry out, "*But He is God.*" Little do they realize they are giving into the evil doctrine of "Docetism." That is, they are denying our Lord's full humanity. Our Lord, in the rigors of life, was very well disciplined. He maximized His every thought and action. He did more in three and a half years than most of us as ministers do in a total life time. And that my friend is no exaggeration.

I think many of us are at awe at Jesus' feeding such a large multitude, and they were all completely full or satisfied. (And indeed, we should be in awe of such an amazing miracle.)

> When Jesus went ashore, He saw a large crowd, and He felt compassion
> for them because they were like sheep without a shepherd; and He
> began to teach them many things.   Mark 6:34

I wonder, do you as a Pastor see people as money or filling the seats, or do you see people that need a shepherd which belong to the Lord? (The people most certainly do not belong to you or your church; though it should be His church not yours.) I am afraid many see people as only numbers or dollar signs ($). Similarly, is your eye more on the building where you worship (a building you hope to have), or are your eyes and mind on people desperately needing the Great Shepherd, the Savior?

We only have one life to "get it right." If you say, "My focus is on people." Well, friend does the evidence in your life and action of your ministry demonstrate you are seeking the lost for Christ in your surrounding community of the church where you serve? Or have you silently endorsed the *electionists* by default? (By default, I mean you are not going out 7/24, 'Go out into the highways and hedges, and compel *them* to come in, that my house may be filled.' Luke 14:23 KJV) Well, at the Bema Seat, it will be evident when the secrets of our hearts are revealed.Rom. 2:16

Footnotes:

1. "Sea of Tiberias:" was changed from Sea Galilee to Tiberias after Herod Antipas built the city of Tiberias in Galilee and Perea region around 18-20 AD. (The name "Sea of Tiberias" was only use for a short time.) For a little while later, Sea of Tiberias was changed back to Sea of Galilee. This might suggest that the Gospel of John might have been written earlier on than what many scholars thought when dating John's Gospel. (Although, it should be noted that Sea Galilee had other names such as: Lake Tiberias, Lake of Gennesaret, and Lake Kinneret.) See Google search.

2. "Manna:" from Google search.

The Fifth miraculous miracle and sign
Jesus Walks on the Sea of Galilee

[16]Now when evening came, His disciples went down to the sea, [17]and after getting into a boat, they *started to* cross the sea to Capernaum. It had already become dark, and Jesus had not yet come to them. [18]The sea *began* to be stirred up because a strong wind was blowing. [19]Then, when they had rowed about three or four miles, they saw Jesus walking on the sea and drawing near to the boat; and they were frightened. [20]But He said to them, "It is I; do not be afraid." [21]So they were willing to receive Him into the boat, and immediately the boat was at the land to which they were going.   John 6:16-21

CHAPTER 12

Jesus walks on the Water

And straightway he caused his disciples to *go*[a] into the ship [*boat*], and to *go* before *into* the other side *unto* Bethsaida, while he sent away the people. [46]Then *as soon* as he had sent them away, he departed into *the mountain* to pray. [47]And when *evening* was come, the ship [*boat*] was in the *middle* of the sea, and he alone on the land. [48]And he saw them troubled [*struggling*] in rowing, (for the *wind* was contrary *to* them) and about the fourth watch [*3 to 6 AM*] of the night, he [*Jesus*] came *to* them, walking *upon* the sea, and [*Jesus*] would *have* passed by them. [49]And when they saw him walking *upon* the sea, they supposed it had *been* a spirit,[b] and cried out. [50]For they all saw him, and were *frighten*: but *immediately* he talked with them, and said *to* them, Be ye of good comfort: it is I, be not *afraid*.   Mark 6:45-50 (GNV)

[a]No words have been changed in GNV Bible; only the spelling has been updated and words in brackets ([] []) are added for clarity.

[b]Many translations use *"ghost"* (GK *phantasma*), though the word means *"apparition* or an *appearance."* No Orthodox Jews would believe in "ghosts;" so, GNV using "spirit" (e.g., demon spirit) is better than "ghost."

Introduction

In the previous miraculous sign, our Lord revealed the awesome power to *recreate* and *duplicate* five barley-cakes and two fishes *instantaneously* and *extremely fast*. Perhaps faster than the eye can see. It seems evident the apostles as well as the crowd were permitted to participate in passing on the *creation* and *duplication of bread and fishes* during the meal. Otherwise, how else how could 20 to 30 thousand people be so quickly feed?

Our Lord shall override the Law of gravity and the natural Law of physics in this marvelous sign. The Lord Jesus is the one who set the Laws of the universe in place, and by virtue of His own authority, He is able to override all natural Laws in creation.

Jesus walked on a very turbulent sea as the violent wind and waves crashed against Him and the disciples' boat. Astonishingly, our Lord permits Peter to experience walking on the water at Jesus' command. So, these two great miracles occurred **at the command** and **will** of Jesus. Let no one foolishly say that Peter walked on the turbulent sea based on his intrinsic faith and will. Peter walked on the sea at Jesus' **command** and **will**.

We should not be surprised that many religious institutions, seminaries, and even some of most prestigious universities have openly denied the Christian Faith upon which they had been founded. Many such groups though they were established by Christians, now openly deny and even hostilely seek to even tear down the Faith they once embraced. So, we should not be surprised at such "*institutions*" that now deny such glorious miracles. Such great learning institutions have given way to rationalism and even to *spontaneous evolution*. The universe did what? The universe created itself? Yes, according such endless theories, the intellectuals eagerly espoused today: the universe harnessed the power to create the big bang. Oh, "Where did such power come from?" The intellectual says, "Uh, I don't know; it was just there?" Friend, this is what the so-called brilliant minds are telling our children.

Spontaneous evolution is one of the wildest evolutionist theories ever to be put forth in years gone by and even today. Spontaneous evolution alleges that humankind is capable change the destiny of humans by shear will and manipulation. Of course, most intellectuals still think and even endorse some form of Charles Darwin's theory [1] of evolution [2]. (Most intellectuals do not endorse *spontaneous evolution* or Erasmus Darwin, but they certain to keep quiet.)

With the madness of these endless theories, some have tacked-on "a *god*" from their depraved and darkened mind. Friend, if you believe life evolved over endless eons, then, you have more faith than me. You have better odds of *spitting off the top the Empire State Building in a furious wind and the spit falling into a cup below* rather than life evolving by itself. All life and all that exist in the universe is extremely too complicated to have evolved or generated itself even if you push evolution back by fifty billion years. Such theories are insanely misled and pushed by madness near infinity. Where did the incredible

146

power and force come from to unleash such an enormous explosion? Where did the build-blocks derive from to generate life?

So, where did all the power come from to unleash such awesome infinite force? Such speculations are nothing more than a fairy tale illusion, a fantasy of darken minds. Allow me to throw in a little tidbit of humor that great minds theorize life emerged by chance. Most of those who are on *"band wagon"* of some form of evolution alleges that when the universe began, (as noted above) started out with an enormous *"LOUD BANG!"*

The intellectuals call it *"THE BIG BANG THEORY."* Friend, you cannot have **"bang"** unless some One hears it. So then, if there was a bang, who heard the **BIG BANG**? Mankind is backed-in (without him realizing it), and he has acknowledged the only logical conclusion. All life and all that is in the universe was created by the Lord is the only logical explanation. All life and all things in the universe exist because all things were wonderfully and marvelously created by Christ the Lord. Hallelujah!

A. There was a violent storm on the sea

The disciples were crossing the Sea of Galilee probably in a relatively small boat from Bethsaida to Capernaum, and the distance was approximately six miles (9.7 km). However, the crossing occurred during the night. The Sea Galilee was not very deep in some places (that is compared to some lakes). During the crossing, a sudden and furious wind came whipping down from Mt. Hermon. These winds instantly caused enormous and violent waves. These huge waves could capsize many boats and especially the disciples' small boat. Then, the fishmen could lose their lives in a moment. Still, traveling in any size boat during a wind storm on the Sea Galilee could be very treacherous, frightening, and deadly even today.

The apostles do not ask, "Lord how will You get from Bethesda to Capernaum?" Walk around would be a long walk. Walking at night on the road would be treacherous and hazardous at night time due to falling and being seriously injured. There was also the real threat of the presence of wild animals or unexpected robbers as well walking on a road alone and at night. Anyway, the disciples did not ask any questions. They just simply did what they were directed to do by our Lord.

Besides, Jesus had not yet dismissed the great multitude. In addition, our Lord would be spending some time on the mountain praying. During the three and half years of ministry, Jesus' frequent praying is likely a typical grueling day for our Lord. (His day began with prayer as well as throughout the day, and Jesus ended His day with fervent prayer.) He ministry was so exhausting and demanding each day. I doubt many really realize the pressures of life continued crushing and pressing down upon Him. Keep in mind, our Lord was in a body humiliation like ours. He pushed His body no doubt to the full limit. Keep in mind the Hebrews writer says of Jesus' life and ministry,

> [7]During the days of Jesus' life on earth, he offered up prayers and petitions with fervent cries and tears to the one who could save him from death, and he was heard because of his reverent submission. [8]Son though he was, he learned obedience from what he suffered.
>
> Heb. 5:7, 8 (NIV)

The Bible says,

> [45]Immediately Jesus made His disciples get into the boat and go ahead of *Him* to the other side to [*from*] Bethsaida [*to Capernaum*], while He Himself was sending the crowd away. [46]After bidding them [*multitude*] farewell, He left for the mountain to pray. [47]When it was evening, the boat was in the middle of the sea, and He was alone on the land. [48]Seeing them straining at the oars, for the wind was against them, at about the fourth watch of the night-
>
> Mark 6:45-48

The Lord sees the huge waves from where He is praying, and the disciples were no doubt very frightful due the danger of capsizing their small boat. Note again,

> When it was evening, **the boat was in the middle of the sea**, and **He was alone on the land.** [48][*Jesus*] **seeing them straining** [*being battered as they rowed, HSB*] **at the oars, for the wind was against them**, at about the fourth watch of the night [*3 to 6 AM*].
>
> Mark 6:47, 48

Yes, many of these men were expert fishmen on the Sea of Galilee. But listen, these disciples were very much aware of violent waves crashing into their small boat, and lives could be lost in a moment's time. This was indeed a *hair-raising* experience for the apostles.

The disciples knew they were indeed in a frightening situation and lives could be lost. Matthew adds,

> Meanwhile the **boat, already far from land**, [*their small boat*] **was taking a beating from the waves** because **the wind was against it.**
>
> Matt. 14:24 (NET)

As I have said, this must have been one *hair-raising* experience. The disciples were in very grave danger of losing their lives, and they knew it. The disciples must have felt helpless to do anything.

What is easy to overlooked is the source of their danger. The danger could have been caused by Satan or one of the demons. Think for a moment! In the same way, the saints battle with our arch-enemy, the devil.[Eph. 6:10-18; 1 Peter 5:8] Sadly, many of us are unaware of the origin of storms in our life In these times in our life, you want to be sure *"you are all prayed up."*

We know from Job that Satan was permitted to cause total destruction of everything in Job's life. Friend, if you think Satan cannot put a storm in your life, well, you are sadly mistaken. Read carefully and think again. If your life is skimpy or anemic of fervent prayer, you may be less than victorious through the storm.

> Now the day came when Job's sons and daughters were eating and drinking wine in their oldest brother's house, [14]and a messenger came to Job, saying, "The oxen were plowing and the donkeys were grazing beside them, [15]and the Sabeans swooped down and carried them all away, and they killed the servants with the sword! And I— only I alone— escaped to tell you!" [16]While this one was still speaking, another messenger arrived and said, "The fire of God has fallen from heaven and has burned up the sheep and the servants— it has consumed them! And I— only I alone— escaped to tell you!" [17]While this one was still speaking another messenger arrived and said, "The Chaldeans formed three bands and made a raid on the camels and carried them all away, and they killed the servants with the sword! And I— only I alone— escaped to tell you!" [18]While this one was still speaking another messenger arrived and said, "Your sons and your daughters were eating and drinking wine in their oldest brother's house, [19] and suddenly a great wind swept across the wilderness and struck the four corners of the house, and it fell on the young people, and they died! And I— only I alone— escaped to tell you!"   Job 1:13-19 (NET)

So, we do not know that Satan may have been allow to cause such furious gale-force winds upon the disciplines in their small boat. There is little anyone can do against furious winds and especial if it is demonically induced.

Also, what is sometimes easily overlooked is Jesus and the apostles faced similar terrifying experiences on the Sea of Galilee.

> Leaving the crowd, they took Him along with them in the boat, just as He was; and other boats were with Him. [37]And **there arose a fierce gale of wind,** and the **waves were breaking over the boat** so much that **the boat was already filling up** [with water]. [38]Jesus **Himself was** in the stern, **asleep** on the cushion; and they woke Him and said to Him, "Teacher

[*Rabbi*], do You not care that we are perishing?" [39]And **He** got up and **rebuked the wind** and said to the sea, **"Hush, be still."** And the **wind died down** and it became **perfectly calm**. [40]And He said to them, "Why are you afraid? Do you still have no faith?" [41] They became very much afraid and said to one another, **"Who then is this**, that **even the wind** and the **sea obey Him**?"   Mark 4:36-41

The charlatans, the quacks, and the fake practitioners of *the Name and Claim* or *Prosperity Gospel* have no clue who Christ the Lord really is. *The hecklers* and *fault-finders* of Jesus and the Gospel have no awareness of the actual identity of Christ the Lord. However, when they stand before Him, and stand they shall; then, they will understand what it means, "the fear of the Lord."

B. Jesus comes walking on the water

As we have noted, each Gospel writer brings his own unique contribution and insight. Only Matthew gives us the extended aspect of Peter's experience in the furious gale on the Sea of Galilee. (This we shall examine in the next chapter.) For now, let us look into the unique account as given by Mark which is slightly expanded and with a little more detail.

Immediately Jesus made His disciples get into the boat and go ahead of *Him* to the other side to Bethsaida, while He Himself was sending the crowd away. [46]After bidding them farewell [*to the multitude*], He left for the mountain to pray. [47]When it was evening, the boat was in the middle of the sea, and He was alone on the land. [48]Seeing them straining at the oars, for the wind was against them, at about the fourth watch [between 3 to 6 PM] of the night He came to them, walking on the sea; and He intended to pass by them. [49] But when they saw Him walking on the sea, they supposed that it was a ghost[c] [GK *phantasma, apparition, phantom, spirit*], and cried out; [50]for they all saw Him and were terrified. But immediately He spoke with them and said to them, "Take courage; it is I, do not be afraid." [51]Then He got into the boat with them, and the wind stopped; and they were utterly astonished, [52]for they had not gained any insight from the *incident of* the loaves, but their heart was hardened.[d]   Mark 6:45-52

[c]"Seeing a ghost:" likely the disciples may have thought it was "a spirit;" that is, supposing it was a demon. Jews didn't believe in ghosts, but the disciples have encountered demons before.

d"—their heart was hardened:" meaning disbelief of the truth even when before their very eyes.Heb. 3:7ff; 4:7

The Lord knew that the disciples were safe and that they would arrive at the shore without harm. The texts in the Holman Standard Bible reads,

> He saw them being battered as they rowed, because the wind was against them. Around three in the morning He came toward them walking on the sea and wanted to pass by them.   Mark 6:48 (HSB)

Jesus probably told them that He would meet them on the other side Sea of Galilee. Jesus realized that the disciples had been overcome with fear in their present situation. (Panic was starting overtaken the disciples.) Thus, the apostles had become *overly anxious* and *gripped with fear*.

Our Lord has assured us that *He would never leave us nor forsake us*,[Heb. 13:5] but as humans, we tend to be fickle, fearful, and deficient in the assurance of our faith. As reassuring of the Great Shepherd of the sheep, our Lord is full of compassion and empathy in tending and keep close watch over His sheep. Jesus is watching over us, but so are His angels watching over us.Heb. 1:14 Still, many of us give into unwarranted fears.

Our Lord Jesus hearing the disciples *scream out* in terror when the disciples first seen sight of Him on the sea (though the apostles did not realize it was Jesus). Our Lord realized their panic and fears had apparently consumed the disciples. Well, wouldn't you know, our own fears often cause many us to worry about things that will never occur. The problem or worry just seems to gradually disappear and nothing happens. We are like a *ping pong ball*, we bounce our unwarranted fears and worry on others around us.

Listen, do not misunderstand me. Fear is indeed a paralyzing emotion. There is nothing funny about overloaded or burdened down with fear or worry. Too much worrying can take a serious toil on our health. Some have such hazardous jobs. Some people that have hazardous jobs do not last long on the job due to intense stress and anxiety. For example, airport control tower workers at O'Hare Airport in Chicago have from 60 to 120 seconds for planes landing or taking off. (A fraction of that time may occur during very busy hours.) This does not take into account all the other small airports and innumerable planes flying in the area. In addition, Midway Airport in Chicago is no small airport. Midway Airport is one of the busiest airports in the United States as well. The control tower workers' stress, anxiety, and worry are burnt-out after five years, and they must resign.

Therefore, the Great Shepherd of sheep decides to approach the small boat and tend to the frightened disciples.

> [48]And he saw them trying to urge forward [*in their boat*], for the wind was contrary to them: and about the fourth watch of the night he comes to them walking upon the sea, and he would pass by them. [49]And having seen him walking upon the sea, they thought it was an apparition, and cried out:
> Mark 6:58, 49 (SLT)

As I mentioned earlier, this was a typical day in the ministry of our Lord, and His ministry was filled to the max and even overflowing. His ministry was indeed unbelievingly extremely exhausting and rigorously demanding. Unfortunately, while many recognize rightfully His **eternal Deity** in the incarnation, many Christians fail to grasp that our Lord was also **fully human** and feeling all the pain and exhaustion of His body. Furthermore, our Lord continues forever as God but also as a man (fully human). Still, He is one person, God and man.

In one account, the Pharisees said of Jesus,

> Then the Jews said to Him, "You are not yet fifty years old, and have You seen Abraham?"
> John 8:57 (NKJ)

Does the above verse allude to how exhausted Jesus might have been and aged by rigorous of the demands of a true Pastor (Shepherd)? Did our Lord have the appearance as though He was approaching fifty due to His rigorous and demanding schedule? Though He was physically about thirty-three? If you have ever noticed anyone working heavy and extremely hard labor, such people tend to live a short life. I mean some people putting in eighteen hour a day have short lifespans.

Dr. Adrian Rogers initially took over a church of 9,000. When he retired, they had near 25,000. Although he retired in his 70s, he reportedly died three months later. Dr. Rogers put so much of himself in the labor of the ministry that he was probably just exhausted and worn out.

It is difficult to find any Pastors putting in just eight full hours for the Lord in genuine rigorous labor in the ministry nowadays today. Still, praise the Lord, there are some men of God that "burn the candle beyond mid-night," [3] and their life is cut short.

So, I think many expositors and Christian teachers minimize or tend to overlook the intense rigors of our Lord's ministry and particularly as it relates to His humanity. They tend to give too much emphasis on His Deity but dismiss the weariness of His humanity. This is why I think some Christian (without realizing it) give way to semi-Docetism (wrongly only emphasizing His Deity) and minimize that our Lord was also human. (He took on the full nature man, and yet, He was full God in one person, Jesus.) Do you recall Hebrews exhortation concerning our Lord's earthly ministry?

> Who, in the days of His flesh, when He had offered up prayers and supplications, with **vehement cries** and **tears** to Him who was able to save Him from death, and was heard because of His godly fear, [8]though He was a Son, *yet* He **learned obedience by the things which He suffered**. [9]And having been perfected, He became the author of eternal salvation to all who obey Him, [10]called by God as High Priest "according to the order of Melchizedek,"   Heb. 5:7-10 (NKJ)

It is this same blessed Lord who intended to meet the disciples on the other side the Sea Galilee. Yet, Jesus decided to join the fearful disciples in the small boat.

> [47]And evening having come, the ship [*boat*] was in the midst of the sea, and he [*was*] alone upon land. [48]And he saw them trying to urge forward [*straining with oars*], for the wind was contrary to them: and about the fourth watch of the night he comes to them walking upon the sea, and he would pass by them. [49]And [*the disciples*] having seen him walking upon the sea, they thought it was an apparition, and cried out: [50]For all saw him, and were troubled [*terrified*]. And quickly he spake [*spoke*] with them, and says to them, Take courage: I am; be not afraid. [51]And he went up to them to the ship [*boat*]; and the wind ceased, and they were greatly affected in mind above measure and wondered [*utterly astonished* NAS].   Mark 6:47-51 (SLT)

We should not be too harsh with the apostles under their circumstances. As we already noted, the Sea Galilee can become very treacherous and extremely dangerous. This was a night, and I doubt any of apostles had much sleep in the small boat. They were very tense, edgy, and certainly exhausted from the day before. (Keep in mind this was a typical day in our Lord's ministry.)

Like sheep that can become edgy and very tense when wolves and bear come near them, the apostles became intensely anxious and fearful in a violent storm on the sea. Therefore, the Great Shepherd decided to join the apostles in their small boat.

Friend, do you see the tenderness with which our Lord calms the disciples (His sheep) with the ensuring words,

> For they all saw him and were terrified. But immediately he spoke to them: "Have courage! It is I. Do not be afraid."   Mark 6:50 (NET)

Jesus is so very faithful in His tender care watching over us. Yes, even when we have no cause to worry. The arm of the flesh gives way to unwarranted fear and worry. That my friend is true of all us. We sometimes worry when there is no cause to worry. Jesus is continually giving His unwavering assurances. (Look now at some of the assurance in God's Word.Deut. 31:6; Josh. 1:8f; 2 Chro. 32:7; Isa. 54:4; Ezek. 2:26; Jer. 30:10; 42:11; 46:27)

The Lord Jesus said,

> "Are not five sparrows sold for two cents? *Yet* not one of them is forgotten before God. Indeed, the very hairs of your head are all numbered. Do not fear; **you are more valuable** than many sparrows."   Luke 12:6, 7

> "Let not your heart be troubled; you believe in God, believe also in Me. ²In My Father's house are many mansions; if *it were* not *so*, I would have told you. I go to prepare a place for you. ³And if I go and prepare a place for you, **I will come again and receive you to Myself**; that where I am, *there* you may be also. ⁴And where I go you know, and the way you know." ⁵Thomas said to Him, "Lord, we do not know where You are going, and how can we know the way?" ⁶Jesus said to him, "I am the way, the truth, and the life. No one comes to the Father except through Me."   John 14:1-6 (NKJ)

The psalmist said,

> ¹³As a father has mercy on sons, YHWH has mercy on those fearing Him. ¹⁴For He has known our frame, Remembering that we [are] dust. ¹⁵Mortal man! His days [are] as grass, He flourishes as a flower of the field; ¹⁶For a wind has passed over it, and it is not, And its place does not discern it anymore. ¹⁷And the kindness of YHWH [is] from age even to age on those fearing Him, And His righteousness to sons' sons, ¹⁸To those keeping His covenant, And to those remembering His precepts to do them.   Psa. 103:13-18 (LSB)

Yes, the apostles knew all the above even as we also know or ought to know those things in Scripture. There are many, many other such promises in Scripture. Yes, like disciples, we too are but dust and we worry. We worry because like apostles, we do not get the insight of the feeding 20 to 30 thousand people. This is why Jesus also said,

> Because they had not understood [the miracle of] the loaves [how it revealed the power and *Deity* of Jesus]; but [in fact] **their heart was hardened** [being oblivious and indifferent to His amazing works].

> Mark 6:52 (AMP)

My friend, don't you see that we too are so fickle in our faith? We say with all our gusto, "I believe," but we come up short of demonstrating our faith with concrete and firm actions. We just come up short without continuing to follow through in completion. This is why Jude says,

> But let us keep ourselves in the love of God as we **look for the mercy of our Lord Yeshua** The Messiah unto our eternal life.
>
> Jude 1:21 (ABPE)

Conclusion

Sometimes we are so ambivalent in our walk of faith. We at times are bubbling over with joy and excitement, and there are other times we tend to be despondent and seemingly as though we are lifeless. Friend, Jesus is the Great and Wonderful Shepherd. He does not change, [Heb. 13:8]. He will never leave us or forsake. He has promised,

> "Go therefore and make disciples of all the nations, baptizing them in the name of the Father and the Son and the Holy Spirit, teaching them to observe all that I commanded you; and **LO, I AM WITH YOU ALWAYS**, even to the end of the age."　　　　Matt. 28:19, 20

Please tell me, why are we not being obedient and going into the world (especially to the community surrounding the church) making disciples just as our risen Lord of Glory instructed us to do? Is our love for the world robbing us of our love and zeal for the Lord? Have we become too fearful? Maybe some never had any zeal in the first place for the Lord? Maybe some only had a profession of faith; they never really had a possession of saving faith?

As I have said so many times, we have only one life to live for Jesus. Friend, let us make the days we have left count for the glory and praise our Lord.

> And let the peace of God rule in your hearts, to which also you were called in one body; and be thankful. [16]Let the word of Christ dwell in you richly in all wisdom, teaching and admonishing one another in psalms and hymns and spiritual songs, singing with grace in your hearts to the Lord. [17]And whatever you do in word or deed, *do* all in the name of the Lord Jesus, giving thanks to God the Father through Him.
>
> And whatever you do, do it heartily, as to the Lord and not to men.
>
> Col. 3:15-17, 23 (NKJ)

Let the last words of Revelation be our focus,

He who testifies to these things says, "Yes, I am coming quickly." Amen. Come, Lord Jesus. The grace of the Lord Jesus be with all. Amen.

Rev. 22:20, 21

Footnotes:

1. Charles Darwin's grandfather: "Charles Darwin's grandfather, Erasmus Darwin, was an evolutionist who proposed theories of life's modification and adaptation to the environment in his writings. While Charles publicly downplayed the influence, his own work shows evidence of his grandfather's impact and shared interest in concepts like sexual selection-"

   "The Temple of Nature": In his posthumously published poem *The Temple of Nature* (1803), Erasmus Darwin described the process of organic life arising and changing over vast periods."

   "Influence on Charles": While Charles Darwin developed the mechanism of natural selection, evidence suggests he studied his grandfather's work, with annotations found in his copy of *The Temple of Nature* showing shared interest in topics like competition for reproduction." (From Google search.)

2. Darwin's theory of Evolution": Charles Darwin's theory of evolution, also known as evolution by natural selection,' proposes that species change over time through a process where organisms with advantageous traits, naturally occurring variations within a population, are more likely to survive and reproduce, passing those traits on to their offspring, resulting in gradual changes within a species over generations and the emergence of new species from a common ancestor-" Google search

3. "*Burn the candle at night*," I mean to work very long hours, and sometimes, working longer than doing double shifts. In the eighteen hundreds, such labor was common throughout the world. Men, women, and even children worked horrific and dangerous long hours. A person's life span was short and very painful.

CHAPTER 13

At Jesus' authority,
Peter walks on the sea

(This miracle is not in John)

28And Peter answering Him said, "Lord, if it is You, command me to come to You on the waters"; 29and He said, "Come"; and having gone down from the boat, Peter walked on the waters to come to Jesus, 30but seeing the vehement wind [*on the seas*], he was afraid, and having begun to sink, he cried out, saying, "Lord, save me!" 31And immediately Jesus, having stretched forth the hand, laid hold of him and says to him, "Little faith! For why did you waver?" 32And they having gone into the boat, the wind stilled, 33and those in the boat having come, worshiped Him, saying, "You are truly God's Son."   Matt. 14:28-33 (LSV)

Introduction

Peter's walking on the Sea of Galilee was certainly an amazing miracle, but Peter did not perform the amazing miracle by his own intrinsic faith, power, or authority. Our blessed Lord is the one who created the miracle to happen in the first place. Granted, Peter exercised tremendous faith in stepping out and down from the boat on to the turbulent sea. Peter demonstrated tremendous faith in the power of Christ the Lord. So, Peter's tremendous faith was relying on the power of the Lord Jesus, but the miracle was not in Peter's intrinsic faith. I think there are few who would actually exercise such obedience as Peter today. Peter was a man that often *put his foot in his mouth*[1] (*so to speak*) even at Jesus' command. Yet, Peter's heart was indeed at the right place in the presence of our blessed Lord Jesus.

There are many men like Peter who lived a rough life as a fisherman. Fishermen worked long hours and did very hard labor. To be a fisherman like Peter, you needed to be physically and mentally strong, and with outstanding stamina. In simple language, you needed to be in excellent condition to do the kind of work he and his fishing partners were doing day after day for life. Some fishermen made moderately good livings, but the hard work probably paid heavy toll on their bodies. Their hands and feet took a tough beating, and the hot sun beating down them took its toll on them. Still, these men showed wisdom in working close together. In this way, the men could keep close watch on one another for safety and peace of mind as well as share in their reward of fishing together and building comradery.

I doubt many realize that these fishermen were also "*scrappers*." By being *scrappers*, these men were fighters, and they could stand their ground and stand "toe to toe" against most any adversary. Let me tell you, they would not be easily intimidated or threatened. If anyone threatened them, those who made such threats might seriously regret it in the long run. These were indeed mighty men of God!

For example, you might recall when the Jewish authority came to arrest Jesus, Peter was first to draw his sword, and he was ready to take on Roman soldiers. (However, I dare say this was true of many men following Jesus.)

> [3]Judas, therefore, having taken the band and officers out of the chief priests and Pharisees, comes there with torches and lamps, and weapons; [4]Jesus, therefore, knowing all things that are coming on Him, having gone forth, said to them, "Whom do you seek?" [5]They answered Him, "Jesus the Nazarene"; Jesus says to them, "**I AM,**"[a] and Judas who delivered Him up was standing with them. [6]When, therefore, He said to them, "**I AM,**" they went away backward, and fell to the ground. [7] Again, therefore, He questioned them, "Whom do you seek?" And they said, "Jesus the Nazarene"; [8] Jesus answered, "I said to you that **I AM,**[a] if, then, you seek Me, permit these to go away"; [9]that the word might be fulfilled that He said, "Those whom You have given to Me, I did not lose even one of them." [10]Simon Peter, therefore, having a sword, drew it, and struck the chief priest's servant, and cut off his right ear—and the name of the servant was Malchus—[11]Jesus, therefore, said to Peter, "Put the sword into the sheath; the cup that the Father has given to Me, may [shall] I not drink it?"
> John 18:3-11 (LSV)

ᵃ The "*He*" [vv 5, 6, 8] is not in the GK though some think it is implied. "**I AM** is literally the name for the Lord our God, **YHWH**.Exodus 3:13-15

When Peter swung his sword [v10], he was not going for the ear; he was going to cut off his head.

It ought to be noted that from the outset that our Lord was in complete charge and excising total control over the situation. (Though there were no doubt a host of angels surrounding our Lord and His faithful eleven apostles.) Normally, the Roman soldiers would have arrested all of them. Yet, at Jesus' direction, the soldiers did not arrest anyone but Jesus. Amazingly and so awesome indeed, the Lord Jesus was in complete control of the arrest and dismissed the apostles without any incidents. Even though Peter cut off Malchus' ear. Incredibly, Jesus put the ear back on the slave and healed the ear: "And He touched his ear and healed him."Luke 22:51

Jesus' apostles were indeed valiant and fearless men of faith. How desperate the church is in need of valiant and fearless men of faith totally committed to Christ the Lord and His mandates with zeal, ardent obedience, and action. Hallelujah! However, many men today talk bold and tough in the church, but in reality, it is all nothing but a "bag of wind." They cannot backup their words with *action* and *fearless obedience of faith*. Many men may stand, but they stand like women in labor!

A. Only Peter stepped out of the boat

I guess the fault-finders are good at finding fault with Peter. Well, let me tell you, the day of reckoning is coming for the fault-finders. Believe me, the fault-finders will be terrified and infinitely fearful and overcome with dread that has no end. So, before you point your finger at Peter, I remind *you that the rest of your fingers are pointing back you*. Hello! Listen, if you enjoy finding fault, keep in mind that Peter was the first to recognize the Lord Jesus. Matt. 16:16ff Also, I am reminded that when Peter stepped out of the boat on the turbulence sea against violent storms and high waves, there were eleven others who remained in the boat. In addition, the boat was small, yet the Bible says,

> Then Peter **got down out of the boat**, walked on the water and came toward Jesus. Matt. 14:29 (NIV)

Some of the fishermen's boats sat a little higher and slightly bigger in the water than some others. Peter may have had to step up, then step over the topside of the boat, and then he had to then step down into the sea. I don't know about you, but just going through the motions of getting out of the boat was indeed an awesome exercise of faith in Christ in the treacherous wind and ferocious waves at night. I doubt many of us would be willing to demonstrate such awesome faith towards Christ. If you say you would boldly step out of the boat, then I call you a liar! As I have said, "the church is in desperate need of such godly men." (Pay attention: the church does not fight a great spiritual war with women and children. The church needs **men, godly men**!) The fact Pastors are pursuing to get *women* and *children* to get in the church. Instead, we must seek out men for Christ. That is, we ought to be men. I mean seeking out men who are willing to put their life on the line for Jesus, men of war. Let me tell you my friend, the apostle Peter demonstrated extraordinarily courageous faith in action numerous times.

Don't be stupid and think to yourself that you would step out by faith at night in a stormy sea. Until you are in the exact scenario as Peter's, you do not know what you would do: *run, freeze,* or *fight*. If the truth be known about ourselves, we would likely freeze and remain huddled in the boat.

As you continue to read about Peter after Jesus' arrest, we know he closely followed behind our Lord. (Peter was willing to die for Christ.) Yes, Peter initially denied knowing Christ at beginning of Jesus' arrest, but Peter is the only man that stayed close to our Lord and was willing to risk his own life. I think we have a lot "big mouth" people, who are all *talk but have no show*. Many *big mouth* men are often all talkers. They demonstrate **little or no action in their faith**. As I have said, *it is difficult to find any Pastor putting in eight solid hours of laboring* for Christ and His Kingdom five or even six days in a week. I mean the Pastor does not sit behind a desk most of the day. Listen, I mean Pastors are going out *knocking on doors compelling people to come Jesus as Lord and Savior* 7/24. They are too fearful. (Sadly, many Pastors and church leaders do not even know how to give the Gospel invitation and draw in the net.) Why? As I have said, many ministries and Christian workers are too fearful rather than be full of faith with action.

As we noted above, Peter had a sword with him. Peter was willing to fight for the Lord against the odds. I think the same was true of the other ten apostles, excluding Judas Iscariot. As I have said, Peter proved himself by cutting off the servant ear. He was willing go against the Roman cohort of soldiers. Peter was willing to die for the Lord Jesus. Therefore, careful what to say about Peter or the other ten apostles.

Yes, Peter likely knew well how to swim. However, this is during a violent wind storm with monsterous waves and during the night. Galilee is known to have *sudden* and very *violent gales* without warning coming down from Mt. Hermon, even today. The Sea Galilee was not excessively deep as compare other large bodies of water. Still, the Sea Galilee is said to be at least 140 deep in some places. The boat was halfway or more across the sea. So, Sea Galilee was still dangerous and deep. This was also at night, and I doubt that anyone could see very clearly at that time of night. (They had no lighting, such as flood lights we have today.) Besides, tension must have been very great in the boat among the disciples. Therefore, let us be careful what you say about Peter. He was an extraordinary man of faith and obedience. He was more than willing to put his faith into full action at any moment and for any cause for our Lord. This alone put Peter extremely higher in his walk of faith than many of us today. Therefore, the Word of God says concerning Peter,

> [28]And Peter answering Him said, "Lord, if it is You, command me to come to You on the waters"; [29]and He said, "Come"; and having gone down from the boat, Peter walked on the waters to come to Jesus, [30]but seeing the vehement wind [*on the seas*], he was afraid, and having begun to sink, he cried out, saying, "Lord, save me!"   Matt. 14:28-30 (LSV)

Let us keep in mind, Peter did not know for sure it was the Lord Jesus. This why the Scripture says,

> And Peter answering Him said, "**Lord, if it is You**, command me to come to You on the waters."   Matt. 14:28 (LSV)

Yes, Peter *put his foot in his mouth* so to speak. However, Peter was also willing back up his words with action, this more than I can say of many us as Pastors today. Well, as I have said, there are people with a lot talk, but there are few men that can back up what they say. Nevertheless, Peter was a man who was willing and could back up his words with fighting action. I dare say that this was definitely true of most of the apostles and thousands of other men that believed in Christ and were men of faith in action. But the churches are bankrupt in many places because of the lack of *"faith in action:"* many men are bankrupt with Scripture and too lazy!

I know a man who traveled from Luzon Island to the southern part Mindanao Island where very hostile and very militant Muslims lived. (These are Muslims that kill Christians, and they still do.) Those Pastors in Luzon said behind his back, "He is crazy; he is going to get killed." Well, the man that went to southern Mindanao saw many people make professions of faith in Christ, even the wife of a Muslim religious leader. (There were many people turning from Islam to Christ.) Hallelujah!

Let us note the text again,

[28]And Peter answering Him said, "Lord, if it is You, command me to come to You on the waters"; [29]and He said, "Come"; and having gone down from the boat, Peter walked on the waters to come to Jesus, [30]but seeing the vehement wind [on the seas], he was afraid, and having begun to sink, he cried out, saying, "Lord, save me!"   Matt. 14:28-30 (LSV)

I do not know what actually and fully happened to Peter once on the sea. However, I surmise that Peter got *distracted*. He *took his eyes off Jesus*. Friend, what a spiritually application for the saints today. Listen to me, if you want victory in your life, then take your eyes off of the people or the situation. Stop finding fault or worry, and *keep your eyes on Jesus*. Friend, *don't you know Jesus has His eyes on you*? As the Hebrews writer says,

Therefore, since we are surrounded by such a great cloud of witnesses [a reference to Heb. 11], let us throw off everything that hinders and the sin that so easily entangles [us]. And let us run with perseverance the race marked out for us, **FIXING OUR EYES ON JESUS**, the pioneer [GK archegos, author NAS] and perfecter [GK teleiotes, completer, completionist] of faith. For the joy set before him he endured the cross, scorning its shame, and sat down at the right hand of the throne of God. Consider him who endured such opposition from sinners, so that you will not grow weary and lose heart.

Heb. 12:1-3 (NIV)

Regrettably, the churches have lost their focus. Yes, many churches have abandoned the prime directive from the risen Lord. They are no longer reproducing sheep [especially men Matt. 4:19] as we are instructed. In some places, the Gospel is only being given out by women and children. Men are omitted because either they are too fearful or just disobedient to Jesus' command. Then, there is nothing but *trickling down evangelism*. (There is no systematic and thorough door to door evangelism.) Evangelism is almost abandoned in many churches. Friend, I am not joking. It's true. The churches doing evangelism is nothing more than dripping faucet. Even invitation to the Gospel is "is far and few between." I ask you, "How sad it that?"

Even among the saints, there are few sheep reproducing sheep. Instead, many goats and wolves have entered among the fold of the sheep wearing sheepskins and scattering the sheep. As Jude says,

For certain individuals whose condemnation was written about long ago have secretly slipped in among you. They are ungodly people, who pervert the grace of our God into a license for immorality and deny Jesus Christ our only Sovereign and Lord.   Jude 1:4 (NIV)

There are fewer faithful shepherds reproducing the sheep. (The Pastor ought to lead from the front by going "door to door," and be godly men following the example.) Christians are not being trained in evangelism. There is little example among the leadership. People are out to *grab all the gusto they can*. As I have said, the shepherds are *no longer going out into the highways and byways compelling people to come to the Savior*. Some shepherds are following the delusion of the *electionists*. The shepherds no longer look for the lost sheep who have wondered off the Gospel path. For shame!

The shepherds are busy filling the pockets with ungodly gain and focusing on retirement. (Pastors are worthy of their pay, amen, but the Pastors are also expected to put in an honest week of fervent labor for the Master and His glory.) Many like playing church: "I'm the Pastor." The shepherds are fearful and immoral and very wicked. Their god is the belly.Rom.16:18; Phi. 3:19; Jude 1 12,13 Others are too *"lazy"* or too busy *"hobnobbing"* [2] with other Pastors or going to other churches while people are going to Hell.

The problem is too many ministers sit behind their *office desk* or just sit at home. Others sit in *front of the TV, internet,* or even the *radio* or *cell phone*. Still others are busy *jibber jabbering* with others or in fruitless meetings. It certain that they are spending less time **on their knees** or **going door to door** compelling people to come to the Savior.

There are those who say, "The Gospel is for everyone," but in truth, their actions prove they are following *electionists* who do not go out seeking the lost. In addition, the truth of the matter is that many spend no time in God's Word for their own spiritual enrichment. They have little or no spiritual devotions. There is no personal study or devotion. They no longer have ears to hear the Lord. Even when His Spirit speaks to our heart, let us not harden our hearts, Heb.3:8; 4:7. Hearts have been hardened or callused by sin of disobedience. There is no repentance anymore. What, no one sins any longer? Many voices are empty or silent in the halls of Heaven. They are full of fear and very short on faith. Obedience is a lost word nowadays.

Therefore, from my perspective, Peter was indeed a very mighty man of God. Peter showed a very deep commitment. Let me tell you, if you have been tempted to belittle Peter's faith in action, then stand in front of the mirror and look at yourself and honestly tell the truth. Then you will hang down your head in shame. Praise God for Peter and his unwavering faith in Christ the Lord.

B. Peter loses his focus

Now, let's look at Peter as he loses his focus on Christ the Lord. For surely, this is the case of many of us today.

And Peter answered him, "Lord, if it is you, command me to come to you on the water." ²⁹He said, "Come." So Peter got out of the boat and walked on the water and came to Jesus. ³⁰But when he saw the wind [*blowing and causing high waves*], he was afraid, and beginning to sink he cried out, "Lord, save me." ³¹Jesus immediately reached out his hand and took hold of him, saying to him, "O you of little faith, why did you doubt?" ³²And when they got into the boat, the wind ceased. ³³ And those in the boat worshiped him, saying, "Truly you are the Son of God."

Matt. 14:28-33 (ESV)

We must remind ourselves as I have said that there were eleven others still huddled together in the boat. Peter was the only one that spoke up and asked, 'Lord, is that You?' Then, he said, amazingly, 'Lord, if it is you, command me to come to you on the water.' He said, 'Come.'ᴹᵃᵗᵗ· ¹⁴ː²⁸, ²⁹ ᴱˢⱽ

Peter climbs down from the boat on to the turbulent sea and at night. Then, Peter is actually walking on the sea that is very tempestuous water plus he walks in furious winds from Mt. Hermon. Keep in mind that this is night time; so, visibility was very limited. (It is hard to stand in the turbulent water, but with the furious winds, it was doubly difficult.) Peter wisely asked, 'Lord, if it is you, command me to come to you on the water.'

Friend, what the text tells us that Peter exercised extraordinary faith, and much more faith than most of us today. You can say what you want, but for me, Peter is exercising an enormous amount of faith in Christ and His power. He is not exercising faith in general; he is placing reliance in Christ the Lord and His power alone. He is not exercising his faith in himself. No! Peter was placing his confidence in Jesus and His power. Peter was demonstrating a tremendous quantity of confidence in Christ. Oh, would to God there might be men with such awesome and fearless faith today among the churches.

What happened to Peter? Alas, Peter seemingly *lost his focus*. He was aware he was walking on the Sea Galilee in a furious gale. It was night, and Peter was doing what is physically impossible. Peter was walking on water. We ought to know that such actions are humanly impossible. Peter certainly knew his actions were impossible: he was an expert fisherman. Listen, this was not Peter's debut; his first time to be in ferocious storm on Galilee. Peter had "been in the face of furious storms on the Sea Galilee before." However, this was Peter's first and only time he walked on water.

The Bible says,

³⁰But when he saw the wind [e.g., *blowing and causing high waves*], he was afraid, and beginning to sink he cried out, "Lord, save me." ³¹Jesus immediately

164

> reached out his hand and took hold of him, saying to him, "O you of
> little faith, why did you doubt?" Matt. 14:30, 31 (ESV)

What many people never realize is that Jesus was carpenter by trade. Carpenters often cut their own trees down and cutting and planing the wood themselves. Our Lord was therefore amazingly physically a strong man. This is very evident when He life Peter (a full-sized man) out of the sea with one hand. Hallelujah, what a wonderful and glorious Savior we have.

Peter could not see the wind, but he most assuredly could see the winds effect and feel the force of the wind against him. Additionally, he could see and feel the high waves crashing against him. Friend, seeing the high waves and feeling the furious wind blasting again him and high waves ought to frighten most of us. It is certain Peter must have struggled to maintain his balance on the turbulent sea and vehement wind as he walked on water.

There are at least four things to note particularly concerning Peter's situation, which also has much to teach us today.

✓ He became **fearful**.

✓ He **lost** his **focus**.

✓ He took his **eyes off of Jesus**.

✓ He began to **doubt**.

1). He became fearful.
Fear is a paralyzer. The text says,

> But seeing the wind, he **became frightened**, and beginning to sink, he
> cried out, "Lord, save me!" Matt. 14:30

When fear grips any of us, one of three things will happen.

a). *Freeze:* Fear can literally cause people to freeze. A person can become immobile or petrified. The person cannot do anything. Almost everything completely shuts down. We lose our bearings and everything within us just shuts down.

b). *Panic:* Also, we can panic, and when panic sets in, we are likely to just run. (In this state of mind, we may not even know where we are running; we are just running to get away.) This is when we can only react, "Get away from this situation." So, we just run and hope we can escape the situation.

It is certain that Peter had no place to run. Sometimes that is what can happen to us: we are in such a dreadful situation, but we can only react by running from the circumstance. We are not thinking rationally; we are just reacting.

    c). Fight: Lastly, our adrenaline kicks-in and we fight. This is where heroes emerge from the frightening danger. Some people have done such amazing actions that it is impossible to comprehend the action was real. For example, a mother's child is under a car; there is little time to waste. Then, incredibly the mother lifts the car and saves her child. We cannot explain it; we can only know it happens. It is possible in such moments when people do incredibly miraculous feats or actions. Well, did an angel(s) somehow intervene in their behalf in assistance? You tell me.

In Peter's situation, he seemingly *froze* for the moment. Then, he started to sink. Sometimes, we can face the situation against all the odds, and we go against the odds.

2). He lost his focus.

Once we lose our focus, we begin to bounce around like a *ping pong ball*. **We lose the edge** of the moment and we no longer remain focused on the task at hand. The sharper our focus and concentration, the more productive we will be. We cannot attempt to do our maximum productivity while doing other things. We cannot give our attention to the desired task and do other things. For instance, we cannot prepare for a sermon or read the Scripture and at the same time watch TV, listen to the radio, or be part someone's conversation. Our Lord was very, very focused on His tasks at any given moment. Jesus was very focused whether He talking with others, teaching people, praying, or listening of others. (When the Lord listen to our prayers, we can be confidence we have His 100% attention!) Jesus was awfully focused on His given task at any time. (Therefore, remember, when we pray, we can be fully certain He is totally focused listening to our prayers.) The church for certain has lost it focus and lost its edge.

The churches would do well to stay focused on whatever their given task they are working on at the time. We can get easily distracted. It is certain that the churches need to give more attention to ongoing *evangelism* and *discipling* and *training*. You read me correctly: it is time to train, train, and to continue with on-going training. Listen, we must keep steam rolling forward: continue with ongoing.

Evangelism in the community has come to a *screeching halt* with many churches in their community. Evangelism is virtually nonexistent both **in the pulpit** and **door to door**. If you ask some Pastors, "Are you aware of Evangelism 7/24?" They may look at you dumbfounded, as if to say: "What's that?" Evangelism 7/24 is zero today in many churches or a *dribble* or a *little trickle* of a few hours a week. Yet, it is the highest command given to the churches and every Christian by the risen Lord.

3). He took his eyes off of Jesus.

We have already noted this before, but it is important to once again to get this emphasis,

> Therefore, since we have so great a cloud of witnesses surrounding us, let us also lay aside every encumbrance and the sin which so easily entangles us, and let us run with endurance the race that is set before us, **FIXING OUR EYES ON JESUS**, the author and perfecter [completer or completionist] of [our] faith, who for the joy set before Him endured the cross, despising the shame, and has sat down at the right hand of the throne of God. Heb. 12:1, 2

The apostle Paul also says,

> So then, my dear ones, just as you have always obeyed [my instructions with enthusiasm], not only in my presence, but now much more in my absence, continue to work [living] out your salvation [that is, cultivate it, bring it to full effect, actively pursue spiritual maturity] with awe-inspired fear and trembling [using serious caution and critical self-evaluation to avoid anything that might offend God or discredit the name of Christ]. For it is [not your strength, but it is] God who is effectively at work in you, both to will and to work [that is, strengthening, energizing, and creating in you the longing and the ability to fulfill your purpose] for His good pleasure. Phi. 2:12, 13 (AMP)

If we keep our eyes on Jesus, we are less likely to get distracted by the world, the flesh, or the devil. Jesus ought to be our plumbline: like a *sharp and pointed arrow directing our path*. As a result, our focus can become razor and lighting sharp. It is like when Peter swung his mighty sword to cut off the head of the high priest's servant head. If Peter had struck Malchus' neck, his head would have rolled off his shoulders. I am sure the servant was thankful Peter missed his head.

The churches need to refocus themselves and get revived and fully charged up by the Holy Spirit. (Revived, what's that? Is that like a revival?) The churches need to keep the plumbline on the risen Lord Jesus and His **prime directives** and **commands**. This means to get your priorities in order. Hello! Many churches have simply lost their focus. In some cases, the churches have abandoned their birthright: going into all the world but especially around the church community, with the urgency of **compelling people to come into the Kingdom of God**. Come to Christ as Lord and Savior. For our Lord promised, 'Lo, Jesus will be with you unto the end of the age.'

4). He begins to doubt.

The last thing we ought to learn from Peter's experience here is that he *doubted*. The Bible says,

> But seeing the wind, he became frightened, and beginning to sink, he cried out, "Lord, save me!" Immediately Jesus stretched out His hand and took hold of him, and said to him, "You of little faith, **why did you doubt**?"   Matt. 14:30, 31

What is doubting? Doubting is simply disbelief. Doubting or disbelief has a crippling effect upon our walk of faith of obedience and action or the things we do. Regardless how much faith one may profess, doubt lets out all the hot air we may boast about in our walk in Christ. With the presence of doubt, we shall very quickly run out of gas.

What a sorrowful situation. Many people allege to belief God's Word, but *"When push comes to shove,"*[3] we have come to a dead-end. We come to a *halt*. We come to a dead-stop! The critical problem is that too many of us says we believe, but inwardly, we have lingering doubts. Upon those that doubt, Jude says,

> And have mercy on some, who are doubting.   Jude 1:22

James says this about doubting, but the application applies to most anything when we are praying.

> And let steadfastness [*perseverance*] have its full effect, that you may be perfect [*fully matured*] and complete, lacking in nothing. [5]If any of you lacks wisdom, let him ask God, who gives generously to all without reproach, and it will be given him. [6]But let him ask in faith, with no doubting, for the one who doubts is like a wave of the sea that is driven and tossed by the wind. [7]For that person must not suppose that he will receive anything from the Lord; [8]he is a double-minded[b] [*ambivalent*] man, unstable in all his ways.   James 1:4-8 (ESV)

168

ᵇ*Double-minded*, the meaning here is the person vacillates becomes indecisive, and unsure in his faith. However, let us also keep in mind what John says in 1 John 5:14, 15.

The professing church today has arrived to where it professes to believe, but in the very next breath, we have lingering doubt. If we are troubled with lingering doubt, how then can we give our best for the Master?

Conclusion

Well, my friend, I don't know about you, but I think we need more men and women like Peter. In simple language, Peter was willing and did step down out of the boat. Ah, but Peter step out at the command of our Lord! This was not being credulous or having blind faith. Peter's faith was relying upon his unwavering faithfulness in the Lord Jesus and 'His Command.' Peter did the impossible! Peter did the impossible because he asked for permission, and he did as he was instructed, *"Step down and out of the boat Peter on the turbulent sea, and walk on water."* Hallelujah, praise the Lord! Peter showed boldness in trusting in the words of Jesus. Do you read me my friend? Peter *showed boldness in trusting in the words of Jesus*! Where is our boldness in trusting the words of Jesus?

Peter placed his trust in Jesus' words with <u>*action of obedience*</u>. Peter demonstrated his unreserved commitment in the power and authority of Christ the Lord. Can you just imagine what the churches might do if we exhibit such unreserved and unconditional commitment of faith and obedience in Jesus' commands?

> ¹⁸And having come to them, Jesus spoke to them, saying, **ALL AUTHORITY** has been given to Me in heaven and upon the earth. ¹⁹**GO** therefore, disciple all the ethnicities (nations), **BAPTIZING** them into the name of the Father, and of the Son, and of the Holy Spirit; ²⁰**TEACHING** them to observe (watch over, guard, keep) all things whatever **I COMMANDED YOU**. And behold, **I AM WITH YOU** all the days until the culmination (consummate coming together of all into the whole) of the age.   Matt. 28:18-20 (LET, 2021)

However, the command begins and continues around the community of the church. What good is there giving to missions but the church fails to go door to door compelling people to enter the Kingdom of God. Get it right: **we do <u>not</u> invite people to a *Bible study*. We do <u>not</u> invite people to *church*.**

Instead, we invite people to <u>REPENT</u> and <u>RECEIVE JESUS CHRIST AS LORD</u> AND <u>SAVIOR</u>!

Yes, Peter got *distracted*, and he took his *eyes off the Lord* of glory. Yes, Peter began to sink, and *he cried to the Lord to save him*. Yes, Peter became *fearful*. Yes, Peter *doubted*. However, my friend, Peter is the only man ever to walked on a turbulent gale on the sea other than our Master, the Lord Jesus. Regardless of what you may say, there is no sinful and moral man that broke the natural Laws of nature and lived to tell about it.

Remember: if you point your finger at Peter because he sunk in Galilee Sea, *all of your other fingers are pointing back at you*. Hello!

Yes, Peter was overcome with fear, but remember, Peter is the only who stepped down from the boat in the mist of the furious storm. There were elven others that remained huddled in the boat.

There is a lot we can learn from Peter's experience. He was an extraordinary man that put his complete trust in Jesus' command, "Come on Peter step down and out the boat." And Peter did it! What if the Christians would put their complete trust in Jesus' command and begin knocking on door to door around the church? Do you my friend think that community would radically change for better and change for glory and praise of God?

Footnotes

1.   "Put his foot in his mouth:" while the expression is often implying a negative connotative, the expression can imply more than you can do. In this sense overstep our bounds, we have invariably embarrassed ourselves without realizing it. However, this shows the brazen deep faith in Jesus our Lord.

2.   "Hobnobbing," socializing among Pastors and particularly socializing with some of the more influential Pastors or churches.

3.   "When push comes to shove:" Google gives this meaning, "when the situation becomes critical or urgent, or as a last resort. It implies a point where action, even if difficult, must be taken."

Sixth miraculous miracle and sign
Jesus Heals a Blind Man from Birth

As He passed by, He saw a man blind from birth. [2]And His disciples asked Him, "Rabbi, who sinned, this man or his parents, that he would be born blind?" [3]Jesus answered, "*It was* neither *that* this man sinned, nor his parents; but *it was* so that the works of God might be displayed in him. [4]"We must work the works of Him who sent Me as long as it is day; night is coming when no one can work. [5]"While I am in the world, I am the Light of the world." [6]When He had said this, He spat on the ground, and made clay of the spittle, and applied the clay to his eyes, [7]and said to him, "Go, wash in the pool of Siloam" (which is translated, Sent). So he went away and washed, and came *back* seeing. John 9:1-7

CHAPTER 14

Healing a man that had been blind since birth

When He had said this, He spat on the ground, and made clay of the spittle, and applied the clay to his eyes, and said to him, "Go, wash in the pool of Siloam" (which is translated, Sent). So he went away and washed, and came *back* seeing.   John 9:6, 7

Introduction

This is one of the most unusual miracles or signs recorded of Jesus. The complexity and healing of a blind person from birth is ever so unique and astounding. I dare say that only a well-trained physician like an optometrist would be able to explain the incredible and amazing extraordinary miracle. This miracle must by necessity require the *reconstruction of the human brain* (as I understand the miracle) in order to see. Yes, you read correctly, the *reconstruction of the brain* is necessary to accomplish such amazing miracle. As I have said, this miracle is indeed one of most incredible miracles to take place. This is more than opening the eyes of a blind in order to see. (Even if such had his eyes open, blind since birth, they could understand what they were seeing.) Hear me, the brain of a blind man from birth must have some type of reconstruction that must occur in the brain in order to see. Otherwise, the healing of the eyes the blind person from birth still would not be able to understand what he was seeing for the first time. Amazing!

Only as we are in this present era of medicine, we are just now gaining insight and beginning to understand the very complexity of this tremendous and astounding miracle. No soothsayer, charlatan, or so-called counterfeit miracle worker is able to reproduce this miracle. This is indeed an incredible miracle.

Even with all the knowledge and medical advancement, no one is yet able reproduce the amazing feat. If we understood all the endless complexity of a person seeing who had been blind since birth, maybe we could then begin to understand this most incredible miracle. As it is, most us haven't the faintest clue as the complexity of this awesome miracle.

This miracle or literally "sign" as John refers to it is only found in John's Gospel. The reader ought to keep in mind that the apostle John is giving his emphasis to the southern ministry to Jerusalem and Judea. This was the hub for the zealous hard-core Jewish leaders. This is why John in each of the miracles he stresses amazing miracles as ***SIGNS***. John gives the emphasis of "signs" early in his Gospel. Repetition is a major element in learning; so, let us once again look at John's emphasis with the word "*signs*."

> And He [*Jesus*] found in the temple those who sold oxen and sheep and doves, and the moneychangers doing business. [15]When He had made a whip of cords, He drove them all out of the temple, with the sheep and the oxen, and poured out the changers' money and overturned the tables. [16]And He said to those who sold doves, "Take these things away! Do not make My Father's house a house of merchandise!" [17]Then His disciples remembered that it was written, "Zeal for Your house has eaten Me up [*would consume Me*]."

> [18]So the Jews answered and said to Him, **"What <u>SIGN</u> do You show to us, since You do these things**?" [19]Jesus answered and said to them, **"Destroy this temple, and in three days I will raise it up."** [20]Then the Jews said, "It has taken forty-six years to build this temple, and will You raise it up in three days?" [21]**But He was speaking of the temple of His body.** [22]Therefore, **when He had risen from the dead, His disciples remembered** that He had said this to them; and they believed the Scripture and the word which Jesus had said. [23]Now when He was in Jerusalem at the Passover, during the feast, many **believed in His name when they saw the <u>SIGNS</u>** which He did.   John 2:14-23 (NKJ)

Repetition is the mother of learning, so, we ought to understand that John is writing to many hostile Jews that saw Jesus as false prophet. This is the reason for John to emphasis the word "*sign*." Gentiles were not concerned about signs, but to the Jews, signs were proof (credentials of certification) that Jesus is the real and legitimately Prophet and the Messiah that was to come

173

into the world. Here are examples of sign(s) in John's Gospel: John 2:11, 18, 23; 3:2; 4:48, 54; 6:2, 14, 26, 30; 7:31; 9:16; 10:41; 11:47; 12:28, 37; 20:3. (I only show the emphasis in John, the rest of the Scripture is inundated with the emphasis of signs to Israel.)

Therefore, John is definitely writing his Gospel to Jews that they might believe that Yehoshua is the Messiah and the Redeemer to deliver Israel. Even as the apostle Paul declares concerning Israel as it is clearly given in the NRS,

> And even those of Israel, if they do not persist in unbelief, will be grafted in, for God has the power to graft them in again. ²⁴For if you [*Gentiles*] have been cut from what is by nature a wild olive tree and grafted, contrary to nature, into a cultivated olive tree, how much more will these natural branches be grafted back into their own olive tree. ²⁵So that you may not claim to be wiser than you are, brothers and sisters, I want you to understand this mystery: a **hardening has come upon part of Israel, UNTIL the full number of the Gentiles has come in.** ²⁶And **so all Israel will be saved**; as it is written, "**Out of Zion will come THE DELIVERER; he will banish ungodliness from Jacob.**" ²⁷"And this is my covenant with them, when **I** [*the Lord*] **TAKE AWAY THEIR SINS.**" Rom. 11:23-27 (NRS)

Still, the Jew must come by the way of cross of Christ like everyone else or else they shall perish in their sin of unbelief.

A. Tradition, Superstition, and Prejudice is blinding

If there is one thing that ought to stand out in this text in John is that the blinding effect of *tradition* which tends to override the authority of the truth of God's Word. The man who had been blind from birth testified to the religious leaders, but the religious leaders had already *assumed* that they knew all there was to know concerning the truth of God's Word. (When we think that we know most or all the answers the Scriptures, we ought to realize *we know nothing!*) So, the religious leaders are rebuked by the man who had been healed of his blindness, and this is indeed an astonishing account. *The blind man seeing now said*:

> "Since the world began it has been unheard of that anyone opened the eyes of one who was born blind. ³³If this Man were not from God, He could do nothing." ³⁴They [*the religious leaders*] answered and said to him, "You were completely born in sins", and are you teaching us?" And they cast him out [*of temple*].

[35]Jesus heard that they had cast him out [of temple]; and when He had found him, He said to him, **"Do you believe in the Son of God[a]?"** [36]He answered and said, **"Who is He, Lord, that I may believe in Him?"** [37]And Jesus said to him, **"You have both seen Him and it is He who is talking with you."** [38]Then he said, **"Lord, I believe!"** And **he worshiped Him**. [39]And Jesus said, "For **judgment I have come into this world, that those who do not see may see**, and **that those who see may be made blind."** [40]Then *some* of the Pharisees who were with Him heard these words, and said to Him, **"Are we blind also?"** [41]Jesus said to them, "If you were blind, you would have no sin; **but now you say, `We see.' Therefore your sin remains."**   John 9:32-41 (NKJ)

[a]Some GK text read, "Son of God;" other GK text read, "Son man." The more difficult text "Son of God" is preferred.

[*]v34, the GK word [*hamartiais*] for sin is literally plural, "sins" and not sin.

The above text, while it likely refers to Jewish **blinded by their tradition and superstition**, the text has immeasurable insight to each of our own *excessive baggage of tradition* and our *overlapping of superstitions*. If you do not honestly confess and acknowledge you too are carrying *"excessive baggage of traditions, overlapping with superstitions,* and yes even *prejudices,"* then shame on you. When we fail to acknowledge our blindness, we are in worse condition because we cannot even realize our own blindness.

The churches are plagued with unwarranted and unscriptural practices in and out the churches. Many of these things have their roots is paganism. In many ways, these practices hinder the Gospel though many ignorantly imagine that such practices further the Gospel. Friend, this is not only sad; this is sick! Many of our traditions and superstitions overlap. These things are fueled and greatly distorted by our own **prejudices**. Yes, each of is filled with all types of *prejudices*, which we also conveniently deny.

Philip found Nathanael, and Philip was excited that he and others had found the Messiah, Jesus of Nazareth. Nathanael sarcastically remarked: *"Jesus of Nazareth?"*

"Can any good thing come out of Nazareth?" Philip said to him, "Come and see."   John 1:46

Prejudice is denied by most all of us, but prejudice is all over the world. However, just like Nathanael remarked, this was the sentiment leading Jews in Jerusalem: "There is nothing good that could come out of Nazareth." So, believing Jesus was from Nazareth, this added to the Jews prejudice in Jerusalem and Judea.

First, if you are unwilling to acknowledge you have blinding prejudice, then, I am sorry no one can help you. This is why Solomon said,

> Do you see a man wise in his own eyes? *There is* more hope for a fool than for him.   Prov. 26:12 (NKJ)

> The rich man is wise in his own eyes, But the poor who has understanding sees through him.   Prov. 28:11

> The sluggard is wiser in his own eyes Than seven men who can give a discreet [*discerning judgment*] answer.   Prov. 26:16

Listen, the whole world is immerged and overtaken by prejudice, and friend, that includes *me and you*. So, how can we ever get untangled from the snare of *tradition* or *superstition* or even *prejudice*? We just do not learn or fully understand that *illumination* and *insight* must come from God, but we are so locked down by prejudice that we cannot see the truth. Friend, prejudice blinds truth.

For an example of blinding prejudice, we have the ardent KJV (NKJ), and then, there are those that are adamantly opposite to the KJV. (There is a group that solely endorse the GNV Bible, which was the forerunner for two hundred years before the KJV was finally adopted in America.) This is one of reasons for the multiple uses of translation: *to help open our eyes to the truth of God's Word*. Yes, we need to have godly men translate the Word of God. Yet, the Lord uses the unbeliever even though he/she doesn't realize the Spirit is indeed using even the unbelievers in translation of the Bible.

Another form of prejudice is the "*electionists*." That is, only the elect will be saved. So, there is little zealous of *biblical evangelism* going door to door compelling people to come Jesus as Lord by the *electionists*. (They have the false allusion that God will just bring in the elect.) Many of the *electionists* **do not** do any extensive and ongoing evangelism classes and certainly the *electionists* are void of any ongoing field experience in real evangelism. In addition, the *electionists* rarely do not give the invitation of Gospel in many churches anyone.

There are some people who boast that they believe that the Gospel is available for everyone, but yet, they too are doing little in house to house or door to door evangelism. They are more like the *electionists* that do not evangelize. "How bizarre is that my friend?" That is, there very little evangelism surrounding the community of churches who espouse salvation is for everyone. So, yes, *"the Gospel is available everyone,"* but there **are** **few** going out **7/24** compelling people to come to Jesus as Lord. So, while some allege to believe that the Gospel is for everyone, they too are not going out aggressively **7/24**. What good is it you say that *you believe the Gospel is for everyone* but you do not go into the community of the church and passionately present the Gospel?

It is a fact that they are *sluggards*! There are at least <u>seven</u> <u>reasons</u> why those who believe *the Gospel is available to everyone* but they are not going out **7/24**. Here are some of the reasons some Pastors and churches leaders do not go out into the community surrounding the church to evangelize even though they profess the Gospel is for everyone.

1. They are **too** **satisfied** with the *"status quo."*

2. They are simply **too** **lazy**.

3. They are **too** **afraid**.

4. They are **too** **disobedient** or living in sin.

5. Some leaders are **not** **genuinely** **saved**.

6. Others **follow** **the** **cults** using Bible study.

7. Unskilled in **how** **to** **draw** **in** **the** **net**.

So, do not tell me you believe the Gospel is for everyone, but your church is only doing *trickle down evangelism*, a few hours a week. You are not doing evangelism **7/24**. Jesus said,

> 'Go out into the highways and along the hedges, and **COMPEL** *THEM*
> **TO COME IN,**[b] so that my house may be filled.'   Luke 14:23

> [b]Let me give a word to the *fault-finders*. My friend, I know the above Scripture is a parable, but this does not change the truth whether it is a parable or not.

There are many more such traditions and superstitions that plague the churches. It is incredible the number of holidays and days off that are taking place through the churches or just simple religious days, it is unbelievable. Some people are *"sticking out their chest"* and saying to themselves, "We don't do those things." Well, you are wrong, and we are all too blind as noted above to see it.

Well, just think of the Christmas tree. Some people give Dr. Martin Luther the credit with initiating the Christmas tree. Then people give gifts to one

177

another, but the Real Giver of life, Jesus Christ, is often omitted or only a side-bar at Christmas time. Christ the Lord is not given the preeminent at Christmas; I don't care what you may allege.

Well, again, we tack-on even more. At Christians, there are those who actually roll play "Santa." I am not joking; you know it is true. Some only put on the red hat, but the red hat symbolizes "Santa." Christian parents sing or tell their children: "You better watch out Santa knows if you been good or bad; so, be good for goodness sake." Let me tell you, only Christ the Lord our God has the attribute to know whether we are good or bad. Just change one letter around the word Santa and see what you get: Santa = **Satan**.

Another example, the Bible never uses the word "_Easter_" except in the 1611, [Acts 12:4] JKV (which derived from the Romanist). Actually, the GK word is "_pascha_," Passover. (This demonstrates the Roman Catholic's influence on the KJV, which many are unaware or in denial of Romanist's direct influence.)

The churches eradicated and removed all the glorious Passover which is connected to Communion, but Luke put Passover and Communion Service side by side.

> [Passover] "For I say to you, I will no longer eat of it until it is fulfilled in the kingdom of God." [17]Then He took the cup, and gave thanks, and said, "Take this and divide _it_ among yourselves; [18]for I say to you, I will not drink of the fruit of the vine until the kingdom of God comes."

> [Communion] [19]And He took bread, gave thanks and broke _it_, and gave _it_ to them, saying, "This is My body which is given for you; do this in remembrance of Me." [20]Likewise He also _took_ the cup after supper, saying, "This cup _is_ the new covenant in My blood, which is shed for you.[c]   Luke 22:16-20 (NKJ)

> [c]The _fault-finders_ argue that Luke does not put things in actual sequence or in order. I will leave that to the Lord to judge; I am simply pointing out a personal observation.

To top off the blinding traditions and superstitions do not forget, we have "the Easter Bunny," and the Easter Bunny that lays eggs? (A bunny lays eggs?) At Easter time, some Christian men actually buying new suits, and this is for "Easter?" They may say, "What? this reminds them of the resurrection and new life in Christ." My friend, get real.

We ought to be amazed that anyone is saved nowadays due to wholesale corruption and wickedness that has blanketed the churches. Paul was so right when he said, "where sin increased, grace abounded [GK *huperperisseuo, super-abounded*] all the more.^Rom. 5:20 Keep in mind that the apostle continues by saying,

> What shall we say then? Shall we continue in sin, that grace may abound? God forbid. How shall we, that are dead to sin, live any longer therein? Rom. 6:1, 2 (KJV)

B. Opening the eyes of the blind since birth

This is amazing and puzzling miracle or sign ought to leave most of us stunned and stupefied. **Twice** the man that was blind from birth attempted to answer the religious leaders who were relentlessly and callously interrogating him. Unfortunately, their traditions and superstitions blanketed their reception along with their prejudices which kept them from hearing the man.

Even the disciples were following tradition and superstition of the religious leaders,

> Now as *Jesus* passed by, He saw a man who was blind from birth. And His disciples asked Him, saying, **"Rabbi, who sinned, this man or his parents, that he was born blind?"** John 9:1, 2 (NKJ)

Yes, in one sense of the word, the Pharisees did hear the man's testimony in how he was healed. Still, the blind man who had been healed and now could see did not know who Jesus was. He was blind, and he only knew that he was once blind but now his eyes were opened and he could see for the first time in his life. Now he could see the awesome beauty of creation. The blind man that was healed tried to explain to the religious leaders, but Pharisees' own **religious-filters** and **ardent prejudices** hindered them from receiving the truth of whatever the man was saying. In simple language, their own religious prejudices blinded them from the true. How sad is that my friend?

Most regrettably, this is true of me and you and everyone else in this world. You read me right! We are so encumbered by our own prejudices (religious prejudices and non-religious prejudices). This is prejudice from years of traditions, and yes, superstitions as well. More than that, we are *bogged down* with prejudices do to our old nature. (Anyone who denies their multiple prejudices, then they are lying to themselves.) Unfortunately, we may try to deny such influences on each of us, but this is still very true. Listen, this is true even with husbands and wives; we do not honestly hear one another. We do not fully seek to hear the other person. We often assume that we know what they saying before they even finish their sentence. Friend, whether you are aware of your acts of prejudice or not, we are all actually very prejudiced.

179

The religious leaders in Jerusalem apparently couldn't stand hearing the man especially as he corrected them. The religious leaders were so full of themselves. I find it incredible that the religious leaders ask the blind man second time how is that he now sees. The Pharisees were so engulfed by their *traditions, superstitions,* and even *prejudices* that they were unable hear or listen to the man. It is a wonder that they didn't attempt to stone him. I think this is especially true since the religious leaders became so enraged with the man. Ironically, the religious leaders became blinded and overwhelmed by their *traditions, superstitions,* and *prejudices.* How warped is that?

It is easy to find fault as the religious leaders did with the man. This is because like many religious leaders (then and now) they are filled with their traditions and superstition and overtaken by their prejudices. The religious leaders were not asking the man questions to gain the truth. Listen to me, the religious leaders were "*interrogating him.*" The Pharisees were *interrogating* the man to determine the error of the man since he was born in sin.

Do you know what is so ironic today? Many so-called religious leaders today do not even believe the miracles of Jesus even though they allege that they believe the Bible. The truth is that they are liars and counterfeiters of the truth of God. So, in a sense, the Pharisees are no worse than the charlatans that flood the electronic churches, air ways, and other places today. Many of the so-called religious leaders do not realize that when they declare error with God's Word; friend, they are finding fault with the Lord and calling God a liar.[1 John 5:10] Friend, God cannot lie![Titus 1:2] They have joined "*the father of lies.*"[John 8:44] Yeah, they have joined ranks of ***the fault-finder's club.***

Friend, in the same way today, many of us do not want hear the truth. We want people to tell us what we want to hear. Yes, we want have our ears *tickled.*[2 Tim. 4:2-4] In reality, many of us, like many of the Pharisees, cannot stand the truth. If we can no long endure hearing the truth, how in the world do we expect to honestly hear and practice the truth?

How can we explain this about ourselves today? One of the mysteries is that many church leaders are falling away even though they allege to speak the truth. I think the departure or falling away is likely due to "*demon oppression.*" I said, *demon oppression* **not** demon possession. According to 1 John 4:4, I do not think a true Christian, born from above, can be demon possessed.

There are men **that were** seemingly sound in the faith, **but** for some reason, these men are now **introducing heresies** into the churches, and I mean *damnable heresies.* As Peter says as given by the KJV,

But there were false prophets also among the people, even as there shall be false teachers among you, who privily shall bring in **damnable** [GK *apoleia, destructive*] heresies, even denying the Lord that bought them, and bring upon themselves swift **destruction** [GK *apoleia*].   2 Peter 2:1 (KJV)

Now, here is Jesus' response to Pharisees; consider carefully what our Lord says.

[35]Jesus heard that they cast him forth outside [*cast out of the temple*], and having found him, He said to him, "Do you believe in the Son of God?" [36]He answered and said, "Who is He, Lord, that I may believe in Him?" [37]And Jesus said to him, "You have both seen Him, and He who is speaking with you is He"; [38]and he said, "I believe, Lord," and worshiped Him. [39]And Jesus said, **"I came to this world for judgment, that those not seeing may see**, and **those seeing may become blind."** [40]And those of the Pharisees who were with Him heard these things, and they said to Him, "Are we also blind?" [41]Jesus said to them, "If you were blind, you were not having had sin, **but now you say—We see, therefore your sin remains."**   John 9:35-41 (LSV)

If we want more illumination in God's Word, we need to first confess we are blinded by our excessive baggage due to *ecclesiastical traditions, superstitions*, and *prejudices* that we have accumulated. If we lie to ourselves and say that this is not true of us ("I am not prejudice") and that we think we are open to the truth, then I dread to tell you: we are unable to bear the truth.

Truth is only available when we are willing to shed ourselves of the things that are blinding us from the truth. The same is true as we are indoctrinated and strongly influenced by the big three:

1). **The world** around (everything we hear, see, feel, smell, and even taste) us feeds our corrupt lower nature and minds.

2). The **carnal nature** that feeds our wicked heart (emotions, will, and thought processes) that is continually bent on evil.

3). **Demonic forces** that is introducing and feeding evil thought into our lives, and demons inducing evil thoughts without us fully realizing its source or origin. Listen, evil spirits use every area of life to lead us astray. So, let us remain on our spirit toes.

Conclusion

Most of what has been discussed in this chapter will be regrettably pushed aside, dismissed, or even denied. However, we are all overloaded with excessive baggage which we have accumulated over the years. We have accumulated a lot more than we realize or are willing to admit. We live in a surrounding environment which unfortunately plays a vital role that formulated our established traditions, superstitions, and even prejudices which helps to govern our point of view.

As Peter says, concerning Lot,

> (for by what he [Lot] **saw** and **heard** *that* righteous man, while **living among them**, felt *his* righteous **soul tormented day after day** by *their* lawless deeds). 2 Peter 2:8

Do you still think the world around you is having no negative effect in your life?

This does not mean all our influences are negative or bad. Some of our influences have been very good. Yes, some influences have been very productive and beneficial along the way. However, when our guard is down or when we do not remain alert, we might be unaware of the things that seem to attach themselves like a *blood sucking leech* along with the good influence that might be dangerous and harmful to us. (Does that make sense to you? I hope so.)

Evil spirits masquerade themselves as godliness in our minds, and sometimes we are unaware of it.

> For such people are **false apostles, deceitful workers, masquerading as apostles of Christ**. And no wonder, for **Satan** himself **masquerades as an angel of light**. It is not surprising, then, if his [Satan's] **servants also masquerade as servants of righteousness**. Their end will be what their actions deserve. 2 Cor. 11:13-15 (NIV)

Listen and pay attention: Jesus warns us that many will follow the road to destruction, which is Hell.[Matt. 7:13-15, 21-23] Yes, even sadder, some of these workers became enemies of the cross of Christ,

> For **many live as enemies of the cross of Christ**; I have often told you of them, and **now I tell you even with tears. Their end is destruction; their god is the belly; and their glory is in their shame**; their minds are set on earthly things. Phil. 3:18, 19 (NRS)

Listen, if the apostle Peter can be seduced by the evil one, then, friend we are easy money (easy prey by the devil), [see Matt. 16:21-23]. The battle is with our mind.[2 Cor. 11:3] Therefore Paul says to bring every thought in captivity to the obedience of Christ.[2 Cor. 10:4, 5]

So then, while Satan is not able to possess a believer, the evil one is able to seek to seduce a believer. The evil one may **overtly** indwell unbelievers. Satan cannot indwell a believer because of the indwelling the Holy Spirit.[1 John 4:4]

Listen to this warning: Satan is also **covert**. The evil one is able to **conceal, cloak,** or **disguise** himself from believers. Satan is able to deceive believers and even induce thoughts into the mind to tempt them or to lead them estray as they are **demon oppression** (but no demon is permitted to possession a genuine believer.) This means evil spirits may attack the mind. A word to the wise,

> For the weapons of our warfare *are* not carnal but mighty in God for pulling down strongholds, casting down arguments and every high thing that exalts itself against the knowledge of God, **bringing every thought into captivity to the obedience of Christ.**
>
> 2 Cor. 10:4, 5 (NKJ)

Seventh miraculous miracle and sign
Jesus Raises Lazarus from the Dead

So Jesus, again being deeply moved within, came to the tomb. Now it was a cave, and a stone was lying against it. [39]Jesus said, "Remove the stone." Martha, the sister of the deceased, said to Him, "Lord, by this time there will be a stench, for he has been *dead* four days." [40]Jesus said to her, "Did I not say to you that if you believe, you will see the glory of God?" [41]So they removed the stone. Then Jesus raised His eyes, and said, "Father, I thank You that You have heard Me. [42]"I knew that You always hear Me; but because of the people standing around I said it, so that they may believe that You sent Me." [43]When He had said these things, He cried out with a loud voice, "Lazarus, come forth." [44]The man who had died came forth, bound hand and foot with wrappings, and his face was wrapped around with a cloth. Jesus said to them, "Unbind him, and let him go."   John 11:38-44

CHAPTER 15

Lazarus was dead for four days

Jesus said, "Take away the stone." Martha, the sister of him who was dead, said to Him, "Lord, by this time there is a stench, for he has been *dead* four days." ⁴⁰Jesus said to her, "Did I not say to you that if you would believe you would see the glory of God?" ⁴¹Then they took away the stone *from the place* where the dead man was lying. And Jesus lifted up *His* eyes and said, "Father, I thank You that You have heard Me. ⁴²"And I know that You always hear Me, but because of the people who are standing by I said *this*, that they may believe that You sent Me." ⁴³Now when He had said these things, He cried with a loud voice, "Lazarus, come forth!" ⁴⁴And he who had died came out bound hand and foot with graveclothes, and his face was wrapped with a cloth. Jesus said to them, "Loose [GK *luo*, also *unbind, untie*] him, and let him go." ⁴⁵Then many of the Jews who had come to Mary, and had seen the things Jesus did, believed in Him. John 11:39-45 (NKJ)

Introduction

The raising of Lazarus from the dead is indisputable and irrefutable. First, the false prophets and lying charlatans may declare they can do the same or even great miracles, but they are liars and counterfeiters and lightyears from the truth of God's Word. There is **no** power by man that can regenerate or recreate life that is in decomposition and corruption for four days. Listen, only the Lord our God is able to create and sustain all life. The Lord is the only one that can give life after the body is in decomposition and in the process of rotting and *immediately* restore it.

Anyone can deny the miracle of raising Lazarus who had been dead for four days, but let everyone know you cannot dispute the incredible miracle. (The evidence remains forever indisputable!) Therefore, the disbelief of the raising of Lazarus after being dead for four days does not remove the reality of the amazing miracle.

To our Jewish brethren, the truth is here. Yehoshua, the Ben Elohim, (Jesus the Son of God) is the only explanation and truth of the matter. There is no other logical explanation. Deny the marvelous sign if you will, but the truth stands forever and ever. Amen and glory to God.

To the rest of the deniers of the miracle of the raising of Lazarus, Hell awaits you. Laugh, if you wish, but I warn you, God knows your heart and the inner thoughts of your mind. At the Judgment, the Lord shall judge the secrets of the heart,

> - on the day when, according to my gospel, God will judge the secrets
> of men through Christ Jesus.   Rom. 2:16

The apostle John devotes chapters 11 through 21 of his Gospel to Jesus' last week of His public ministry and His resurrection. One week later after Lazarus' being raised from the dead, our Lord was crucified on cross. Our Lord laid down His life and died; He was placed in a grave; and three days later, He Himself raised His physical body from the grave.

The resurrection of Jesus Christ like the raising of Lazarus is irrefutable. **The resurrection Jesus Christ is an historical fact**, and it is not an innuendo or an inference. Yes, there is more evidence that Jesus arose from the dead than Julius Caesar ever lived. This again is fact! The resurrection of Jesus Christ is **concrete fact** and **clearly evident**. The evidences are so concrete, as I have said, that there are more evidences that Jesus arose from the dead than Julius Caesar ever lived.

Gilbert West and George Littleton lived during 1800s. They did not believe the resurrection of Jesus Christ or the conversion of Saul of Tarsus, which they through were the two strongest arguments for the Gospel. As a wealthy man, West agreed spend two years researching the resurrection and disproving it, and Littleton would do the same with so-called conversion of Saul (Paul) of Tarsus. These men also agreed not to collaborate with one another during two year of research. When they met two years later, they both were now believers. These men discovered the evidences were too overwhelming that they could no longer deny the historical facts. Both men also wrote a book stating their findings to be irrefutably true.

So, go ahead and deny the evidences of the raising of Lazarus or even resurrection of Jesus Christ the Lord, but know this also, you will be the one *putting the nails in your coffin*.[1] People also deny the resurrection by rejecting the physical resurrection of Jesus Christ. Some allege that Jesus arose from the dead, but He arose only in a spiritual body and not literal physical body. Friend, Jesus raised His own physical body from the dead just like the Bible plainly declares.[1 Cor. 15:3, 4] So, important is the physical resurrection of Jesus Christ that if our Lord did not rise from the death, we who believe are still in our sins.[1 Cor. 15:17-22]

Careful that you do not mock the Scriptures and the wonderful evidences that the Bible plainly presents. Some foolish people died before their time for mocking our Lord. So, I am warning you that the Bible declares,

> [7]Do not be deceived, **GOD** **IS** **NOT** **MOCKED**; for whatever a man sows, that he will also reap. [8]For he who sows to his flesh will of the flesh reap corruption, but he who sows to the Spirit will of the Spirit reap everlasting life. [9]And let us not grow weary while doing good, for in due season we shall reap if we do not lose heart.   Gal. 6:7-9 (NKJ)

(Those Pastors reading this book: I am warning you as well. Do not be foolish or even mock God in your heart or declare His Word untrue.)

> Indeed, let God be true but every man a liar. As it is written: "That You may be justified in Your words, And may overcome when You are judged."   Rom. 3:4 (NKJ)

A. Lazarus' body was in the process of decomposition

As we have seen in other miracles or signs by our Lord, Jesus did not need to be present if He wanted to cure or heal Lazarus. Our Lord did not even need to says a word; **He only needed to will it so**. There was no faith on Lazarus' part. Lazarus had been dead four days. So then, let us remind ourselves that there was no faith involved by Lazarus. Lazarus' physical body was dead, and his body was rotting in the tomb. Today's charlatans and fake healers allege faith is required to be healed. These so-called healers are liars and deceiving over six hundred million people world-wide. Please listen my friend, these con men and women are like a fake sideshow and carnival acts. There is no truth in them.

Friend, if it is the will of God, He will heal the person. That is a fact. The con men and women say if you have enough faith you can *be healed* and even *become very rich*. **Liars, liars, liars your pants us is on fire**! This is why the medical professionals are often baffled. There are people who had Christians praying for them, and they recover though doctors declared that they ought to be dead. Many of these people exhibited no faith, but still, they miraculously recovered. So, let us remind ourselves that our Lord had the absolute power and authority to heal anyone. So then, God may truly heal some people, but if He does heal anyone, friend, it by His mercy and grace alone in Christ. For example, there was a centurion Gentile who realized Jesus' power and authority, and he went to Jesus. The servant in whom the centurion sought out Jesus did not exhibit any faith; it was the centurion who sought Jesus who exhibited faith.

> The centurion answered and said, "Lord, I am not worthy that You should come under my roof. But **only SPEAK A WORD**, and **MY SERVANT WILL BE HEALED**. [9]"For I also am a man under authority, having soldiers under me. And I say to this *one*, `Go,' and he goes; and to another, `Come,' and he comes; and to my servant, `Do this,' and he does *it*." [10]When Jesus heard *it*, He marveled, and said to those who followed, "Assuredly, I say to you, I have not found such great faith, not even in Israel! [11]"And I say to you that many will come from east and west, and sit down with Abraham, Isaac, and Jacob in the kingdom of heaven. [12]"But the sons of the kingdom will be cast out into outer darkness. There will be weeping and gnashing of teeth." [13]Then Jesus said to the centurion, "Go your way; and as **you have believed**, *so* **let it be done for you**." And his **servant was healed** that same hour.
>
> Matt. 8:8-13 (NKJ)

As we consider the raising of Lazarus from the dead, our Lord deliberately delayed going to Lazarus for four days. This delay establishes conclusively that Lazarus was not only dead but his body began to rot.

> So when He heard that he [Lazarus] was sick, He then **stayed two days longer** in the place where He was.   John 11:6

> [*Jesus said to His disciples*:] "Our friend Lazarus has fallen asleep; but I go, so that I may awaken him out of sleep." [12]The disciples then said to Him, "Lord, if he has fallen asleep, he will recover." [13] Now **Jesus had spoken of his death**, but they thought that He was speaking of literal sleep. [14]So Jesus then said to them plainly, "**Lazarus is dead.**
>
> John 11:11-14

> Jesus said, "Remove the stone." Martha, the sister of the deceased, said to Him, "Lord, **by this time there will be a stench**, for he [Lazarus] **has been *dead* four days**."   John 11:39

188

The critics can say, "I do not believe Lazarus was actually dead." Of course, what else could skeptic say. This is because if it is true (which it is true) that they acknowledged the truth that Lazarus' has been raised from the dead, then they would have to acknowledge that Jesus is the Messiah, the Son of God.

Yes, anyone can deny truth, but when truth is indisputable like it was with West and Littleton who were honest men, they submitted to the truth. Those that deny the truth prove they are like the religious leaders in Jerusalem, dishonest men. Some people are so dishonest that even to themselves they cannot bear the thought that they are wrong and that the Gospel is really true.

> But some of them went to the Pharisees and told them the things which Jesus had done. ⁴⁷Therefore the chief priests and the Pharisees convened a council, and were saying, "What are we doing? **For this man is performing many signs.** ⁴⁸"**If we let Him** *go on* **like this, all men will believe in Him**, and the **Romans will come and take away both our place** and our nation." ⁴⁹But one of them, Caiaphas, who was high priest that year, said to them, "You know nothing at all, ⁵⁰nor do you take into account that it is expedient for you that **ONE MAN DIE FOR THE PEOPLE**, and that the whole nation not perish." ⁵¹Now he did not say this on his own initiative, but being high priest that year, **he prophesied that JESUS WAS GOING TO DIE for the nation,** ⁵²and **not for the nation only, but in order that HE MIGHT ALSO GATHER TOGETHER INTO ONE THE CHILDREN OF GOD WHO ARE SCATTERED ABROAD**. ⁵³So from that day on they planned together to kill Him.   John 11:46-53

It is so amazing that the Lord put the words into the mouth the high priest which gives even greater glory to God. Hallelujah! As humans, we do not even realize their very own words will condemn themselves.

> "I tell you that on the day of judgment, people will give an account [even] for every worthless [idle, careless] word they speak. For **by your words you will be justified**, and **by your words you will be condemned**."
>
> Matt. 12:36, 37 (NET)

Solomon sums up Ecclesiastes this way,

> ¹¹The words of the wise are like cattle prods—painful but helpful. Their collected sayings are like a nail-studded stick with which a shepherd drives the sheep. ¹²But, my child, let me give you some further advice: Be careful, for writing books is endless, and much study wears you out.

[13]That's the whole story. Here now is my final conclusion: **Fear God** and **obey his commands**, for this is everyone's duty. [14]God will judge us for everything we do, including every secret thing, whether good or bad.   Ecc. 12:11-14 (NLT)

Unfortunately, there are many even in churches that have <u>no</u> fear of God today. (Shocking but true!) Friend, I am not joking. There are many professing believers in the churches, Bible believing churches, that believe in the living God, but like the fool [Psa. 53:1-3; Prov. 3:3-7], they do not fear the Lord. However, Jesus said as He refers to Himself, the Judge of all flesh,

Do not fear those who kill the body but cannot kill the soul; rather fear him who can destroy both soul and body in hell.   Matt. 10:28 (NRS)

Millions who profess faith in Jesus have been deceived by having received a **DIFFERENT JESUS** and a **DIFFERENT GOSPEL**. As result of them having been deceived and misled, they shall sorrowfully perish forever in Hell.

People have hardened their hearts due the wickedness of their sin and unbelief. They do not realize God has been testifying to them by His Holy Spirit. Just as Stephen said of Israel, it is true of those have hardened their hearts against God and His Word,

"You men who are stiff-necked and uncircumcised in heart and ears are always **resisting the Holy Spirit**; you are doing just as your fathers did."   Acts 7:51

The raising of Lazarus is a very great miracle. Friend, this is truly an astonishing miracle. The Lord wants you in His Kingdom as a son or daughter, but you need to repent of your sins and believe and receive Jesus as Lord and Savior right now. Otherwise, you shall surely perish in your sins in Hell.

B. Lazarus exhibited no faith; he was dead

Again, the Bible describes the miraculous miracle of the raising of Lazarus from the dead as given below,

And some of them said, "Could not this Man, who opened the eyes of the blind, also have kept this man from dying?" [38]Then Jesus, again groaning in Himself, came to the tomb. It was a cave, and a stone lay against it. [39]Jesus said, "Take away the stone." Martha, the sister of him who was dead, said to Him, "Lord, by this time there is a stench, for he has been *dead* four days." [40]Jesus said to her, "Did I not say to you that if you would believe you would see the glory of God?" [41]Then they took away the stone *from the place* where the dead man was lying. And Jesus lifted up *His* eyes and said, "Father, I thank You that You have heard Me. [42]And I know that You always hear Me, but because of the people who are standing by I said *this*, that they may believe that You sent Me." [43]Now when He had said these things, He cried with a loud voice, "Lazarus, come forth!" [44]And he who had died came out bound hand and foot with graveclothes, and his face was wrapped with a cloth. Jesus said to them, "Loose him, and let him go." John 11:37-44 (NKJ)

Sometimes overlooked is Jesus calling him by his name, '**LAZARUS, COME FORTH!**'[John 11:43] Otherwise, everyone in the grave would have risen. Hallelujah! Jesus said,

> Don't be so surprised! Indeed, the time is coming when all the dead in their graves will hear the voice of God's Son,[a] and they will rise again. Those who have done good [b] will rise to experience eternal life, and those who have continued in evil will rise to experience judgment.
>
> John 5:28, 29 (NLT)

[a]The phrase "*God's Son*" (of "*the Son of God*") does not appear in the GK text, but the context conclusively establishes the inference.

[b]The "done good" is for those who made the right decision for Christ in their life. The Bible is unequivocally clear there is none good, and certainly, there is none righteous before God.

Jesus' discussion with a rich religious ruler, is a point to not to be overlooked: there is no one good before God.

> A ruler questioned Him, saying, "Good Teacher [*Rabbi*], what shall I do to inherit eternal life?" [19]And Jesus said to him, "Why do you call Me good? No one is good except God alone. [20]"You know the commandments, 'DO NOT COMMIT ADULTERY, DO NOT MURDER, DO NOT STEAL, DO NOT BEAR FALSE WITNESS, HONOR YOUR FATHER AND MOTHER.'" [21]And he said, "All these things I have kept from *my* youth." [22]When Jesus heard *this*, He said to him, "One thing you still lack; sell all that you possess and distribute it to the poor, and you shall have treasure in heaven; and come, follow Me." [23]But when he had heard these things, he became very sad, for he was extremely rich. Luke 18:18-23

The young man only recognized Jesus only as a *good* "Rabbi," but he did not acknowledge Him as the Son of God. (He was unaware that Jesus is Messiah and the Lord.) The same today: many Jews and others genuinely acknowledge Jesus as *"a good teacher" (true)*, but they fail to recognize that **Jesus is LORD of all**.

Here is where the young ruler came up short in his dialogue with Jesus:

➢ First, the rich young ruler, Jesus is explicit that there is only One that is good. God is the only one good.

➢ Second, no one is able to obey the Law because all are sinners in Adam.[Rom. 5:12; 1 Cor. 15:22]

➢ Third, Jesus points out the man's sin of covetousness (he coveted his wealth.) The man thought he actually fulfilled or obeyed the Mosaic Law. Thus, rich young ruler was self-righteous.

➢ Fourth and most important, the young ruler failed to realize, like many others then and even today, we are all sinners deserving the wrath of God before the Lord who is a holy and righteous God.

➢ Fifth, God shall judge our sins and each one outside the redemption in Jesus Christ.

➢ Sixth, no one can be justified by works of the Law, [Gal. 2:16-21]. The Law is holy and good, but the Law is only like a mirror: the Law points out our sin but the Law does not impute righteousness. Also, the Law reveals the righteousness and holiness of God.

➢ Seven, the young ruler missed out on the greatest opportunity of his life to serve the Lord. Jesus said, "give your money to the poor (you will be rewards in Heaven);" then, Jesus invited him to *join His ministry*. Wow! (Jesus said that we cannot serve to masters. 'You cannot serve both God and money.'[Matt. 6:24 NIV])

[21]And he [*the young ruler*] said, "All these things I have kept from *my* youth [e.g., he had *obeyed the Law*]." [22]When Jesus heard *this*, He said to him, "One thing you still lack; sell all that you possess and distribute it to the poor, and you shall have treasure in heaven; and come, follow Me." [23]But when he had heard these things, he became very sad, for he was extremely rich.   Luke 18:18-23

Except for our Lord Jesus, all have sinned and come short of the glory of God.[Rom. 3:10-12, 23] Friend, this is exactly why we need a Savior (a Redeemer), to save us for the penalty of sin.[Rom. 6:23]

Many of us miss the point concerning the young rich ruler. This is especially true with the rich young ruler who was a *covetous person*, and he was *self-righteous* in his own eyes. Yet, Mark's Gospel adds that our Lord, "-looking at him, loved him, and said to him, 'You lack one thing: go, sell all that you have and give to the poor, and you will have treasure in heaven; and come, follow me.'"Mark 10:21 ESV Friend, make no doubt about it: Jesus is offering His love to you also right now. Don't miss out on greatest opportunity even in this life believe in and follow Jesus. Christ Lord will forgive you of all your sins, and praise God, Jesus will make you a citizen of Heaven right now, **today**. Yes, Jesus will make you a citizen of Heaven **today** if you will only trust Him.

Unfortunately, most of us like the rich young ruler deny we are *covetous* or *self-righteous* persons and wretched sinners. The sin of covetousness is a behavior many of us do not like to think is "true of ourselves." The truth is that we are indeed a selfish and egocentric more the we realize or are willing to admit.

There is only one way to Heaven and this is through Jesus as Lord and Savior. There are very many religious and non-religious roads, but all these roads will surely put a person in Hell forever. Salvation or redemption in Jesus Christ is a call by grace. We are saved by grace. We continue or sustained by grace. Friend, listen carefully, we shall ultimately reach the portals of Heaven by His grace and grace alone though genuine saving faith in Jesus Christ as Lord and only Redeemer.

Nevertheless, let me be very clear: Heaven is **not** attained by a *hope so*, *think so*, or *maybe so*. I tell you that you had better **KNOW SO**. If you do not know Jesus as your Lord and Savior, I assure you that you will indeed end up in Hell. Hell is paved with sincerity, which means thinking that maybe or wishing you are saved will not put you into Heaven. Jesus is explicitly clear,

> "Truly, truly, I say to you, **he who hears My word, and believes Him who sent Me, HAS ETERNAL LIFE**, and [he] does not come into judgment [condemnation], but [he] **HAS PASSED OUT OF DEATH INTO** [eternal] **LIFE**."   John 5:24

When you truly trust Christ Jesus as Lord, Jesus said that you have now already passed from death into eternal life.

This is where unfortunate the *electionists* go awry. There is indeed a definite point when a person genuine places their complete trust solely in Christ as Lord, and praise God, the person is then genuinely saved. If you do not know for certain that you have passed from death unto new life in Christ, friend, you better make sure right now. Because the Bible gives us this assurance,

If we receive the testimony [GK *marturia, witness*] of men, the testimony [*witness*] of God is greater; for the testimony [*witness*] of God is this, that He has testified [*witnessed*] concerning His Son. [10]The one who believes in the Son of God has the testimony [*witness*] in himself; the one who does not believe God has made Him a liar, because he has not believed in the testimony [*witness*] that God has given concerning His Son. [11]And the testimony [*witness*] is this, that God has given us eternal life, and this life is in His Son. [12]He who has the Son has the [*eternal*] life; he who does not have the Son of God does not have the [*eternal*] life. [13]**These things I have written to you who believe in the name of the Son of God, SO THAT YOU MAY KNOW THAT YOU HAVE ETERNAL LIFE.**   1 John 5:9-13

Friend, yes, the Lord wants you in Heaven, but you need to know for certain that you have made a definite and decisive commitment and completely trust in Jesus as Lord and Savior. John says,

Yet to all who did receive him, to those who believed in his name, he gave the right [GK *exousia, legitimate authority*] to become children of God— children born not of natural descent, nor of human decision or a husband's will, but born of God.   John 1:12, 13 (NIV)

If you are not sure, pray right now and declare to the Lord you want to be sure. (If you have doubts or even disbelief, the Lord understands. Share you doubts or disbelief, He will make Himself known to you very plainly.) Below is a prayer you can pray if you desire to genuinely receive Christ as Lord and Savior, and if you truly do, friend, He will wonderfully change your life for the better and make you a citizen of Heaven **TODAY**.

> *Tell the Lord you are a sinner and unable to save yourself from your sin. Then, tell Him you believe with your whole heart and mind Jesus died for your sins, buried, and arose from dead on the third day. (If you have doubts, be honest and tell Him of your doubts; He will understand.) Right now confess that you are a sinner and you are asking Him to forgive you of your sins. Declare that you believe in Jesus as your Lord and Savior, and you want to truly receive Jesus as the Lord of your life and Redeemer who is coming again. The Lord will save you right now.*

Here is God's promise to you:

⁹Because if you confess with your mouth that Jesus is Lord and believe in your heart that God raised him from the dead, you will be saved. ¹⁰For with the heart one believes and thus has righteousness and with the mouth one confesses and thus has salvation. ¹¹For the scripture says, *"Everyone who believes in him will not be put to shame."*ᶜ ¹²For there is no distinction between the Jew and the Greek, for the same Lord is Lord of all, who richly blesses all who call on him. ¹³For *everyone who calls on the name of the Lord will be saved.*   Rom. 10:9-13 (NET)

ᶜNote: the italics by the NET is used to alert the read that the text is a quotation from the OT.

Friend, this is a promise that comes from God who cannot lie.[Titus 1:2; Heb. 6:17-20] Hallelujah! It is true; believe on the Lord Jesus and you shall be saved.[Acts 16 31]

Conclusion

The raising of Lazarus from the dead (after he had been dead four days and his body was in process of rotting) is indeed an incredible and amazing miracle. Today, the false prophets, the deceiving charlatans, and the lying fake healers claim even greater miracles. But my friend, only the Life-Giver Himself, the Lord our God, He is the only One that can give life to a rotting corpse. Therefore, only the Lord our God can give eternal life. If you want eternal life in Heaven, this eternal life is only in Jesus Christ as your personal Lord and Savior. Friend, do not mock it. Hell is real, and there are no atheists in Hell. Do read me? There are no atheists in Hell. Those in Hell know the Gospel is true. Friend, it is too late for them, but it is not too late for you if only you will believe and receive Jesus right now. At death, the atheist realizes Hell is real, but there is no turning back. It is too late!

There is **no** religious institution that can give anyone eternal life. There is **no** church or place of worship that can give eternal life. There is **no** person on the face of this earth that can give you an eternal life and a home in Heaven. If you are trusting anything other than Jesus Christ as Lord to go to Heaven, I am sorry and dread telling you but you are on the road to Hell. Furthermore, it is not Jesus plus the person's so-called *good works*. Friend it is all by Jesus' grace and grace alone, [Rom. 11:6].

If you end up in Hell, it is your own disbelief that will surely put you in Hell. Jesus came to save you from the penalty of sin. Jesus did not come to condemn you. Do not be deceived. Friend, you will surely die in your sin without Jesus as your Lord and Savior, [John 8:24].

Jesus Christ is the only one that is able to save you. There is no other name given whereby we may be saved and redeemed from our sin.[Acts 4:12] Sincerity will not get you into Heaven! But I tell you right now that sincerity will surely place you into Hell without Jesus Christ as your personal Lord and Savior.

The raising of Lazarus who had been dead for four days is irrefutable evidence that Jesus is the Christ, the Son of the living God.[Matt. 16:16] Again, there is no other name given under Heaven whereby we must be saved.

If you will by faith reach out to the Lord, repent of your sins, and place your complete trust in Jesus Christ and receive Him as your Lord and Savior, God's Word declares that He will save you unto the uttermost. God will save you all the way into Heaven itself and even make you a citizen of Heaven right now, **today**.

> [24]And He, because of His remaining throughout the age [forever], has the inviolable [perpetual] priesthood, [25]from where also He is able to save [anyone] to the very end [to uttermost][d], those coming through Him to God—ever living to make intercession for them. [26]For also such a Chief Priest was fitting for us—holy, innocent, undefiled, separate from the sinners [sinless], and having become higher than the heavens, [27]who has no daily necessity, as the chief priests, to first offer up sacrifice for *his* own sins, then for those of the people; for this He [Jesus] did once, having offered up Himself [for our sins].   Heb. 7:24-27 (LSV)
>
> [d]"The very end" [v 25], is the GK word *panteles*. Hence, the Lord Jesus saves to the *uttermost*. He will save us all the way *to the end* even into Heaven itself. So, "*very end*" is indeed an excellent translation. The word simply means "*to full completion*."

Footnotes:

1. "Putting the nails in your coffin" means to [fail] to take actions or [fail] to make decisions that will ultimately lead to someone's or something's downfall or failure. (Google search.)

CHAPTER 16

Where did Lazarus go at death?

Jesus answered and said to them, "Are you not therefore mistaken, because you do not know the Scriptures nor the power of God? [25]"For when they rise from the dead, they neither marry nor are given in marriage, but are like angels in heaven. [26]"But concerning the dead, that they rise, have you not read in the book of Moses, in the *burning* bush *passage*, how God spoke to him, saying, 'I *am* the God of Abraham, the God of Isaac, and the God of Jacob'? [27]"He is not the God of the dead, but the God of the living. You are therefore greatly mistaken."

Mark 12:24-27 (NKJ)

Introduction

This chapter has been added due to questions that may emerge from the time-period of the death of Lazarus but before Jesus raises Lazarus' body from the dead. "Where was Lazarus while his body laid in the tomb?" This discussion will be hard to overcome for some that are very "*steeped in*" ecclesiastical doctrine or ecclesiastical tradition of the elders. False tradition can mislead or blind any of us from the truth of God's Word. Tradition is much harder to overcome than many of us are willing to admit. So, it is easier to simply deny our prejudices and blind spots rather than acknowledge them.

The natural question that may arise in the mind of some, though the thought is not always verbally asked is, "Where did Lazarus go once he died and his body was put into the tomb?" Was Lazarus still in existence once his body died, or did Lazarus ceased to exist once his body died? A similar question some may asked, "What constitutes the makeup of mankind?" (What constitutes or distinguishes human from angels or even animals)? Does a person exist only in a body, or does a person continue to exist even after the body dies? Given the immaturity and lack of insight into God's Word today by some, these issues must be addressed. Please stay focused as we probe these questions.

However, this is much more than immaturity or lack of insight to God's Word when considering such questions as noted above. Church tradition has unfortunately *muddied the water* and plays a very big role in influencing the minds of many people. In addition, the inroads of the cults and those on the fringes of orthodoxy have had major influences today on the saints in Christ. Others are *spiritually bankrupt* in Scripture and void of any sound theological reading or training. These are people that are analogous to the "barnstorming.[1]" Those who fly by "barnstorming" do not use "the *instrument panel*" in flying a plane. This is analogous to some people behind the pulpit and many among the electronic church. They fly by *"the seat of the pants,"* and they are likely to spiritually crash.

These are people who had little or no training in the Word of God. Please hear me! A person does not have to go to seminary, Bible College, or Bible Institute to prepare for the ministry. Charles Spurgeon did not have any traditional seminary training as far as I know, but Spurgeon was a well-read man. He vigorously spent long hours in the study of the Faith in the Scriptures and reading many theological works. Unfortunately, some who are in the ministry nowadays do not pattern themselves after Spurgeon, but many follow the carnal ways of the natural man.

Therefore, there are many today that have given themselves over to following the world. Some are foolishly unaware of the *three strikes law* that wars against the saints:

➢ The *world influence-*

➢ The deception of the *carnal nature-*

➢ Satan and the *evil forces* that <u>blind</u> and *bind* people from the truth of God's Word.

Therefore, let us give heed to the apostle Peter's warning,

> And God will exalt you in due time, if you humble yourselves under his mighty hand by casting all your cares on him because he cares for you. Be sober and alert. Your enemy the devil, like a roaring lion, is on the prowl looking for someone to devour.   1 Peter 5:6-8 (NET)

A. Where was Lazarus after his body died?

You might think to yourself, "Of course, Lazarus was dead!" Lazarus' body was in the grave four days, true? Martha said to Jesus when He asked to roll the stone from the grave of Lazarus,

> Jesus said, "Remove the stone." Martha, the sister of the deceased, said
> to Him, "Lord, by this time there will be a stench, for he has been *dead*
> four days."   John 11:39

Some *"electronic preachers"* (unbelievably) deny Lazarus was dead. It is hard to believe, but there are a few *electronic preachers* that do not think Lazarus was dead. In denying Lazarus was dead, they have joined the ranks among the cults and unbelievers. This is because they imagine, "One must have faith to be healed." What a blatant insult the Scriptures and the discreating of marvelous miracle of Jesus in raising Lazarus from the dead.

Mary Baker Eddy, the founder of the Christian Science Religion, denied the raising Lazarus from the dead. She denied Lazarus was ready dead. At any rate, Christian Science is neither Christian nor Science. It is a cult!

However, there are others that believe Lazarus was not in Heaven after he died. These are alleged Christians that maintain that Lazarus and the rest of the believers at death were in a compartment for the redeemed in Hades. Such groups allege that *"Abraham's bosom"* is supposedly part of or what they characterize as *"Paradise"* which they allege further that this is part Hades. The other compartment of Hades is a place of suffering, awaiting the final judgment when the unsaved shall be cast in the Lake of Fire.^{Matt. 10:28; Rev. 20:10ff} The idea that the redeemed are in Hades (not Heaven before resurrection of Jesus Christ) is a monstrous form of eisegesis. This kind of thinking follows some of the erroneous hyper-dispensationalists.

There are two things that helped to faulter this erroneous notion of the OT redeemed waiting in Hades. There is a text in Scripture in part (not the whole verse) particularly in the Byzantine Greek text or also known as the Majority text. The other influence is hyper-dispensationalism (mentioned above) and all those that may "tag alone with ecclesiastical tradition."

1. The text is John 3:13

Here is the Scripture as compared to several other translation of the text.

KJV	NAS	NET	NIV
And no man hath ascended up to heaven, but he that came down from heaven, *even* **the Son of man which is in heaven**.	"No one has ascended into heaven, but He who descended from heaven: the Son of Man."	No one has ascended into heaven except the one who descended from heaven — the Son of Man.	No one has ever gone into heaven except the one who came from heaven—the Son of Man.

The phrase *"even the Son of man which is in heaven"* is not strongly supported by older GK texts. In addition, the phrase brings into question the inner-workings with the blessed Trinity and the persons within Godhead. The phrase (*even the Son of man which is in heaven*) does not harmonize with the rest of the Scripture, and for this reason, this is sufficient basis to denying the authenticity of the phrase.

The tense must be examined and carefully read and thought through: 'No **one has ascended into heaven,** but **He who descended from heaven**: the Son of Man.'[v 13] (You should not attempt to dissect the verse. These two clauses must be examined or seen interlinked together since each clause supplement each other.)

Jesus is not saying no one has ascended to Heaven. So, please get it right! This is a declaration concerning Christ Himself. Therefore, the declaration is a comparative of Christ *ascending* and His *descending* from Heaven Himself. There is no denial of others who had already ascended to Heaven alive such Enoch or Elijah as noted below. Neither is there denial of the believer going immediate to Heaven upon the death in the OT, which Jesus clearly declares in Luke 16:22. Jesus is very explicit that the Lord God is *the God of the living*. Luke 20:38 There is nothing implied that "Abraham's bosom" was part of Hades.

The account of the poor man at death (was also named Lazarus) is an actual event in the life of a believer and is literally true. Also, keep in mind, the account is among the list of other parables in Luke 15 and 16. (Yet, the account in Luke 16:19-31 is not called a parable.) However, there are metaphors being used here in Luke 15 and 16. So my friend, careful that you do not take every word literally. Furthermore, even if Luke 16:19-31 is a parable, a parable does not mean the event was a story and untrue event. Parables can be the true account or historically genuine but in story narrative.

First and foremost, we must understand that God is One! There is no other God but the Lord our God.

"Hear, O Israel! The LORD is our God, the LORD is one! You shall love the LORD your God with all your heart and with all your soul and with all your might."   Deut. 6:4, 5

"Declare and set forth *your case*; Indeed, let them consult together. Who has announced this from of old? Who has long since declared it? Is it not I, the LORD? And there is no other God besides Me, A righteous God and a Savior; There is none except Me. Turn to Me and be saved, all the ends of the earth; For I am God, and there is no other."

Isa. 45:21, 22

So, while many people worship *a god*, many people are **not** worshipping the Lord. *God* is not the Creator's name; His name is the **Lord** or **I AM** [Ex. 3:13-15] forever. As Jesus told the Samaritan woman, the same applies to many people in the world today. Jesus said to the woman, 'You Samaritans worship what you do not know.' [John. 4:22 NIV]

God is indeed omnipresent. Yet, God is omnipresent through the Holy Spirit. David said,

Where can I go from **Your Spirit**? Or where can I flee from Your **presence**? [8]If I ascend into heaven, You *are* **there**; If I make my bed in hell [HEB *sheol, an unseen world*]a, behold, You *are* **there**. [9]*If* I take the wings of the morning, *And* dwell in the uttermost parts of the sea, [10]Even there Your hand shall lead me, And Your right hand shall hold me. [11]If I say, "Surely the darkness shall fall on me," Even the night shall be light about me; [12]Indeed, the darkness shall not hide from You, But the night shines as the day; The darkness and the light *are* both alike *to You*. Psa. 139:7-12 (NKJ)

aThe HEB is *Sheol* is not "*Hell*." *Sheol* has a very wide range of meanings in the HEB Scriptures. So, careful, this is an old ENG translation. The word hell does carry the same meaning of a "literal Hell" then or today, let us avoid pagan background influences.

God is omnipresent. So, the Father and Son are omnipresent **through the Holy Spirit**. The Father and Son need not be omnipresent themselves. There is no need for the Father and the Son to be omnipresent since "God is One." The blessed Trinity share in only **One essence of being**. Yet, there are three persons within the Trinity of God: the Father, the Son, and the Holy Spirit.

Therefore, there is indeed a legitimate cause to question the last clause [John 3:13 KJV]: '*even* the Son of man which is in heaven.'[v 13b] Christ can be on earth and at same time in Heaven by the Holy Spirit.

Still, the verse [v13] is indeed very difficult as you examine the verse as a unit or a single thought.

> "No one has **ascended into heaven**, but **He who descended from heaven**: the Son of Man." John 3:13

Paul refers to the complete makeup of mankind as: body, soul, and spirit.[1] Thess. 5:23 (*We shall discuss what constitute mankind's being or what is the total makeup of mankind a little later.*) As noted above, the Lord is referring to Himself.[John 3:13] Jesus is **not** comparing Himself with anyone else. The parallel or the comparison of "ascended and descended" in the tense is one single action. The action centers in Christ Himself. So then, Enoch was translated into Heaven without experiencing death, and the prophet Elijah went to Heaven in a whirlwind without dying.Gen. 5:24; 2 Kings 2:11, 12 Moses and Elijah appeared to Jesus during His transfiguration.Matt. 17 Moses' appearance with Elijah, but Moses' body was buried by God.Duet. 34:5-7 So, where did Moses come from to be at the transfiguration? Elijah came from Heaven for transfiguration of Jesus.

Pay attention and think with me. Are we going say that Elijah went directly from Heaven, but Moses came from Hades? To say Elijah came from Heaven but Moses came from Hades is nonsense. No! Elijah and Moses both came from Heaven. (This alone proves the error of the idiotic notion that OT saints went in Hades.) Scriptures declares that all the saints are in Heaven.2 Cor. 5:8 or Phi. 1:21-23 The promises Paul declares do not belong exclusively to NT saints. The promise is to all saints of all dispensations. Jesus is very clear, and His statement stands for all dispensations,

> [29]Jesus answered and said to them, "You are mistaken, not knowing the Scriptures nor the power of God. [30]For in the resurrection they neither marry nor are given in marriage, but are like angels of God in heaven. [31]But concerning the resurrection of the dead, have you not read what was spoken to you by God, saying, [32]'I am the God of Abraham, the God of Isaac, and the God of Jacob'? God is not the God of the dead, but [*He is the God*] of the living." [33]And when the multitudes heard *this,* they were astonished at His teaching. Matt. 22:29-34 (NKJ)

Concerning the saints in Heaven after they die, Jesus was abundantly clear that He saw Abraham in Heaven. (Jesus did not see Abraham in Hades, *Abraham bosom.*) But if you follow the tradition of Dispensationalism you are going to have to say that the father faith, Abraham, went to Hades and not Heaven? This is as bad as the cults that say Abraham was non-existent after he dies. Our Lord saw Abraham in Heaven.

Listen to me, Abraham was very much alive when his body died. Upon his death, Abraham went to his people, the redeemed.

> "Then Abraham *yielded* the spirit, and died in a good age, an olde man, and of great *years*, and was **gathered to his people**." Gen. 25:8 (GNV)

Where did Abraham and Sarah go after they each died? The Bible says, Abraham, as well as Sarah, '**was gathered to his people**.'[Gen. 25:8] Where were Abraham and Sarah at death: in Heaven and in Hades? They were in Heaven! Jesus said of Abraham,

> Your father Abraham was overjoyed that he would see my day. **HE SAW IT AND WAS HAPPY**." [57]"You aren't even 50 years old!" the Jewish opposition replied. "**HOW CAN YOU SAY THAT YOU HAVE SEEN ABRAHAM**?" [58]"I assure you," Jesus replied, "before Abraham was, I AM." [59]So they **picked up stones**[b] **to throw at him**, but Jesus hid himself and left the temple.   John 8:56-59 (CEB)

> [b]When Jesus uses the phrase '**I AM**' the Jews instinctively knew Yehoshua was identifying Himself as the Lord God.[Ex. 3:13-15] Thus, we read, So, they **PICKED UP STONES TO THROW AT HIM** since Jesus uses the sacred Name **I AM** concerning Himself. "Jesus hid Himself and went out of the temple, **going through the midst of them, and so passed by**."[v59 NKJ]

This is one of the times angels probably assisted Jesus in getting away. The time was not yet for our Lord to completely reveal Himself. He did not use His intrinsic Divine power. So then, angels likely intervened since Christ's identity was to remain concealed at this time. Jesus kept His true identity hidden. So, He uses His angels.

2. Hyper-dispensationalism

Some dispensationalists have put forth the notion that there were two parts to Hades particularly before Jesus Chrisrt's resurrection. They allege that the saints were freed from Hades after Jesus arose. There is absolutely **no** biblical basis for the conjecture that Abraham's bosom or Paradise was ever part of Hades or that Abraham's bosom was part of Hades. Such notion is pagan not biblical. Unfortunately, many have swallowed this conjecture that Abraham's bosom was part of Hades. Listen, there is no warrant or inference to such a notion. This shows how strong tradition can interfere in sound biblical exegesis. Tradition just seems to override the explicit teaching of Scripture.

Yet, in the lesson of the poor man dying [Luke 16:19ff]: unregenerate cannot see the redeemed, and the redeemed cannot see the unregenerate. The expression '- he lifted up his eyes and **saw Abraham** afar off, and [*saw*] **Lazarus in his bosom**.' [Luke 16:23 NKJ] is metaphoric language. The event is a portrait of the poor man is comforted in Heaven, but the poor man was not literally lying on Abraham's bosom in Hades is alleging like holding a baby. Any Orthodox Jew knows the difference between literal and figurative language. If you are a Pastor or teacher of God's Word and you do not know the difference between the literal and figurative language, shame, shame on you!

This is like Solomon said, "- the dead know nothing."[Ecc. 9:5] He does mean a person is nonexistent at death. (The cults say we are nonexistent at death.) Solomon is referring the body. You can think what you want about the redeemed at death, but I am telling you that you had better be careful what you say and think. We shall give account not only of the words and deeds we did (good or bad), but we shall be held accountable for every idle word spoke and even the things we harbored in our hearts and minds.[Rom. 2:16; Rev. 2:22] If you do not fear God's examination, then you are a fool!

One text used by dispensationalists to allege Jesus took Paradise or Abraham' bosom to Heaven is Eph. 4:8-11. The dispensationalist's teaching is based upon misreading of the text in Eph. 4. It is alleged that when Christ arose from the dead and ascended to Heaven He liberated those held in Hades. Here is the text:

KJV	GNV	NET	NAS
Wherefore he saith, When he ascended up on high, **he led captivity captive,** and gave gifts unto men. [9](Now that he ascended, what is it but that he also descended first into the lower parts of the earth? [10]He that descended is the same also that ascended up far above all heavens, that he might fill all things.) [11]And he gave some, apostles; and some, prophets; and some, evangelists; and some, pastors and teachers.	*Wherefore* he saith, *When* he *ascended upon high,* **he led** *captivity captured,* and *gave* gifts *unto* men. [9](*Now,* in that *he* ascended, what is it but that he had also descended first into the lowest *partes* of the earth? [10]He that descended, is *even* the same that ascended, *far above* all *heavens,* that *he* might fill all things) [11]*He* therefore gave some to be Apostles, and some Prophets, and some *Evangelists,* and some *Pastors,* and Teachers	Therefore it says, "When he ascended on high HE **CAPTURED** **CAPTIVES**; he gave gifts to men." [9]Now what is the meaning of "he ascended," except that he also descended to the lower regions, namely, the earth? [10]He, the very one who descended, is also the one who ascended above all the heavens, in order to fill all things. [11]It was he who gave some as apostles, some as prophets, some as evangelists, and some as pastors and teachers.	Therefore it says, "WHEN HE ASCENDED ON HIGH, **HE LED CAPTIVE A HOST OF CAPTIVES**, AND HE GAVE GIFTS TO MEN." [5](Now this *expression,* "He ascended," what does it mean except that He also had descended into the lower parts of the earth? [10]He who descended is Himself also He who ascended far above all the heavens, so that He might fill all things.) [11]And He gave some *as* apostles, and some *as* prophets, and some *as* evangelists, and some *as* pastors and teachers.

Note: in GNV only the spelling is updated, but no words are changed.

The phrase in Eph. 4:8 GNV is very clear (even though it is over 500 years old), '*When* he *ascended upon high,* **he led** *captivity captured,* and *gave* gifts *unto* men' as well in the other three versions. People are **not** being liberated; people have been **captured**. This declaration of victory by the army is under the Lord. The text is a translation of Psa. 68:18, 19. Paul is likely paraphrasing Psa. 68:18, 19 (but *Psa. 67:19* in Septuagint, the GK OT, LXX.)

The King, which is the Lord, is the victor. As the Victor of war, the King shares the booty by giving gifts to His men of war. So, this is a triumph capturing the enemy and sharing the spoils or plunders of the victory among the King's faithful troops.

Let us refocus on the issue once a person dies-

I have already established that saints go directly to Heaven upon death. By the way, this is one of reasons believers bury the dead and do not cremate the body. The body is part of the redemption.[Rom. 8:23] Sadly, many Christians are cremating the bodies of loved-one simply because it is cheap. Well, if you chose to cremate a loved-one's body that my friend is on you.

As to the phrase or the words "Abraham's bosom" or "Paradise," these are words or phrases that refer to Heaven and not a compartment in Hades. The apostle Paul was explicit that he went to Heaven likely when he was stoned, but apparently, Paul was revived after the stoning. (This occurred probably at Lystra, Acts 14:19, but Paul was uncertain whether he was in his body or out of the body.)

> And I know that this man (whether in the body or apart from the body I do not know, God knows) was **caught up into PARADISE** and **HEARD THINGS TOO SACRED TO BE PUT INTO WORDS, THINGS THAT A PERSON IS NOT PERMITTED TO SPEAK**.
>
> 2 Cor. 12:3, 4 (NET)

There is a very important observation to note here in the above verses. No one has ever gone to Heaven and returned except the apostles Paul and John. Neither Paul nor John were permitted to reveal anything about Heaven. So, all those individuals that have claimed to have gone to Heaven or even Hell and came back to tell us are one of three possibilities: they are either: *spiritually deluded*; or they are *in grievous error*; or they are *bold face liars*!

Paul is explicitly referring to Heaven as "Paradise" and not Hades. Those given over to tradition will says that "Paradise" was taking up to Heaven when Jesus ascended. "Friend, get real!" I wonder from which "Cracker Box Candy [2]" someone got this idea?

Jesus told the thief on the cross who believed in Him,

> And Jesus said to him, "I tell you the truth, today you will be with me in **PARADISE**."
>
> Luke 23:43 (NET)

Jesus is not referring to Hades. My friend, Jesus is definitely referring to Heaven. Of course, the cults are quick to pervert the Scripture to their own destruction. As the apostle Peter brilliantly describes many in our day as given by the NAS,

> Therefore, beloved, since you look for these things, be diligent to be found by Him in peace, spotless and blameless, [15]and regard the patience of our Lord *as* salvation; just as also our beloved brother Paul,

according to the wisdom given him, wrote to you, [16]as also in all *his* letters, speaking in them of these things, in which are some things hard to understand, which the untaught and unstable distort, as *they do* also the rest of the Scriptures, to their own destruction. [17]You therefore, beloved, knowing this beforehand, be on your guard so that you are not carried away by the error of unprincipled men and fall from your own steadfastness, [18]but grow in the grace and knowledge of our Lord and Savior Jesus Christ. To Him *be* the glory, both now and to the day of eternity. Amen.   2 Peter 3:14-18

Therefore, the Scripture definitely declares that all believers go to Heaven upon death. The promise of 2 Cor. 5:8 applies to all dispensations. So, while Lazarus died during the Old Covenant and under the Mosaic Economy, he went directly to Heaven when his body died. Whether or not he was permitted to recall things he saw and heard in Heaven, Scripture is silent. But from Paul words, he said,

> [*I*] was caught up into paradise and heard things too sacred to be put into words, **things that a person is NOT PERMITTED TO SPEAK**.
>   2 Cor. 12:3 (NET)

Therefore, be careful, do not give into those who claimed to have gone to Heaven or even Hell and came back to tell us about it. Whether sincere or in pretense, they have been deceived. Do not believe them.

B. Humankind consists of corporeal and non-corporeal elements

Where was Lazarus the person when his body laid in the tomb? This raises the question of what then constitutes the elements of humankind? That is to say, are humans *dichotomous* or *trichotomous*? These are the only two biblical or orthodox positions. The cults and many unbelievers do not believe human beings possess a soul or soul/spirit. So, when a person dies, they cease to exist according many cults and those that reject God's Word.

Just so you know, I lean towards the *trichotomous position* though slightly modified. However, man is not a soul or just a person in a live body, but human beings possess a soul (soul/spirit) which dwells within the body. Scripture does refer to mankind as "a soul" (meaning he/she is a person) in distinguishing him from the animal kingdom.

The animal kingdom has life if they are alive, but God did not breathe into animals *the breath of life*. So, animals do not possess non-corporeal element; that is, animals do not possess a soul or soul/spirit. The Bible teaches that God breathed into Adam, and Adam became a "living soul." (By the way, one of the HEB words for man is literally, '*adam*': meaning man or mankind). The other HEB word is '*ish*' meaning a married man, an adult male, or for example, "a man of God (*ish Elohim*)."

> And the LORD God formed man ['*adam*'] of the dust of the ground, and breathed into his nostrils the breath of life; and man became a living soul.^c   Gen. 2:7 (WBT)

> ^cThe HEB word for "soul" is "*nephesh*" (GK *psuche*). Be very careful here: yes, *nephesh* does imply *a living being*, but when God breathed in Adam, he also became a *living soul*. Mankind possesses a soul or soul/spirit. Mankind possess a soul (which is the nonmaterial or non-corporeal of his makeup). This distinguishes mankind from all other living things in creation, even angels are not spoken of as possessing a soul or soul/spirit. So, only man possesses a soul (or soul/spirit.)

The Bible is very, very explicit that the saints will enter Heaven when they die.[2 Cor. 5:8; Phi. 1:22f] The Lord Jesus declares this promise,

> '- everyone who lives and believes in me **SHALL NEVER DIE**."
>   John 11:26 (ESV)

The cults and unbelievers declare that a person no longer exists at death. Those with such thinking are in very grievous error. Again, Jesus said,

> '- everyone who lives and believes in me **SHALL NEVER DIE**."
>   John 11:26 (ESV)

> "Most assuredly, I say to you, he who hears My word and believes in Him who sent Me **HAS EVERLASTING LIFE**, and shall not come into judgment, but [*he*] has **PASSED FROM DEATH INTO** [*eternal*] **LIFE**.   John 5:24 (NKJ)

> ⁴⁷Truly, truly, I say to you, he believing in me **has eternal life**. (v 47)

> ⁵⁰This is the bread which coming down from heaven, that whoever should eat of it, and he **should not die**. ⁵¹I am the living bread which having come down from heaven: if any one eat of this bread, **he shall live forever**: and also the bread which I shall give is my flesh, which I shall give for the life of the world.   John 6:47, 50, 51 (SLT)

The cults like Seventh Day Adventist and JWs are notorious liars as we noted above, such groups which the apostle Peter rebukes [2 Peter 3:14-18]. The cults and other unregenerate distort the Word of God to their own destruction. If you know or associate with such groups, friend, run hard and fast and avoid them like a plague lest you become ensnared with them.

Finally, Jesus warns the unbelievers that death does not end all.

> Do not be afraid of those who kill the body but cannot kill the soul. Rather, be afraid of the One who can destroy both soul and body in hell.[d]   Matt. 10:28 (NIV)

> [d]The word translated "hell" is the GK word "geenna." Geenna is the final abode of the unregenerate, the Lake of Fire.[see Rev. 20:10-15] The word hell has many meaning, but in this connect that Jesus is referring to is the eternal wrath of God upon the unsaved without Christ.

In case you miss the point here, Jesus warns that a person consists of a **body** and **soul**, and the body and soul will be cast into *geenna*, which is the Lake of Fire. This again shows that mankind possesses two elements. Mankind possesses a *material aspect* which is tangible in this present world, the *body*. Humankind also possesses a *nonmaterial aspect* which is intangible to this world. Intangible, the *soul* or *soul/spirit* is not a physical body. Jesus said, '- for a spirit does not have flesh and bones as you see I have.'[Luke 24:39]

Wait, don't rush to get ahead of me! So, what constitutes the makeup of all humankind. Is man a *dichotomous* or a *trichotomous*? That is, is a person consisting of only a *body* and *soul*, which is a *dichotomous*? Or is a human a *trichotomous* consisting of having a body, soul, and spirit?

The difficulty with the *dichotomous* is that they maintain the words *soul* and *spirit* are <u>always</u> interchangeable. Hence, *soul* and *spirit* mean the same thing. First, these two words "*soul* and *spirit*" do not always mean the same thing when compared in Scripture. Also, in a rare text in Ecclesiastes man possesses a spirit, but Solomon seems to question whether animals' spirit go at death," (HEB *ruwach*, GK *pneuma*.)

> Who really knows if the human spirit [ruwach] ascends upward, and the animal's spirit[e] [ruwach] descends into the earth?   Eccl. 3:21 (NET)

> [e]The above text is the only place in Scripture where *spirit* (HEB *ruwach*, GK *pneuma*) is used of humans and animals. So, careful with your conjectures.

Jesus in Matt. 10:28 declares unquestionably that all humankind possesses a body and a soul. Also, what is interesting is that the Bible clearly declares that the soul is divisible into a soul and spirit.

> For the word of God is living and active and sharper than any two-edged sword, and piercing as far as the **division of soul and spirit**, of both joints and marrow, and able to judge the thoughts and intentions of the heart. Heb. 4:12

When Paul declares our complete salvation in Christ, he says,

> Now may the God of peace himself make you **completely holy** and may your **spirit** and **soul** and **body** be kept **entirely blameless** at the coming of our Lord Jesus Christ. 1 Thess. 5:23 (NET)

Therefore, I think it is reasonable to conclude that the _soul_ and _spirit_ of man are the "non-corporeal" elements. That is, the *spirit* and *soul* do not consist of a material substance like that of the human body. The *spirit* and *souls* are made of a substance but the substance is "non-corporeal" and created by God. Jesus declares two elements: body and soul. The Hebrews writer declares the soul and spirit somehow together, but the soul and spirit is divisible.

I hesitate to use "_spirit_" here for many reasons. Nevertheless, the non-corporeal of mankind has substance, but who can describe that substance? I warn you, do not think of the non-corporeal solely as "spirit," and then, try to compare the *spirit* of man analogous to "the Spirit" of God such as 'God is Spirit.'[John 4:24] These two, "the *spirit within man*" and "the *Spirit of God*" are incomparable! The spirit man and the Spirit of God are not the same. So, do not attempt to parallel them. The spirit of man and the Spirit of God are not the same. The spirit of man and the Spirit of God do have the same meaning. God's substance is eternal, everlasting, and without beginning or end. On the other hand, man's "_spirit_" is of this creation, finite, and only exists and is sustained by the Creator.

However, *trichotomous* go a little too far as well. Trichotomous often fails to recognize the unity of the nonmaterial aspect of a person. Still, there is a definite division according to Heb. 4:12 between the nonmaterial aspect of the soul and spirit. Yet, admittedly, the explanation or the description is not easily delineated as some may allege.

In addition, Jesus is very clear; He only notes two aspects that make up humans: body and soul.[Matt. 10:28] Therefore, it seems logical to say, "Yes, humankind is a *trichotomous*:" he possesses a body, a soul, and a spirit.[1 Thess. 5:23] Yet, man is made up of only two aspects or it seems to me: "corporeal and non-corporeal elements."[Matt. 10:28]

Therefore, when an unsaved person dies, he goes Hades to await the judgment in soul/spirit.[Luke 16:22f] If he/she is unregenerate (unsaved), he/she will be Judged when their body/soul/spirit are united. Then each person shall stand before the Lord.^{Rev. 20:10ff} If the person is redeemed in Christ, then, they go to Heaven in their soul/spirit. However, the body/soul/spirit will be united either at the rapture or when the Lord units the body/soul/spirit.[1 Cor. 15:51ff]

As final exhortation and closure to this section, let us be careful to keep in the forefront of our minds that we do **not** worship a *generic* Creator called "*God.*" We worship the Lord! The Lord God is one, and there is no other God but Him. Yes, the Lord God is one, but He is in three persons: the Father, the Son, and the Holy Spirit.[Matt. 28:18-20] The Trinity of God is co-equal, co-eternal, and one in essence and being.

So, those who lean, in one form or another to the *ubiquity*[3] of Christ, careful that you neither compromise the humanity of our Lord nor back-in into "*Tritheism.*" Conversely, others ought to watch out in teaching that the Father has *a difference essence of being* than that of the Son and the Holy Spirit. Also, careful if you allege that the Son and the Holy Spirit were *begotten* by the Father; lest you find yourself stepping into "*Unitarianism.*"

C. The Lord God is the God of the living

The notion that the dead are <u>non-existent</u> according to the cults and according to the endless number of unbelievers ought to raise the wrath of the saints. Yet, the saints are rarely speaking out against the false notions. What a *crying shame.*

The Seventh Day Adventists and JWs allege the person is "*<u>asleep</u>*" at death. I suppose they think that using "*<u>soul sleep</u>*" that this somehow *softens* their teaching on the departed dead. Pay attention, the cults don't believe that the dead are somehow "*the soul is asleep.*" The idea of "soul sleep" after a person dies is a **blatant** and **deliberate outright lie** by such cults!

The Seven Day Adventists and other cults like the JWs do **not** even believe mankind possesses a nonmaterial aspect such as a soul. To them, the spirit means *breath* and *soul* just means a person has *life* (alive.) At death, the person is nonexistent according to such cults. So, when a person dies according to the Seventh Day Adventists and the JWs, the person vanishes. At death, the person is gone. The person at death does not exist anymore.

The dead only exist in the mind of *their God.* That is, the person only exists in the memory of God, but the person that dies no longer exist. (You got it: *soul sleep* means you only exist in the mind of God.) The JWs and others cults also endorse or hold to such anti-biblical and evil doctrines. Actually, the Seventh Day Adventists continued that doctrine, the same doctrine, which they derived from the JWs. Hence, according to such cults, no one exists after they die. The above groups are in full agreement with the atheist. How weird is that?

Such above groups have no immediate hope at death of their loved-one. At death, their loved-one no longer exists. The dead only remain in memory of God, and God will recreate them again in final resurrection. This even includes the so-called saved and the lost in their so-called theology. Consequently, according such cults, a person in order to exist must have a body. There is no soul, and there is no spirit. It is certain the atheists have no hope beyond the grave as well. Sadly, the churches are being devoured by such cults and the carnal imagination unregenerate.

Therefore, it is most important that we once again note the words of our Lord to the Sadducees who did not believe the Bible or believe in eternal life. The Sadducees did not believe even in the resurrection or life after death. Like the cults, there is no life once a person dies.

> Jesus replied, "Are you not in error because **you do NOT KNOW THE SCRIPTURES** or [*you do not know*] **THE POWER OF GOD**? [25]When the dead rise [*a reference to the body*], they will neither marry nor be given in marriage; [*but*] they will be like the angels in heaven. [26]Now about the dead rising [*the body*— have you not read in the Book of Moses, in the account of the burning bush, how God said to him, '**I am the God of Abraham, the God of Isaac, and the God of Jacob**'? [27]He is not the God of the dead, but [*He is the God*] **OF THE LIVING**. You are badly mistaken!"   Mark 12:24-27 (NIV)

Here is a little tidbit and kicker to boot. The discussion begins in Matt. 22:23 through 46. In the section with the Sadducees,[Mark 12:18-27] the Sadducees are much like liberals today except that the Sadducees did not believe in life after death. Yet, the Sadducees claim to believe the Torah, the Law which is the five books of Moses, Genesis through Deuteronomy. Ironically, the Sadducees use the question whose wife will she be in the resurrection among the seven brothers. (To the Sadducees, there is no resurrection: so, when a person dies, life is gone forever.)

Jesus use the burning bush incident with Moses [Exodus 3:1-15] to demonstrate that the believers are alive and well even after the body is dead. The Sadducees missed this point which is clearly declared in the Torah.

> [26]"But concerning the dead, that they rise, have you not read in the book[s] of Moses, in the *burning* bush *passage,* how God spoke to him, saying, 'I *am* the God of Abraham, the God of Isaac, and the God of

Jacob'? [27]He is not the God of the dead, but **the God of the living.** You
are therefore greatly mistaken." Mark 12:26, 27 (NKJ)

So, do not miss the humor here. Let me clarify the pun! Sadducees assume
that there is nothing concerning *the afterlife* in the Torah. Jesus not only
declares there will be a resurrection of the body yet to come, but for now, any
believer who dies goes to Heaven. For Jesus said,

> "**'I *am* the God of Abraham, the God of Isaac**, and **the God of Jacob'**?
> [27] He is not the God of the dead, but the **GOD OF THE LIVING**. You
> are therefore greatly mistaken." Mark 12:26b, 27 (NKJ)

You can laugh now. Not only did the Sadducees miss it: 'I *am* the God of
your father-- the God of Abraham, the God of Isaac, and the God of Jacob.'[Exodus]
[3:6] Our Lord pointed out the Sadducees they missed the burning bush, which
clearly reveals that the saints are alive after death. The saints indeed continue
to exist after death in their souls (or souls/spirits.) How ironic. neither do the
cults today still get it as well. Do you get it now? These are the blind leading
the blind.

Friend, if you have a loved-one that died but was definitely saved, he/she
is home with the Lord. The Lord is not God of the dead. Hallelujah; the Lord
our God is indeed the God the living.

> When the Lamb broke the fifth seal, I saw underneath the altar[the souls
> of those who had been slain because of the word of God, and because of
> the testimony which they had maintained; [10]and they **cried out with a
> loud voice,** saying, "How long, O Lord, holy and true, will You refrain
> from judging and avenging our blood on those who dwell on the earth?"
> [11]And **there was given to each of them a white robe;** and they were
> told that they should rest for a little while longer, until *the number of*
> their fellow servants and their brethren who were to be killed even as
> they had been, would be completed also. Rev. 6:9-11

> The phrase "under the altar" is a metaphor; these are believers "covered
> by the blood of Jesus Christ." These are alive in their souls in Heaven.
> Is God giving robes to nonexistent people?

Friend, you would be surprised to know of the professing believers that
mock the above phrase "under the altar," but some mock the Scripture here
to their own destruction. Hell awaits them. The living saints in their souls are
asking the Lord,

> How long, O Lord, holy and true, will You refrain from judging and
> avenging our blood on those who dwell on the earth?   (v 10)

As I said, the metaphor is used as "the souls under the altar" **redeemed
by the blood**.[1 Peter 1:18, 19] These are the believers that are *covered by the blood*
of our Lord. It is through the blood the saints overcome. "Under the altar" is
indeed a very holy expression, meaning they have been redeemed by the blood
of Jesus Christ. It is like the Passover: *when the Lord see the blood of the lamb
on the doorposts and lintel, the Death Angel will pass over them.* Praise the
Lord! Yes and amen:

> And they overcame him [*devil*] by the blood of the Lamb, and by the word
> of their testimony; and they loved not their lives unto the death.
>
> Rev. 12:11 (KJV)

Therefore, my brother and sister, please do not let anyone mock the *souls
under the altar*. Please rebuke their insult. Hebrews terrifyingly warns,

> Anyone who has violated the law of Moses dies without mercy "on the
> testimony of two or three witnesses." [29]How much worse punishment
> do you think will be deserved by those who have
>
> **SPURNED THE SON OF GOD**,
>
> **PROFANED THE BLOOD** of the covenant by which **they were
> sanctified**, and
>
> **OUTRAGED THE SPIRIT OF GRACE**?
>
> [30]For we know the one who said, "Vengeance is mine, I will repay." And
> again, "The **Lord will judge his people**." [31] It is a **fearful thing** to fall
> into the hands of the living God.   Heb. 10:28-31 (NRS)

Do you see the three rebukes?

1. Spurned the Son of God

2. Profaned the blood

3. Outraged the Spirit of grace

My friend, the above warning includes the believers. No believer will lose
his salvation, but believers can lose their reward. Sometimes over looked, they
can be put to shame at the Bema Seat of Christ. Some have died before their
time, and others their judgment follows them.

²⁴The sins of some men are obvious, going ahead of them to judgment [*at the Bema Seat*[2 Cor. 5:10]]; but the sins of others do not surface until later [*at the Bema Seat*]. ²⁵In the same way, good deeds are obvious, and even the ones that are inconspicuous cannot remain hidden.

1 Tim. 5:24, 25 (MSB)

I know there are many that ignorantly mock Scripture, even some believers mock the Scripture. They do such foolish things not only because they *lack biblical understanding*, but some also do it because they have little or *no fear* of the living God. As Job said of his miserable comforters (his three friends), "'Without a doubt you are the people, and wisdom will die with you.'"[Job 12:2 NET]

The point we do not want to miss is that God is indeed the God of the living. The saints are alive and well in Heaven once they die. The apostle Paul was very clear concerning when believers die in Christ,

Yes, we do have confidence, and we would rather be away from the body and at home with the Lord. 2 Cor. 5:8 (NRS)

But if *I am* to live *on* in the flesh, this *will mean* fruitful labor for me; and I do not know which to choose. ²³But I am hard-pressed from both *directions*, having the desire to depart and be with Christ, for *that* is very much better. Phil. 1:22, 23

Conclusion

I am hopeful this added chapter has been helpful for you clarifying some points on the death the saints. I say this because what Jude says concerning his day, which is doubly true in our generation:

Beloved, although I was very eager to write to you about our common salvation, I found it necessary to write [*in*] appealing to you to contend for the faith that was once for all delivered to the saints. For certain people have crept in unnoticed who long ago were designated for this condemnation, ungodly people, who pervert the grace of our God into sensuality and deny our only Master and Lord, Jesus Christ.

Jude 1:3, 4 (ESV)

Since this was truly troubling to Jude in his day, then, how much more is it in our day? The departure from the faith is a grave and serious warning necessary for our generation today to stay alert and watch out for the false teachers or orthodox teachers that have *skewed off center* and have gone into serious error of the faith.

It is not surprising that our Lord put forth this stirring question,

> However, when the Son of Man comes, will He find faith on the
> earth?"   Luke 18:8b

Jesus was clear that humans possess a body and soul (soul/spirit). The Lord Jesus warns us that He has the authority and power to throw both body and soul in the Lake of Fire. Therefore, walk humbly before the Lord and fear God.

While humankind possesses a body and soul, the soul continues to exist even after the body lays in the grave. The soul goes to Heaven if they are saved, but unregenerate soul goes to Hades to await the judgment. In addition, soul consists of soul and spirit, which is very clear in Scripture.[Heb. 4:12] This is likely the non-corporeal aspect of humankind, the soul/spirit, which is the nonmaterial aspect of the human makeup. Therefore, man is a trichotomous and not a dichotomous.

Finally, let us take comfort that the Lord our God is *"the God of the living."* The Lord is not the God of the dead. Therefore, we have this assurance from God Himself who cannot lie,

> Yes, we are of good courage, and we would rather be away from the
> body and at home with the Lord.   2 Cor. 5:8 (ESV)

Even as Stephen said as he was being stoned just before he died, he said,

> While they were stoning Stephen, he prayed, "Lord Jesus, receive my
> spirit."   Acts 7:59 (NRS)

Footnotes:

1. Flying as *"barnstorming:"* as I am using the phrase "barnstorming" here, I mean a pilot that is unable to fly a plane by the instrument panels. The person flies a plane by observing the ground below him. But if the pilot is unfortunately caught in a cloud, the pilot loses all sense of his bearings and directions. He experiences what is known as *"vertigo."* Then, he is likely to crash the plane. This is analogous to individuals who do not read theological works and other biblical studies and void of any biblical training in Scripture. They base their reality on their senses around them.

2. "Cracker Box" is an American candy of *popcorn and peanuts covered in caramel.* Inside the Cracker Box is found small a *toy* or a *trinket.* The metaphor is to demonstrate false notion that "Abraham bosom" or "Paradise" was theologically part of Hades. Such theory is utter nonsense.

3. *Ubiquity* of Christ: this is the doctrine that Christ Himself is omnipresent. While this doctrine is particularly noted in Communion or Lord's Supper, the doctrine of the ubiquity of Christ overlaps in other areas. The endorsing of the ubiquity of Christ bring to question the full humanity of Christ in His present ministry as High Priest who sympathize with our human weakness because Christ possesses a human nature.[Rom. 8:26-30; Heb. 2:17f; 4:14-16; 5:2; 1 John 2:1, 2] In endorsing the ubiquity of Christ, there is an inference that Christ's Humanity was absorbed, enthralled, or even compromised in the doctrine of the ubiquity of Christ. The present priesthood of Christ is very important because of our Lord's Humanity. He understands and fully empathizes with our weaknesses. In His Humanity as High Priest, He possesses a human body that is separate and distinct from His Eternal Deity. Hence, Christ the Lord is fully Eternal God and fully man, but these two natures (God and man) remain separate, distinct, unmixed, uncompromised, and undiminished in one person, Jesus Christ our Lord and Savior.

Eighth miraculous miracle and sign
Jesus Raises His Body from the Dead

[6]He [Jesus] is not here, but He has risen. Remember how He spoke to you while He was still in Galilee, [7]saying that the Son of Man must be handed over to sinful men, and be crucified, and on the third day rise *from the dead.*" [8]And they remembered His words, [9]and returned from the tomb and reported all these things to the eleven, and to all the rest. [10]Now *these women* were Mary Magdalene, Joanna, and Mary the *mother* of James; also the other women with them were telling these things to the apostles. [11]But these words appeared to them as nonsense, and they would not believe the women. [12]Nevertheless, Peter got up and ran to the tomb; and when he stooped and looked in, he saw the linen wrappings only; and he went away to his home, marveling at what had happened.   Luke 24:6-12

CHAPTER 17

Jesus' resurrection, the greatest poof of the Gospel

Then they drew near to the village where they were going, and He [Jesus] indicated that He would have gone farther. ²⁹But they constrained Him, saying, "Abide with us, for it is toward evening, and the day is far spent." And He went in to stay with them. ³⁰Now it came to pass, as He sat at the table with them, that He took bread, blessed and broke *it*, and gave it to them. ³¹Then their eyes were opened and they knew Him; and He vanished from their sight. ³²And they said to one another, **"Did not our heart burn within us while He talked with us on the road**, and while He opened the Scriptures to us?" ³³So they rose up that very hour and returned to Jerusalem, and found the eleven [apostles] and those *who were* with them gathered together, ³⁴saying, "The Lord is risen indeed, and has appeared to Simon!" ³⁵And they told about the things *that had happened* on the road, and how He was known to them in the breaking of bread. ³⁶Now as they said these things, Jesus Himself stood in the midst of them, and said to them, "Peace to you." ³⁷But they were terrified and frightened, and supposed they had seen a spirit. ³⁸And He said to them, "Why are you troubled? And why do doubts arise in your hearts? ³⁹"Behold My hands and My feet, that it is I Myself. Handle Me and see, for **a spirit does not have flesh and bones** as you see I have."   Luke 24:28-39 (NKJ)

Introduction

The truth of Christ Jesus our Lord is that He was crucified and died for our sin; He was buried and raised Himself from dead on the third day; and

He is gloriously going to return and judge the world in righteousness. These are facts that are self-evident as Gilbert West proved to himself Christ Jesus is indeed risen from the dead. Therefore, the resurrection, though denied by the critics, scoffers, and unbelievers, the facts are indisputable for the genuine truth seeker.

However, being intellectually convinced of the facts concerning the Gospel has no redeeming value just knowing the historical facts to be true. Intellectualism will not get anyone into the Kingdom of God. We must be **born from above by Spirit of God**. Being **born from above by the Holy Spirit** is the only way to enter Heaven's Gate. Each person must be regenerated by the Holy Spirit through personal commitment and trust in Christ the Lord. Else, I am warning every person shall without Christ shall indeed perish in their sin in Hell. There is no other Name whereby we can be redeemed, [Acts 4:12].

The *haters*, *scoffers*, and *ardent critics* shall surely object to referring to Hell since they think this is a human ploy to frighten people. **No**! The truth is frightening in itself as our Lord Jesus warns.[Matt. 10:28] My only rejoinder is I wish to say, "*Why should you object and think Hell is a ploy? You do not believe there is a Heaven or Hell?*" Well, when eternity opens its door for you, then, reality shall remove all doubt. However, when you close your eyes in death, your disbelief shall become reality as you wait the judgment in Hades.

Ah, but to the one seeking the truth, the resurrection of Jesus Christ the Lord is the irrefutable and absolute assurance of the Gospel and saving grace of the Lord. God has witnessed to this truth [1 John 5:9-13]: Christ's saving grace is availability to everyone in the world regardless of the depths of their sin. Friend, there is no sin that is too great that our Lord cannot surely pardon and forgive you. Believe on the Lord Jesus Christ and you shall be saved![Acts 16:31]

Do you know what I find to be so amazing? Jesus told those believers as well as the unbelievers concerning His crucifixion and resurrection. However, the truth of the Gospel was *providentially concealed* from the believers until God's appointed time to reveal the truth of the Gospel. Yet, most amazingly, the unbelieving religious leaders and the cynics actually remaindered Jesus' prediction of His death and resurrection. How ironic is that?

However, *tradition, superstition*, and *prejudice* rob many of us from seeing and believing the truth of God's Word. Listen, the Lord Jesus is a loving and merciful Savior. Jesus said of Israel (due to her disbelief), whom He greatly loves,

> At that very hour some Pharisees came and said to him, "Get away from here, for Herod wants to kill you." [32]He said to them, "Go and tell

that fox for me, 'Listen, I am casting out demons and performing cures [*healings*] today and tomorrow, and on the third day I finish my work. [33]Yet today, tomorrow, and the next day I must be on my way, because it is impossible for a prophet to be killed outside of Jerusalem.' [34]Jerusalem, Jerusalem, the city that kills the prophets and stones those who are sent to it! How often have I desired to gather your children together as a hen gathers her brood under her wings, and you were not willing!

Luke 13:31-34 (NRS)

Regrettably, many in Israel and in the world are unable perceive and receive Yehoshua (Jesus) gentle beckoning or calling of Israel,

"How often have I desired to gather your children together as a hen gathers her brood under her wings, and you were not willing!"

Luke 13:34 (NRS)

Our Lord sets forth a paradox that is beyond human and even the angels understanding. On one end of the paradox is the sovereignty of God that declares Israel's unbelieve. On the other end of the spectrum, is the free will of man to choose to rebel and not obey God's Word. Man is now alienated and under the pending wrath of Almighty God,[John 3:36] and only the blood of Jesus Christ (His sacrifice for our sin on Calvary) will deliver anyone from the terrifying wrath and judgment of God.[Rom. 5:8-11]

All the unregenerate shall learn there is a God of Heaven, the Lord our God. He is a holy and righteous Judge. Since He is indeed infinitely holy and righteous, His wrath will be poured out upon all unregenerate and without mercy and forever and ever. Friend, it is a fearful thing to fall into the hand of the living God in which there will be no mercy.[Heb. 10:31]

As we turn to the last chapter in this study, I cannot warn you strong enough. Friend, you had better be certain that you are genuinely redeemed in Christ, possessing saving faith in Christ. If you have even the slightest doubt of your regeneration in Christ, then I beg you to reexamine your faith just as the Bible warns every professing believer to do.[2 Cor. 13:5] For once the door into eternity closes behind you, it will be too late; there is no turning back.

A. The disciples did not remember nor believe

There are many references to Jesus' prediction of His death and resurrection in the four Gospels. Yes, the critics say, "Why didn't the *Jesus'* followers *believe He had risen from the dead* then, especially His apostles?" I am sure such similar questions have entered the mind of the skeptics or cynics. The

221

electionists would enjoy answering such questions, but my reply to cynics will be more compassionate.

First, please allow me to give you several text that ought to be self-explanatory. This is concerning our Lord's foretelling of His coming death and resurrection.

> "Let these words sink into your ears; for the Son of Man is going to be delivered into the hands of men." But they **did not understand this statement**, AND **IT WAS <u>CONCEALED</u> <u>FROM</u> <u>THEM</u>** so **THAT THEY <u>WOULD</u> <u>NOT</u> <u>PERCEIVE</u> <u>IT</u>**; and they were **afraid to ask** Him about this statement. Luke 9:44, 45

> Then He took the twelve[a] aside and said to them, "Behold, we are going up to Jerusalem, and all things which are written through the prophets about the Son of Man will be accomplished [*fulfilled*]. For He will be handed over to the Gentiles, and will be mocked and mistreated and spit upon, and after they have scourged Him, they will kill Him; and the third day He will rise again." But the **disciples <u>UNDERSTOOD</u> <u>NONE</u> <u>OF</u> <u>THESE</u> <u>THINGS</u>**, and *THE MEANING OF* **THIS <u>STATEMENT</u> <u>WAS</u> <u>HIDDEN</u> <u>FROM</u> <u>THEM</u>**, and they **<u>DID</u> <u>NOT</u> <u>COMPREHEND</u> <u>THE</u> <u>THINGS</u>** that were said. Luke 18:31-34

> [a]What is overlooked is that Jesus' predictions were probably **not** providentially concealed from Judas Iscariot, but the statement may have escaped his awareness at time. Judas Iscariot likely recalls the predictions later and shared the information to the Jewish authorities. The crucifixion was concealed from all believers. Purpose of the crucifixion was even hidden from demons (yes, evil spirits). Satan was unaware of the purpose of the cross until the Lord's appointed time to revel the intention, see 1 Cor. 2:6-8.

Let us also keep in mind that if God had not revealed Himself through the written Word of God the Bible and provided the proclamation by men of God (such as prophets/apostles), how would anyone know God or know His will apart from His revelation? Mankind is unable to comprehend and have a personal relationship with the living God by reason or carnal works. Without divine revelation, God is unknowable, and humankind can only grope for a god of darkened mind.

Mankind is in utter in darkness without light from God. Humankind is alienated from the very life of God due to his utter wickedness and sin of rebellion. So, it is very evident though God has revealed Himself through creation as the Designer and Maker of all things [Psa. 19; Rom. 1:18-22], mankind is unable know God through carnal reason due his darkened mind. So, the natural man is void of the Holy Spirit: for it is from the Spirit of God that illumination is gained. So, the unregenerate is unable to receive the things of God. Even the redeemed are unable hear God's Word due to the hardened and stubborn hearts and minds. Listen, the spiritual things of God can only be discerned through the illumination of God Himself.[1 Cor. 2:14]

Finally, this particularly applies to the servants of God's Word though many Pastors ought to know this- So, please hear me, the Bible is **NO** ordinary book. God's Word is not a lifeless book. God's Word is a living book.

> For the **WORD** of God *is* **LIVING** and ***POWERFUL*** [GK *energes*, lit. *energizing* or *active*], and **SHARPER** than any two-edged sword, **PIERCING** even to the division [*dividing*] of **SOUL** and **SPIRIT**, and [*dividing*] of **JOINTS** and **MARROW**, and is a **DISCERNER** of the **THOUGHTS** and **INTENTS OF THE HEART**. Heb. 4:12 (NKJ)

This is exactly why the Bible declares,

> So then faith *comes* by hearing, and hearing by the word of God.[b]
>
> Rom. 10:17 (NKJ)

[b]Some GK MSS read "hearing by the word of Christ."

Again, in simply terms, intellectualism will not get anyone into the Kingdom of God. Knowing and acknowledging the facts of the Gospel are true will not get anyone into the Kingdom of God. Each individual person must be born **from above** by the Holy Spirit through personal commitment and receiving Jesus as Lord and Savior.[John 1:12, 13; 3:1-7]

Jesus declared His death and resurrection multiple times in the Gospels, which is most evident in the four Gospels: Matt. 16:21, 17:22-23, 20:18-19, Mark 8:31, 9:31, 10:33-34, Luke 9:22, 18:31-33, and John 2:18-22. In addition, there is Scripture that indirectly alludes to the cross, e.g., John 2:18, 19; 3:14-18; 6:40; 8:28; 11:25; 12:32-34. (Some have estimated, on an average, the resurrection of Jesus Christ is referred to about every 53rd verse in the NT.) Therefore, truth holds unchanging whether one believes it or not.

So, we should fervently study God's Word and vigorously share His Word with the lost for whom Christ died. When presenting the Gospel, be sure to share the Word with other right out of the pages of God's Word. Let them see God's Word for themselves. Evangelism or sharing the Gospel is not based on logic or reasoning though our faith is logical and rational. Saving faith must be presented through the Word of God. There is power in seeing and hearing the Word of God.

Saving faith is derived from **seeing** and **hearing** the Word of God.[Rom. 10:17; Gal.3:2; 2 Thess.2:13; Heb.4:12] My friend, it is through the Word of God that brings saving faith which leads to regeneration (born from above) and new life in Christ. Saving faith in Christ is not through rationalism or philosophy or any other human reasoning. (Do you want to be an effective soul winner for Christ? **Show it from the Bible**; don't just tell it.) We come to faith in Christ by seeing and hearing the Word, believing the Gospel from the Word of God.[1 Cor. 15:3, 4] Friend, the Word of God has the power within itself to illuminate and lead to regeneration and transformation the new life in Christ [2 Cor. 5:17] since it is powered by the Holy Spirit.

> For this reason we also thank God without ceasing, because when **YOU RECEIVED THE WORD OF GOD** which you heard from us, you welcomed *it* not *as* the word of men, but as it is in truth, the **word of God, which also EFFECTIVELY WORKS IN YOU WHO BELIEVE.**   1 Thess. 2:13 (NKJ)

Yes, the crucifixion and resurrection were divinely concealed from the disciples during our Lord's earthly ministry. This is reasonable to understand because when any person dies and we know it by fact that they died, it is rational to deny when another person says they are alive. We deny the deceased are alive even when we see them face to face. This is what happened to the disciples.

However, the truth of Christ Jesus' death and resurrection was divinely concealed from all believers. More importantly, the cross was the mystery hidden in God. Friend, this is even true of most of God's Word. There are unrecognized or undetected mysteries not understood even though plainly written in the Scriptures. Somethings are only fully understood by divine illumination by the Holy Spirit. (Pastors, you better remember this one!)

We must keep in the forefront of our mind that we are totally dependent on the Lord for *guidance*, *insight*, *illumination*, and especially for *spiritual results*. If only the church, and especially Pastors and teachers of the Word, understood this, there would be more on our knees before the throne of grace.

The perceiving and understanding of the things of God belong to the Lord alone. Do you read me and understand me: "- *perceiving and understanding the things of God belong to the Lord alone*." There are things that are in this present life that we can only know through the Lord's mercy in granting the illumination. Otherwise, some truths would never be known without insight from the Lord Himself. How much more then understanding God's Word? Therefore, many of us as preachers are bankrupted in our understanding and the delivering God's Word. This is because there is little *fervent* and *passionate* prayer in preparation and delivery. We need to seriously wrestle in prayer with the Lord if our praying and preaching and teaching are going to be effective.

> Therefore, confess your sins to one another and pray for one another, that you may be healed. The prayer of a righteous person has great power as it is working. James 5:16 (ESV)

If we really believed that there is **all-out spiritual war** (there is a deadly spiritual war) which we cannot see, hear, or touch, then friend, we would be more on our knees. Then, we would go out door to door compelling people to enter the Kingdom before it is too late. It is further evident few us are thankful and praise the Lord after the delivery of our sermons. Even worse, **there is <u>no</u> urgency in our proclamation of the Gospel**. The urgency of the Gospel has been forsaken and abandoned. Many sermons are not much more than a lecture or at best a nice homily.

Disbelief of the resurrection by the disciples

Therefore, we should not be surprised at various reactions to the declaration of our Lord's resurrection by the saints. Here are some of the disciples' reactions to the news of the Jesus' resurrection:

➢ John 20:11-18: Mary Magdalene was crying at the tomb; when the Lord reveals Himself to her and she tells the disciples, but it is met with disbelief.

➢ Matt. 28:8-10: The other women returning from the tomb, but are met with unbelief.

➢ Luke 24:13-32: Cleopas and another disciple on the road to Emmaus, but when the two disciples share concerning Jesus' resurrection, it is met with disbelief.

➢ Luke 24:33-35; 1 Cor. 15:5a: Appearance to Peter, but Scriptures don't reveal location of the other disciples and their reactions.

➢ John 20:19-25: Appearance to ten apostles but Thomas was absent.

➢ Luke 24:36-49: Appearance to the apostles and other disciples, as they no doubt shared the news of His resurrection, but we do not know the reaction of those who hear eleven.

➢ Mark 16:14: John 20:26-29, Appearance to all eleven apostles; Thomas is present. I am sure there was more skepticism and disbelief.

➢ John 21:1-25: Appearance to seven apostles at Sea Galilee. (As chronology of this event is uncertain when this occurred.)

➢ 1 Cor. 15:6: Appearance to over 500 disciples. No doubt those (among 500 disciples) share the resurrection account, yet, some people probably did not believe them as well.ᶜ

➢ 1 Cor. 15:7a, Jesus appears to James, the other sibling, and likely to the entire family. It certainly the family rejoiced and praised the Lord.

➢ Matt. 28:16-20; Mark 16:15-19; Luke 24:44-52; Acts 1:8-11: Appearance in giving the Great Commission and Ascension.ᶜ

➢ Acts 9:3-5; 22:7-8; 26:14-16; 1 Cor 15:8; 2 Cor. 12:1ff: Jesus appearance to Saul of Tarsus (the apostle Paul). ¹

ᶜThe truth of the resurrection of Jesus is so astonishing that the evidence would stand as true in any honest court of Law anywhere in the world. Therefore, the above evidence of Christ's resurrection stands irrefutable to the honest seekers of the truth.

The information is from Amazon web service. Amazon web service places the Great Commission just after Jesus appears to the seven apostles in Galilee, which is certainly possible. I see the Great Commission and Ascension as a single event. So, I think Matt. 28:16ff and Acts 1:5ff supplementing one another.

As anyone reads through the account of the resurrection, it is very clear that the various reports of Jesus' appearances were not given credence. The various testimonies and accounts given were not believed to be true. This reveals clearly that the condition of our human hearts and minds are indeed hardened like granite stone. Let us not be surprised with the unbelief when sharing the Gospel!

Peter and John run to the tomb hearing that Jesus' body was stolen, but Peter and John are unaware of the resurrection at that particular moment. As noted above, the report by the women was met with skepticism by the disciple,

Their words seemed to them like idle tales, and they did not believe them.   Luke 24:11 (NKJ)

Jesus appears to two disciples on the road to Emmaus, but this was met with skepticism. Ten of the apostles testified that the Lord is risen, but when Thomas heard it, he disbelieved and demanded proof of Jesus resurrection, John 20:19ff.

Many unbelievers imagined declaring resurrection of Jesus to be only a ploy dreamed up by some the disciples. Other critics allege Jesus didn't really die. So, what then? Are we to suppose that the disciples concocted a hoax or a straight out lie to perpetrate the resurrection? My response to such critics is, "Get real."

These were zealous Orthodox Jews. They were very enthusiastic towards the Mosaic Law. There were not just the twelve (after Mathias is chosen), but thousands upon thousands of men went everywhere sharing the wonderful news of the Gospel (the death on the cross, resurrection, and glorious return) and especially after Saul of Tarsus was persecuting Jewish disciples. Acts 8:1-4 These people left everything behind for the risen Christ. Saul was not a believer. Saul (Paul) was like a *wild boar* going after Jewish people who believed in Yehoshua as the Messiah. So, are we to reason that Saul, who was now a believer just had heat stroke?

The most logical conclusion is that the apostles and Jews disciples did in fact meet the risen Christ, and Christ the Lord gloriously changed their lives. Listen, it cost them their lives to believe in Jesus and the resurrection. Jews who believed in the resurrection were adamantly and furiously persecuted by other Jewish leaders and those that followed the unbelieving religious leaders. Even the Roman Government was hostile to Christians. Romans dipped Christians in oil and placed them on poles, and <u>millions</u> were then put on fire lighting skies. Countless <u>millions</u> and <u>millions</u> of Christians are being persecuted throughout the world even to this very day. The Gospel is true. It is no wonder the Hebrews writer is urging some Jews that were struggling in their faith due the intense persecution by other Jews,

> Remember those earlier days after you had received the light, when you endured in a great conflict full of suffering. [33]Sometimes you were publicly exposed to insult and persecution; at other times you stood side by side with those who were so treated. [34]You suffered along with those in prison and joyfully accepted the confiscation of your property, because you knew that you yourselves had better and lasting possessions. [35]So do not throw away your confidence; it will be richly rewarded.   Heb. 10:32-35 (NIV)

227

Roman Government persecuted Christians for the first three hundred years. Millions of Christians suffered and were tortured. In addition, the churches then had to contend with *false teachers, counterfeit preachers, heretical churches,* and *counterfeit epistles* (letters) claiming to be from one of apostles.[2 Thess. 2:3f] Moreover, there were infiltrations: false teachers came into church from outside, and there were even false teachers that even arose within the churches that were teaching false doctrines.[Acts 20:26- 30; 2 Peter 2:1-3; Jude 1:3, 4] Christians then and even now are persecuted by pagan religions all over the world today. Christians are persecuted by secular-minded people and atheistic governments today; this is world-wide. Therefore, to allege the apostles concocted a lie and suffered martyrium for hoax is the most insane proposal I have ever heard.

In addition, the Roman government sought to destroy all the NT manuscripts. True! Romans nearly succeeded in destroying most manuscripts of first three hundred years. This is why even just finding only fragments of epistles of the first three hundred years of the church is a very rare find. Indeed, finding any NT fragments of the first three hundred years is an extremely rare discovery. Nevertheless, the world, the flesh, and the devil could not destroy the church nor the Word of God. No one can destroy the church because the church and the Word of God is built upon the Rock and the gates of Hell shall not prevail. Hallelujah! Besides, the genuine church (which consist of true believers in Christ by the Holy Spirit) is invisible. (*Put that in your pipe and smoke it!*[2])

B. The unbelievers remembered but did not believe

Now, let us turn to the flipside and Jesus' signs to the unbelieving Jewish leaders and rejectors of Jesus Christ as the Lord and Redeemer. I find it astonishing that with all the mighty signs, reactions, and perceptions many Jews still did not believe. So, let us note again Jesus' beginning of His miraculous signs early on in His public ministries to Israel,

> In the temple he found those who were selling oxen and sheep and pigeons, and the money-changers sitting there. [15]And making a whip of cords, he drove them all out of the temple, with the sheep and oxen. And he poured out the coins of the money-changers and overturned their tables. [16]And he told those who sold the pigeons, "Take these things away; do not make my Father's house a house of trade [GK *emporion, place of marketing* d]." [17]His disciples remembered that it was written, "Zeal for your house will consume me." [18]So the Jews said to him, "What sign do you show us for [*You have authority to*] doing these things?" [19]Jesus answered them,

"Destroy this temple, and in three days I will raise it up." [20]The Jews then said, "It has taken forty-six years to build this temple, and will you raise it up in three days?" [21]**But he was speaking about the temple of his body.** [22]When therefore he was raised from the dead, his disciples remembered that he had said this, and they believed the Scripture and the word that Jesus had spoken. [23]Now when he was in Jerusalem at the Passover Feast, many believed in his name when they saw the signs that he was doing. John 2:14-23 (ESV)

[d]The word "trade" [v16] is the GK word *emporion* which is still used today, *emporium*, a place for **marketing**.

Normally, the authorities in the temple would have arrested Jesus for that would constitute disruption in the temple. Yet, we ought to realize that no one put their hands on Christ the Lord until His appointed time. The Triune God is fully in control at all times. (This is overlooked by many Christians.) The fact there was also a **second cleansing** (without any incident) of the temple accentuates even further that the Lord was definitely controlling or orchestrating all things surrounding public ministries of Jesus. This is most notable in the Messianic Psalm,

> For he will order his angels to protect you in all you do. They will lift you up in their hands, so you will not slip and fall on a stone.
>
> Psa. 91:11, 12 (NET)

There were definitely angels guarding our Lord from cradle to cross. The Lord needed no guarding since He was God manifested in flesh. But what escapes many people understanding is that Christ's true identity must be kept concealed until the appoint time. So, there were numerable angels surrounding our Lord during His earthly life and ministry. Holy angels keep everyone and everything at bay.[3] This was done in order that the Messiahship's identity remained hidden and obscured until the appointed time by Triune God. In the same way, there would be no interference by demons or anything else. Hebrews writer also points out angels guard the saints, believers, but sadly, many saints are totally oblivious to the divine watch-care. The NRS gives a more accurately connotative meaning rather than the denotative meaning,

> Are not all angels spirits[e] in the divine service, sent to serve for the sake of those who are to inherit salvation? Heb. 1:14 (NRS)

[e]The phrase is (in GK *leitourgikos pneuma*) literally "*ministering spirits*," but connotative meaning is preferred, "angels or angelic spirits."

Angels were constantly near our Lord when He is tempted. So, Satan knew he had better be very careful in his approaching our Lord and His temptation. (Angels, evil or holy, are still created beings and finite.) Holy angels were at Jesus' every beckoning.[Matt. 4:11; 26:53] (Christ the Lord is the Commander of the Lord of Hosts.) The mockers, fault-finders, and the naive do not understand that Christ remained *incognito* until the fulfilling of Scripture: the crucifixion, His death, and resurrection. Little do unbelievers realize that **the Lord our God IS AN ON TIME GOD**. Hallelujah!

During our Lord's prayers in the Garden of Gethsemane, Jesus was in anguish in His inner-being in His human nature. For He knew that "He who knew no sin was going to be made sin in our behalf."[2 Cor. 5:21] Our Lord did not shrink-back from the cross. If indeed there was a "shrink back" so to speak, it was because the Lord was going to become sin as a substitute for every genuine believer. Jesus *bore our sins in His own body*.[2 Cor. 5:21, 1 Peter 2:24]

Luke tells us that while Jesus was praying in the Garden of Gethsemane, angels came to strengthen Him, and He even had sweat like drops of blood during His praying.

> "Father, if You are willing, remove this cup from Me; yet not My will, but Yours be done [Now an angel from heaven appeared to Him, strengthening Him. And being in agony, He was praying very fervently; and His sweat became like drops of blood, falling down upon the ground].[f]
>
> Luke 22:42-44

[f]As noted by NAS, vv 43, 44 are not found some earlier GK MSS.

Amazingly, the Google search engine is correct in saying, "The hypostatic union, a core doctrine in Christian theology, describes the union of Jesus Christ's divine and human natures in one person, Jesus, who is both fully God and fully man."[4] The Lord did not set aside His infinite power and authority during public ministry (which would be impossible: God cannot be less than who is, the Everlast God blessed forever.). Instead, He chose not to use His prerogative as God.[Phi. 2:9-11]

Our Lord remained very focused on His timetable of the cross. Yet, His humanity struggled like any other human. But His divine nature remained *cloaked* and *incognito* in order to complete man's redemption. The unbelievers do not comprehend or understand the hyperstatic union of Jesus Christ, the two natures of our Lord due to the grave darkness within humankind.

The bottom-line or point to underscore here is if the saints are being watch-over by angels (*which they certainly are*)[Acts 12:15; Heb. 1:14], how much more for Christ the Lord from the cradle to the grave? It is certain therefore, no one could attack or harm the Lord Jesus during His ministry unless they were given permission by the Holy Triune God. Even the tomb of our Lord and His body was heavy guard by a host of holy angels. Believe me, neither evil angels or deprave men could approach His grave. In the same way (due to angels surrounding our Lord), this is why Jesus could bring immediate judgment and cleanse the temple with no one to stop Him. Jesus humanity was guarded by angels. Thus, making His humanity impregnable and invincible.

Therefore, Jesus refers His death and resurrection as a definite sign, 'Destroy this temple, and in three days I will raise it up.'[John 2:19]

Jesus alludes to His death as He talked with Nicodemus, [John 3:14] as lifting up the serpent in the wilderness. The Jewish leaders were not stupid; the leaders clearly understood his analogies.

Jesus tells us that when He is lifted upon on the cross, the Jewish leaders will definite get the point.

> Jesus went on to say, "When you have lifted up the Son of Man, you will know who **I AM.**[g] You will also know that I don't do anything on my own. I say only what my Father taught me. (John 8:28 CEV)

> [g]I need to remind you once again, the "*He*" does not appear in the GK. It is simply, '**Ego Eimi:**' The name for God in the LXX.[Exodus 3:13-15]

Jesus again alludes to his death for His sheep,

> "The thief comes only to steal and kill and destroy; I came that they may have life, and have *it* abundantly. I am the good shepherd; **the good**[h] **shepherd LAYS DOWN HIS LIFE for the sheep.**"   John 10:10, 11

> [h]Again, let us note the word "good" is GK *kalos*. The meaning is here of *kalos* is that the Shepherd does good things for His sheep. Kalos is *not* referring to the intrinsic good of the Shepherd though Jesus is intrinsically good. Kalos definitely means He will do good things for His redeemed, particular those who obey and do His will.

Again in John 10, Jesus refers to the cross,

> This is why the Father loves me– because **I LAY DOWN MY LIFE**, so that **I MAY TAKE IT BACK AGAIN. No one takes it away from me**, but **I LAY IT DOWN OF MY OWN FREE WILL. I have the authority to lay it down**, and **I have the authority to take it back again.** This commandment I received from my Father."

> John 10:17, 18 (NET)

Jesus alludes to His resurrection, and all those standing by to hear Him. So, unbelieving Jews present certainly remembered Jesus' words at Lazarus grave.

> Jesus said unto her, **I AM THE RESURRECTION, AND THE LIFE**: he that believeth in me, though he were dead, yet shall he live:
>
> John 11:25 (KJV)

One week before the crucifixion, Jesus gives a reference to His death and resurrection. (This text is slightly long but essential to note.)

> [32]And when I am lifted up from the earth, I will draw everyone to myself." [33]He said this to indicate how he was going to die. [34]The crowd responded, "We understood from Scripture that the Messiah would live forever. How can you say the Son of Man will die?[i] Just who is this Son of Man, anyway?" [35]Jesus replied, "My light will shine for you just a little longer. Walk in[j] the light while you can, so the darkness will not overtake you. Those who walk in the darkness cannot see where they are going. [36]Put your trust[k] in the light while there is still time; then you will become children of the light." After saying these things, Jesus went away and was hidden from them. [37]But despite all the miraculous signs Jesus had done, most of the people still did not believe in him. [38]This is exactly what Isaiah the prophet had predicted: "LORD, who has believed our message? To whom has the LORD revealed his powerful arm?" [39]But the people couldn't believe, for as Isaiah also said, [40]"The Lord has blinded their eyes and hardened their hearts— so that their eyes cannot see, and their hearts cannot understand, and they cannot turn to me and have me heal them." [41]Isaiah was referring to Jesus when he said this, because he saw the future and spoke of the Messiah's glory. [42]Many people did believe in him, however, including some of the Jewish leaders. But they wouldn't admit it for fear that the Pharisees would expel them from the synagogue. [43]For they loved human praise more than the praise of God.   John 12:32-43 (NLT)

[i]Literally, "must be lifted up" [v34], but the Jews knew He was referring to His death, 'We understood from Scripture that the Messiah would live forever.'

[j][v 35] Literally, 'walk while you have the Light,' but the NLT has captured the connotative meaning, 'Walk in the light while you can.' The intended

meaning is walk with Christ, which is certainly a definite expectation for a godly life in Christ.

ᵏ"Believe" [v 36] is the GK word "*pisteuo,*" which also means "to trust in-"

Finally, when the religious leaders went to Pilate to set guards over Jesus' tomb, this proves beyond a doubt that some unbelievers certainly understood and recalled Jesus' prediction of His resurrection.

> The next day (which is after the day of preparation) the chief priests and the Pharisees assembled before Pilate ⁶³and said, "Sir, **WE REMEMBER** that while that deceiver was still alive he said, '**AFTER THREE DAYS I WILL RISE AGAIN**.' ⁶⁴So give orders to secure the tomb until the third day. Otherwise his disciples may come and steal his body and say to the people, 'He has been raised from the dead,' and the last deception will be worse than the first."   Matt. 27:62-64 (NET)

Yes, the skeptics will deny that such conversation took place between Pilate and the religious leaders. But again, what else can the cynic say? Otherwise, the unbelievers would have to submit to truth that Jesus is the Messiah and Savior of the world and that He is indeed risen from the dead. The unbelievers can deny such conversation occurred, but the fact is that such dialogue did occur. However, why were the Roman soldiers placed to guard the tomb if such dialogue never occurred?

Why a marvelous mystery and an enigma (or *aenigma*). The believers were concealed from grasping or recalling Jesus' predictions of going to the cross. It was only after our Lord reveal Himself and opened the apostles minds they fully understood,

> Then He opened [GK *dianoigo, to thoroughly open* or *to open up completely*] their minds [GK *nous, minds* or *comprehension*] to understand the Scriptures.   Luke 24:45

My oh my, what an amazing point we also must learn from the insight given to us by Luke's Gospel.[v45]

This was the state of Adam and Eve before the fall: their minds were fully opened and having incredible awareness and insight. Solomon was given a brilliant mind to know things. Daniel and his three companions had their minds so expanded that the Bible declares,

> And in every matter of wisdom and knowledge wherein the king questioned them, he found them **ten times wiser** than all the enchanters and sorcerers that were in all his kingdom.   Dan. 1:20 (LXE)

So, here the apostles were given extraordinary wisdom,

> **For I will give you words and a wisdom that none of your opponents will be able to withstand or contradict.**　　　Luke 21:15 (NRS)

Paul says concerning the apostles, they were given **THE MIND OF CHRIST**.[1 Cor. 2:16] It is very evident that the carnal church at Corinth **did not** have the mind of Christ and **neither does anyone else today** have the mind of Christ. Some have misread the above verse and assume that they too have the mind of Christ. No, we do not have the mind of Christ. For those who misread the above text and assume they have the mind of Christ are fools! Unfortunately, the less mature in the Word are blinded to the contextual or exegetical study of Scripture. The carnal believer incorrectly assumes [1 Cor. 2:16] that they too must have the mind of Christ even assuming that the carnal Church at Corinth had the mind of Christ. Perish the thought my brother!

Let us return to the unbelievers remembering:

How amazing is that the unbelievers' recall concerning Jesus' prediction of the crucifixion and resurrection. As we have noted already, the unbelievers clearly understood the predictions of our Lord's death and resurrection. The critics disbelief will be their own undoing at the judgment. Listen friend, let me also remind you again that intellectual acknowledging of the truth of the cross is no assurance for genuine regeneration and saving in faith Jesus Christ. The devil and demons *believe* and *know* well the facts of the cross, but there is no salvation for evil angels. "For it is clear that he [Christ the Lord] did not come to help angels, but the descendants of Abraham."[Heb. 2:14 NRS]

The evil angels therefore cannot be saved since there is no redemption for them. There is no need for redemption of holy angels; they are "sons of God" by relationship, belong to the Lord. As to humans, we must be born from above by the Holy Spirit to enter the Kingdom of God. Jesus said to Nicodemus (a good man, believed God's Word, and a teacher of the Bible and yet he was unregenerated when he initially had a dialogue with Jesus): 'You must **born from above** to enter the Kingdom of God.'[John 1:13; 3:3, 5; 1 Peter 1:3, 23] Friend, you must be born from above by the Spirit of God if you ever hope to enter into the Kingdom of God. If you are not born again by the Holy Spirit through saving faith in Jesus Christ as Lord and Savior, you shall indeed perish in your sin.

C. The necessity of the shed blood and death of Christ

First, let me say that our redemption was completed at the cross. There is nothing to add to Christ's redemption! I say again, *"our redemption was completed at the cross."* The redemption for mankind is complete, and there is nothing that can be added to our redemption in Christ. Jesus alone saves His redeemed completely. There is absolutely nothing man can do to make himself acceptable before God. Even water baptism or taking Communion **adds nothing** to man's acceptance or redemption before the Lord. Therefore, our redemption was fully completed at the cross. Since our redemption was completed at the cross, mankind cannot add anything the work of Christ.

The cross is where our Lord and Savior died in believer's place for their sin. The cross is where He shed His blood and died in our place or in our behalf for our sins. As we shall see the shedding of **His blood** and **His death** of Christ are integrally woven together into our redemption. I say this because many seem to think the blood is not implied in His death. Therefore, some expositors think the shedding of Christ's blood is not necessary in our redemption. According to some expositors, our Lord's death is the salient issue in redemption. However, is the shedding the blood of Christ necessary in our redemption? His shed blood is indeed absolutely necessary. I strongly affirm that both the Christ Jesus' **SHED BLOOD** and **DEATH** are indeed indispensable to our redemption. Friend, I need not have to be able to explain necessity of our Lord's shed blood and death for our redemption. I only need believe and declare what the Scripture explicitly reveals and teaches. If you disagree, well, that's on you!

Before I go any further, let me ask a question, "If the blood is part of the core of the Gospel, why then to we read concerning the initial Passover-"

> "And when **I see the blood**, I will pass over you; and the plague shall
> not be on you to destroy *you* when I strike the land of Egypt."
>
> Exodus 12:13 (NKJ)

The reality is that when discussing redemption in Christ, there is much more written about the shedding of blood. I am not sure if one volume was devoted to the shedding blood in redemption that this would suffice adequately to explain the necessity. Still, for the dissenters who say that shedding blood is not necessary, I shall just reminder you of some Scriptures and leave topic to rest.

> Indeed, under the law almost everything is purified with blood, and
> **without the shedding of blood there is no forgiveness of sins.**
>
> Heb. 9:22 (NRS)

> 'For the life of the flesh *is* in the blood, and I have given it to you
> upon the altar to make atonement for your souls; for it *is* **the blood *that***
> **makes atonement for the soul**.'
> Lev. 17:11 (NKJ)

> "Therefore take heed to yourselves and to all the flock, among which the Holy Spirit has made you overseers, to shepherd the church of God which **He purchased with His own blood.**" Acts 20:28 (NKJ)

> **In whom we have redemption through his blood, the forgiveness of sins**, according to the riches of his grace; Eph. 1:7 (KJV)

> Knowing that you were not redeemed with perishable things like silver or gold from your futile way of life inherited from your forefathers, but [*you were redeemed*] **with precious blood, as of a lamb unblemished and spotless,** *the blood* **of Christ.** 1 Peter 1:18, 19

Here are other Scriptures confirming the same teachings: Lev. 17:10-14 (see the book of Leviticus); Exo.24:8; Rom. 5:9; Eph. 2:13; Heb. 9:14. Friend, as I have said above, I need not know why the shedding blood is necessary in our redemption; I only need believe it and declare it because the shed blood of Christ is so strongly emphasized in the Scriptures:

God said it.

Jesus did it.

I believe it,

That settles it!

Can someone please say, Amen!

Equally important, Christ the Lord laid His life on the cross for our sins. That is, Christ died in our stead (Jesus died on our behalf) on the cross. This is the heart of the Gospel.

> For I delivered unto you first of all that which I also received, how that **Christ died for our sins** according to the scriptures; And that he was buried, and that he rose again the third day according to the scriptures:
>
> 1 Cor. 15:3, 4 (KJV)

> For while we were still helpless, at the right time **CHRIST DIED FOR THE UNGODLY.**

> But God demonstrates His own love toward us, in that **WHILE WE WERE YET SINNERS, CHRIST DIED FOR US.** Much more then, **HAVING NOW BEEN JUSTIFIED BY HIS BLOOD**, we shall be saved from the wrath *of God* through Him. For if while we were enemies **WE WERE RECONCILED TO GOD THROUGH THE**

DEATH of His Son, much more, having been reconciled, we shall be saved by His life. Rom. 5:5, 8-10

He who did not spare His own Son, but **delivered Him up for us all**, how shall He not with Him also freely give us all things? Who shall bring a charge against God's elect? *It is* God who justifies. Who *is* he who condemns? *It is* **Christ who died**, and furthermore is also risen, who is even at the right hand of God, who also makes intercession for us. Rom. 8:32-34 (NKJ)

For the love of Christ controls us, having concluded this, that one [Christ] **died for all**, therefore all [believers] died; and **He died for all**, so that those who live would no longer live for themselves, but for **Him who died and rose** on their behalf. 2 Cor. 5:14, 15

"I am the good shepherd; the good shepherd **lays down His life for the sheep**."

"For this reason the Father loves Me, because **I lay down My life** so that I may take it again. No one has taken it away from Me, but I lay it down on My own initiative. **I have authority to lay it down**, and **I have authority to take it up again**. This commandment I received from My Father." John 10:11, 17, 18

So, we can see that the shedding of Christ's blood and His death are interwoven together. Nevertheless, let each person be persuaded in his own mind.[Rom. 14:5]

The resurrection of Christ is the "*Amen*" to the completion of our redemption on the cross. If Christ is not risen we are still in our sins, we are still in our sins. Therefore, no genuine Christian can deny the resurrection of Jesus Christ and still claim to be in the faith. Impossible!

And if Christ is not risen, your faith *is* futile; you are still in your sins! [18]Then also those who have fallen asleep [died] in Christ have perished. [19]If in this life only we have hope in Christ, we are of all men the most pitiable. [20] But now Christ is risen from the dead, *and* has become the firstfruits of those who have fallen asleep.[j] [21]For since by man *came* death, by Man also *came* the resurrection of the dead. [22]For as in Adam all die, even so in Christ all shall be made alive. 1 Cor. 15:17-22 (NKJ)

[j]"*Fallen asleep*:" the cults just do not understand nor get it; Paul is discussing the physical body and not the soul. Jesus is the God of the

living, not the dead. "- to be absent from the body and to be at home with the Lord."[2 Cor. 5:8 NAS]

No genuine believer can deny the physical and literal resurrection Jesus' body and still claim to be in Christ. The denial of the physical resurrection (Jesus Christ arose in His body) is a blatant denial of the Faith. **Period!** Jesus' resurrected body was definitely physical and not non-material or just spirit. (Our Lord's resurrected body could be *seen, felt, touched*, and *handled*.) Yet, His body was transformed into a glorious body no longer subject to this present physical world.

> That which was from the beginning, which we have **heard**, which we have **seen** with **our eyes**, which we **looked upon** and **have touched** with our **hands**, concerning the **WORD OF LIFE**— [2]the life was made manifest, and we have **seen it**, and **testify to it** and **proclaim to you** the eternal life, which was with the Father and was made **manifest to us**— [3]that which we have **seen** and **heard we proclaim** also to you, so that **you too may have fellowship with us**; and indeed **our fellowship is with the Father** and **with his Son Jesus Christ**. 1 John 1:1-3 (ESV)

> [36]And as they are speaking these things, Jesus Himself stood in the midst of them, and says to them, "Peace to you"; [37]and being amazed, and becoming frightened, they were thinking themselves to see a spirit. [38]And He said to them, "Why are you troubled? And why do reasonings come up in your hearts? [39]See My hands and My feet, that I am He; handle Me and see, because **A SPIRIT DOES NOT HAVE FLESH AND BONES AS YOU SEE ME HAVING**." [40]And having said this, He showed the hands and the feet to them, [41]and while they are not believing from the joy, and wondering, He said to them, "Do you have anything here to eat?" [42]And they gave to Him part of a broiled fish, and of a honeycomb, [43]and having taken, He ate before them.

> Luke 24:36-43 (LSV)

The redeemed shall have a similar glorified body,

> For our citizenship is in heaven [GK *ouranois*][k], from which also we eagerly wait for a Savior, the Lord Jesus Christ; [21]who will **transform the body of our humble state** into **conformity with the body of His glory**, by the exertion of the power that He has even to subject all things to Himself. Phil. 3:20, 21

> [k]The GK word *ouranos* is actually in the plural (*ouranois*), meaning the *Heavens*. Both in HEB and GK the word for "*Heaven*" is used in the singular and plural interchangeably.[k Luke 22:43; 23:43; Acts 1:11; 1 Thess. 1:10; 2 Thess.1:7]

So, while the meaning is literally *"Heavens,"* the meaning is definitely meaning Heaven is the above of the redeemed.

[k]Luke 23:43 uses the word "Paradise" which is the Persian word for Heaven.[2 Cor. 12:4; Rev. 2:7]

However, there is a serious misunderstanding of a text in [Rom. 4:25] that must be address here. The NAS and NJK are more grammatically and theologically correction.

Who was delivered for our offences, and was raised again **FOR our justification.** KJV	who was delivered up because of our offenses, and was raised **BECAUSE OF our justification.** NKJ	*He* who was delivered over because of our transgressions, and was raised **BECAUSE OF our justification.** NAS

Pay attention: the Lord Jesus was **NOT** raised to give us justification. We were justified at the cross! The word *"for"* in the KJV is less precise. The word *"for"* [Rom. 4:25] is the GK *dia*. *Dia* is in the "accusative" form. The grammar is extremely important here. The meaning is *"because of"* or *"on account of-"* That is, all that genuinely believe in Jesus Christ who have personally received and trusted in Lord and Savior now are declared righteous by faith in Christ. Yes, Christ *died for our sins*. Christ Jesus was not raised to justify us. The GK accusative form in [Rom. 4:25] literally means, "**Christ died on the behalf** or **Christ died in our place for sin.**" So, get it right!

> But now apart from the Law *the* righteousness of God has been manifested, being witnessed by the Law and the Prophets, [22]even *the* **righteousness of God through faith in Jesus Christ for all those who believe**; for there is no distinction; [23]for all have sinned and fall short of the glory of God, [24]**being justified as a gift by His grace through the redemption which is in Christ Jesus**; [25]whom God displayed publicly as **a propitiation in His blood through faith**. *This was* to demonstrate His righteousness, because in the forbearance of God He passed over the sins previously committed; [26]for the demonstration, *I say*, of His righteousness at the present time, so that He would be just and the justifier of the one who has faith in Jesus.   Rom. 3:21-26

Therefore, when Jesus died, He laid down his life at the precise hour or time of the Passover lamb was sacrificed. This is why Jesus said in His dying breath,

> When Jesus therefore had received the vinegar, he said, "**It is finished!**" Then he bowed his head and gave up his spirit.   John 19:30 (WEB)

The fact our Lord Jesus arose in His body from the grave proves our redemption is complete and lacks nothing. Now risen, as High Priest, He intercedes on the behalf of the redeemed:

> My little children, I am writing these things to you so that you may not sin. And [But] if anyone sins, we have an Advocate with the Father, Jesus Christ the righteous; ²and He **Himself is the propitiation for our sins**; and not for ours only, but also [*the propitiation*] for *those of* the whole world.   1 John 2:1, 2

> He that spared not his own Son, but delivered him up for us all, how shall he not with him also freely give us all things? ³³ Who shall lay anything to the charge of God's elect? *It is* God that *justifies*. ³⁴ Who *is* he that *condemns*? *It is* Christ that died, yea rather, that is risen again, who is even at the right hand of God, who also maketh intercession for us.   Rom. 8:32-34 (KJV)

> Therefore, He had to be made like His brethren in all things, so that He might become a merciful and faithful high priest in things pertaining to God, to make propitiation for the sins of the people. For since He Himself was tempted in that which He has suffered, He is able to come to the aid of those who are tempted.   Heb. 2:17, 18

> Therefore since we have a great high priest who has passed through the heavens, Jesus the Son of God, let us hold fast to our confession. ¹⁵ For we do not have a high priest incapable of sympathizing with our weaknesses, but one who has been tempted in every way just as we are, yet without sin. ¹⁶ Therefore let us confidently approach the throne of grace to receive mercy and find grace whenever we need help.
>
>   Heb. 4:14-16 (NET)

> Consequently, [*as High Priest*] he is able to save to the uttermost those who draw near to God through him, since he always lives to make intercession for them. ²⁶ For it was indeed fitting that we should have such a high priest, holy, innocent, unstained, separated from sinners, and exalted above the heavens. ²⁷ He has no need, like those high priests, to offer sacrifices daily, first for his own sins and then for those of the people,

since he did this once [e.g., *Christ died once for sin*] for all when he offered up himself.   Heb. 7:25-27 (ESV)

So, if the Lord Jesus interceded on our behalf as believers, we certainly do not need any so-called dead saints praying for us. **Jesus is all we need**. Jesus is risen! He is risen indeed! Hallelujah!

Conclusion

Therefore, the resurrection of Jesus Christ is indeed an established fact of history. Jesus Christ's resurrection surpasses the most minute scrutiny of meticulous ardent critics that examine the historical evidence. The sheer evidence of the resurrection of Jesus Christ is an indisputable fact whether anyone believes in the resurrection of Jesus Christ or not. The truth stands forever and ever. A person's denial does not change the fact of history: Christ Jesus is risen, and He is risen indeed.

Christ Jesus is not risen as spirit, nor as an apparition, nor spiritual-body. Christ Jesus arose in physical body, but His physical body was wonderfully transformed into a glorious body no longer subject the world.

> [36]And as they are speaking these things, Jesus Himself stood in the midst of them, and says to them, "Peace to you"; [37]and being amazed, and becoming frightened, they were thinking themselves to see a spirit. [38]And He said to them, "Why are you troubled? And why do reasonings come up in your hearts? [39]See My hands and My feet, that I am He; handle Me and see, because **a spirit does not have flesh and bones as you see Me having**." [40]And having said this, He showed the hands and the feet to them, [41]and while they are not believing from the joy, and wondering, He said to them, "Do you have anything here to eat?" [42]And they gave to Him part of a broiled fish, and of a honeycomb, [43]and having taken, He ate before them.   Luke 24:36-43 (LSV)

This my friend is the true Gospel. For if Christ Jesus is not risen, we are still in our sins. Fact is that Jesus Christ is indeed risen, and this is the very core of the Gospel.[1 Cor. 15:3, 4, 17-22] Therefore, anyone denying literal and physical resurrection cannot claim to be saved!

Footnotes:

1. Jesus resurrection: the order slightly varies depending expositors. The present order has been modified to serve a possible sequence. An Amazon web service.

   https://bloqs.s3.amazonaws.com/659-9162/355522_ResurrectionAppearancesinOrder.pdf

2. *Put* [stick] *that in your pipe and smoke it*: an idiom meaning, "used to tell someone that he or she must accept what one says is true even though he or she might not like it or agree with it.

   'It's a stupid movie. "Oh really? Well it was just nominated for an Oscar, so *put a stick that in your pipe and smoke it!*'"

3. *Keep things at bay*: "If you keep something or someone at bay, or hold them at bay, you prevent them from reaching, attacking, or affecting you.

   "Eating oranges keeps colds at bay."
   https://www.collinsdictionary.com/us/dictionary/english/to-keep-something-at-bay#google_vignette

4. The hypostatic union: from Google search engine.

Books, tracts, and songs by the author

Books by the author
Understanding Salvation by Faith in Christ
Understanding the Biblical Principles of Bible Study
Understanding the Biblical Principles of Witnessing
Understanding Prayer
Understanding Christian Doctrine, vol. 1: The Doctrine of God
Understanding Christian Doctrine, vol. 2: The Doctrine of Creation
Understanding Christian Doctrine, vol. 3: The Doctrine of Redemption
A Short Outline on Christian Doctrine
Christ's Supreme Sovereignty Over All (Commentary on Hebrews)
The Seven Mandates of Christ
Two of the Greatest Truths in Universe and their Significances
The Greatest Contemplation of Thought Ever!
Christ the Lord, the absolute center of Theology
Meeting the Greatest Friend You'll Ever Have
The Way of the Lord more Accurately
The Lord is Faithful who calls you into His Kingdom
　　(A Study in 1 Thessalonians)
Earnestly Contend for the Faith, (Study of the Epistle of Jude)
Two Doors into Eternity
The Miraculous Miracles and Signs of Jesus,
　　The Study of the Eight Signs in John

Gospel Tracts
Eternal Life, Yours for the Asking
Have You Received the Gift of God?

Songs
"Thou Art Worthy, O Lamb of God" (Chair song set to music)
"Infinite grace and mercy, He died on Calvary" (*new*),
　　adapted to, *"And Can It Be That I Should Gain?"*
"Tis All to Him I Owe" (similar to the tune, "Jesus Paid it All")
"Jesus' Precious Blood Avails for You" (not set to music)
"Mangrove Song"
　　(Filipino children's song in English, to the tune: "I'm in the Lord's Army")

Index